AI to the Rescue: How Machine Learning Can Help Manage Chronic Disease

Verma

Table of Contents

Chapter 1: Introduction

The rising prevalence of chronic conditions like type 2 diabetes poses an overwhelming challenge to the healthcare system. Three of every five adults in the United States live with at least one chronic condition, and chronic disease care accounts for over 70% of US healthcare spending [42,281]. Globally, the total cost of care for diabetes alone is projected to nearly double to over $2 trillion annually by 2030, representing over 2% of global GDP [31]. In addition to the substantial economic toll, chronic conditions carry a high personal cost; individuals living with chronic conditions make countless decisions every day — about what to eat and how to be active — that impact their health status and long-term quality of life [29]. Unlike treatment for an acute illness, where care is delivered within a clinical setting, successful care for chronic disease necessitates helping patients make decisions outside of the healthcare system, or *self-manage* their condition [29].

Artificial Intelligence (AI) and Machine Learning (ML) have been touted for their potential to improve the reach, quality, and overall performance of the healthcare system [68,210]. AI and ML algorithms have demonstrated strong performance in medical tasks like diagnostic imaging or predicting adverse events like unplanned hospital readmissions [105,211]. There is an opportunity to incorporate these advances into innovative interventions that could support individuals with chronic disease self-management. However, there are challenges to designing interactive systems that incorporate ML inferences in a way that can be integrated with individuals' everyday lives and inform their daily choices. Doing so requires a human-centered approach that considers the fit between an individual's needs and the capabilities of an ML algorithm [87].

For chronic disease management and prevention, recent research has highlighted the potential benefits of technologies for facilitating *health coaching* [16,38,96,229]. In-person health coaching can be an effective intervention to support chronic disease management and prevention [72,73]. Coaching aims to cultivate motivation and engagement, and establish accountability in pursuing achievable health goals in a longitudinal relationship between the coach and their client [196]. However, there aren't enough educators and coaches to support the growing population living with chronic conditions, let alone provide preventative care; in practice, most individuals with type 2 diabetes never receive coaching [81].

Technological advancements — including the proliferation of smartphones and advances in mobile health (mHealth) — can help bring novel forms of health coaching support to broader and more diverse populations. Furthermore, the integration of AI and ML can enable more intelligent and automated health coaching interventions that do not depend on the constant availability of healthcare professionals. ML could find patterns in an individual's self-tracking data, for example patterns of association between an individual's diet and blood sugar levels, to make personalized nutrition recommendations. In addition, AI can enable conversational interfaces, sometimes called *chatbots*, which have the potential to emulate some positive aspects of human interpersonal interactions, like establishing rapport, building relationships, and expressing empathy [22,26,82–84,124,159]. However, there are many open questions when it comes to researching and designing effective automated coaching solutions.

The purpose of this book is to identify computational approaches and interactive technology that enable automated health coaching systems. In particular, I focus on designing tools to support the self-management and prevention of chronic conditions like type 2 diabetes which requires changes to daily activities, including meals and exercise. The tools and interventions examined in this book are intended to be usable and useful for individuals from communities that have been historically underserved by the medical establishment, particularly racial and ethnic minorities including black, brown, and indigenous people of color, as well as those from low income and low wealth families and communities [92]. In three specific research aims, I utilize computational approaches that leverage individuals' self-tracking and health data, consider the capabilities and advantages of text-message based interactions for health coaching dialogs, and contribute data, methods, and algorithms towards the development of more supportive and intelligent health coaching interventions.

1.1 Aim I — Identify and evaluate approaches to translate machine learning inferences into recommendations for personalized nutrition goals

The first aim of this book focuses on *health goal setting* as a central and essential component of health coaching. In the context of type 2 diabetes, a key objective of self-management is keeping blood sugar levels within healthy ranges [29]. Nutrition goals can focus on adopting generally healthy behaviors like increasing fruit and vegetable consumption, but can also be specifically targeted at managing blood sugar levels. However, due to high variability between individuals in the way blood sugar levels change in response to daily activities
[167,272], these goals need to be personalized to each individual's pathophysiology and blood sugar regulation [10,15]. Yet, correctly anticipating about the impact of daily activities on blood sugar is challenging for both individuals and health professionals [168] an individual's daily behaviors and their health state, for example characterizing the relationship between the nutritional composition of meals and corresponding fluctuations in blood sugar levels. However, there are challenges in applying ML to small and noisy person-generated health data (PGHD) to

generate reliable insights. Furthermore, deriving *actionable* suggestions and formulating
nutrition goals based on such insights are non-trivial.

To address these challenges, we designed and evaluated a system called GlucoGoalie that
applies an expert system to translate user-specific ML insights into recommended nutrition goals.
An overview of the system is presented in Figure 1. Each suggested goal focuses on the amount
of one or more macronutrients (i.e., carbohydrates, protein, or fat) in a meal, and suggests
individuals increase or decrease to a target amount.

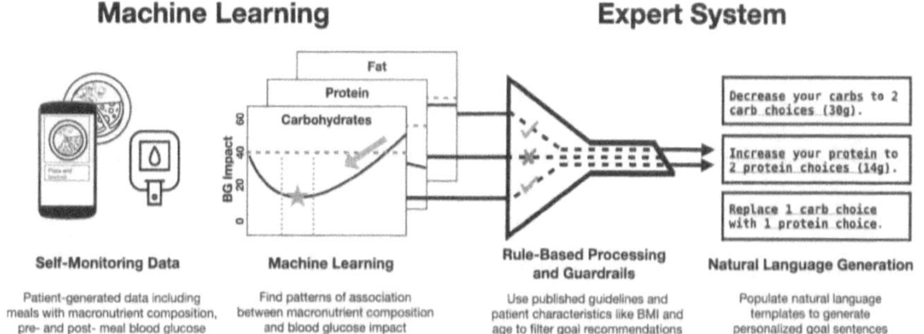

Figure 1. An overview of the pipeline for generating personalized goal recommendations in GlucoGoalie

This approach and the implemented GlucoGoalie system were evaluated in three studies.

In the first evaluation study, I applied an adapted version of attributable components
analysis (ACA), a non-parametric density estimation method based on optimal transport theory
and developed by Tabak and Trigila [243,244], applied it to diabetes self-monitoring data. I
compared ACA with linear regression in an analysis with meal and blood sugar data from 20
individuals with type 2 diabetes. ACA demonstrated a number of characteristics that are useful in

the context of PGHD like identifying non-linear patterns when appropriate, demonstrating robustness to outliers, and producing broader and more informative uncertainty estimates.[1]

In the second evaluation study, I examined the following research question:

Research Question 1.1: Would individuals with type 2 diabetes from medically underserved, low income communities be able to understand and act on computationally generated nutrition goals in a controlled setting?

In a series of simulated meal choice tasks, participants were generally able to understand the goals, but there was a great deal of variation in meeting the macronutrient target amount suggested in the goal.

The third study examined the experience of interacting with ML-derived goal suggestions in the real world, and the impact of the GlucoGoalie intervention on self-management behaviors with the following research questions:

Research Question 1.2: What is the experience of receiving and following recommendations for nutrition goals based on one's own self-tracking data in a smartphone app?

Research Question 1.3: Will individuals with type 2 diabetes report a higher frequency of self-management behaviors after using the GlucoGoalie over 4 weeks?

Research Question 1.4: For individuals who receive personalized goal recommendations, will they change their meal choices — specifically their macronutrient consumption — to more closely align with those goals?

In a deployment study with 20 individuals with type 2 diabetes over 4 weeks, participants made use of the GlucoGoalie smartphone application, improved in self-reported self-management behaviors, and increased their goal attainment over the study period. Eight of

---

[1] The results of this analysis are published in the *Journal of Biomedical Informatics* [179].

twenty participants received at least one personalized goal recommendation, and an analysis of the macronutrient composition of their meals suggests that participants changed their behaviors to be more in-line with their chosen goals. In qualitative interviews with eight participants, users described their efforts to achieve the goals recommended to them by GlucoGoalie. Participants reported a positive experience using the application, and recounted how receiving new suggestions spurred individuals to reflect on their nutrition habits and blood sugar levels. Following goal suggestions was not without challenges, however. Some participants disliked the personalized suggestions or had difficulty incorporating the goals into their eating habits. Participants also described difficulty tracking their meals and blood sugar readings on a sustained basis. Overall, participants wanted more concrete feedback to understand whether they were achieving goals, and more concrete suggestions tied to the specific meals they had eaten.[2]

Together, the results of these evaluation studies suggest that the approach of using an expert system to translate ML inferences into more actionable suggestions is promising, though also carries limitations. In subsequent aims, I build on the findings from these studies to explore more holistic approaches to health coaching interventions.

1.2   Aim II — Compare human-powered and automated health coaching via text messaging

While goal-setting is a foundational aspect of health coaching, there are many other important facets of coaching, like establishing accountability, offering feedback, and building rapport [196]. The second aim of this book expands its lens to a more complete view of health coaching, above and beyond goal setting.

---

[2] The results of this study are published in *Proceedings of the 2021 CHI Conference on Human Factors in Computing Systems (CHI 2021)* [177]

Because of the interpersonal communication at the heart of health coaching, conversational interfaces like chatbots — where users interact with the system through natural language — are a promising candidate [22]. However, some have argued that technological approaches cannot serve the true function of a health coach because they lack the human skills that underlie many aspects of coaching, including flexible contextual thinking and building an interpersonal relationship [218]. Additionally, there may be challenges in adapting coaching practice to a medium like text messaging, which has the advantages of being ubiquitous and widely available, but may also introduce pitfalls because text messages are more constrained and less expressive than live, spoken-word conversations.

To explore the potential and pitfalls of automated text-based health coaching I sought to compare human-powered and automated approaches with the following research questions:

Research Question 2.1: Can a scripted, rule-based chatbot create a positive coaching experience, comparable to that created by a human coach using the same medium (text messaging)?

Research Question 2.2: What aspects of the coaching experience, if any, are uniquely human and do not lend themselves to automated approaches?

Research Question 2.3: What are the potential advantages, if any, of chatbots for virtual coaching?

The first phase of research to address these questions was the iterative design of a scripted chatbot, called t2.coach, following a user-centered process. Chatbots in health-related domains are often scripted or rule-based [146]. In contrast with data-driven dialog modeling approaches that have enabled more dynamic chatbots in other domains like e-commerce or open chit-chat, scripted approaches can be desirable in health because designers have more control over the predictability and accuracy of responses, and the cost of inaccurate responses in health is high. In addition, there is a lack of available data for training data-driven dialog models in health [146]. t2.coach was designed based on an existing protocol for health coaching practitioners, called Brief Action Planning [109], and included functionality for nutrition and physical activity goals setting with daily follow-up conversations to check on goal progress.

The iterative design process for t2.coach included multiple focus groups and feedback sessions with individuals with type 2 diabetes and providers, as well as a deployment study with a partially implemented version of t2.coach and 13 participants. The deployment study utilized an adapted wizard-of-oz (WOz) approach, where an operator works behind the scenes to create the illusion of a fully functioning system, even when it is only partially implemented. I adapted the WOz approach to allow users to interact with the t2.coach prototype over 3 weeks, which led to many important revisions to shorten and clarify dialogs before final development.[3]

The second phase of research examined the primary research questions for this aim through a 3-week study with 23 individuals with type 2 diabetes, split into two groups. One group interacted with the WOz version of t2.coach described above, while the other interacted with an actual health coach over text message. The human health coaches had the same protocol as t2.coach, and tools for sending quick responses, but were encouraged to deviate from the protocol when appropriate.

We identified qualitative themes from post-study interviews with participants using inductive thematic analysis [36], and compared these themes between the two study groups. Importantly, we found that the chatbot created a coach-like experience for participants, who described feeling increased motivation, a sense of external accountability, and support in

---

[3] The fully implemented t2.coach chatbot is currently being evaluated in a 5-year National Institutes of Health funded research project (R01DK113189)

achieving their chosen goals. The results also showed that human-powered coaching had clear advantages, but coaches encountered challenges implementing their usual coaching approach over text message. Coaches described difficulty establishing rapport, as well as knowing when clients would be receptive to receiving messages. The chatbot appeared to have its own distinct advantages, including brief, consistent exchanges that kept goals top-of-mind for participants and spurred proactive changes in behavior, though this repetition verged on annoyance for some participants. Similar to the findings from aim 1, participants in both groups wanted more feedback and suggestions connected to the specific meals they were eating.[4]

Together, these results highlight that human and chatbot coaches have their own complementary areas of excellence, and therefore suggest a set of design goals for automated conversational health coaches that does not directly replicate the human coaches' approach, but instead complements it.

1.3 Aim III — Explore artificial intelligence approaches to enable micro-coaching dialogs

The results of Aim 2 highlight the potential of automated approaches like chatbots to deliver health coaching support while also reiterating the limits of purely scripted approaches. In the third aim of this book, I build on the scripted t2.coach chatbot to make steps towards more intelligent and dynamic conversational coaching tools.

Following on the implications of Aim 2, automated conversational approaches may be well suited to brief conversations with individuals to support specific meal-related decisions. Here, we assume users already have a nutrition goal they are working towards, and explore the design of brief coaching conversations about planned meals in the context of a user's goal. To

___

[4] The results of this study are published in *Proceedings of the ACM on Human-Computer Interaction (CSCW)* [178]

enable these conversations, which we refer to as *micro-coaching* dialogs, the chatbot needs to be able to ***automatically assess whether the user is on track to achieve their goal*** with a planned meal. This assessment enables the coaching system to give ***feedback*** to the user, and offer ***suggestions*** to modify the meal to make it more consistent with the goal. In contrast with in-depth meal logging approaches, micro-coaching dialogs can focus on eliciting the specific details about a planned meal that are relevant to the user's goal, keeping conversations brief and targeted.

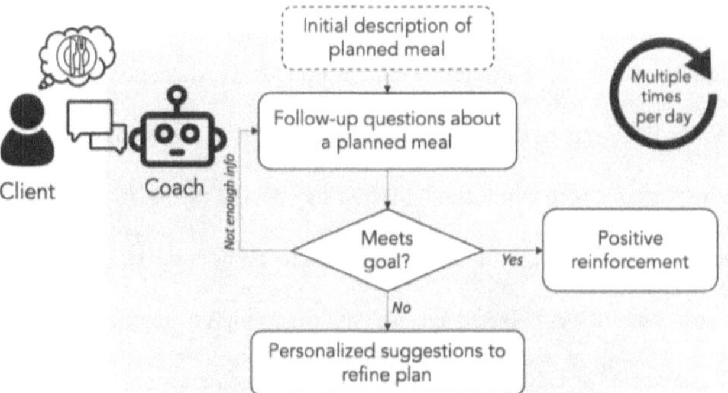

Figure 2. Proposed structure for micro-coaching dialogs.

To enable micro-coaching dialogs, I explored multiple approaches that incorporate various types of Artificial Intelligence mechanisms. The first focused on more clearly mapping the space of questions coaches would ask, with the following research questions:

Research Question 3.1: How do expert coaches formulate follow-up questions about meals their client is planning on eating to understand whether the client is likely to achieve their nutrition goal?

Research Question 3.2: How can existing, structured nutrition knowledge resources be utilized to design and implement a natural language understanding (NLU) system for dialogs about meals and generates a set of follow-up questions?

To address these questions, we completed an interview and structured survey study with health coaches (n=2), and found that there was a limited set of question types that coaches would ask, and that the question types depended on both the meal and the nutrition goal. In addition, the question-asking relied on a great deal of nutrition knowledge. To incorporate nutrition knowledge, we utilized a food-specific natural language processing system (Nutritionix [275]) to identify the components of a user's meal, and a food ontology (FoodOn [75]) to tag each food item with relevant characteristics. These characteristics, for example which foods are lean proteins and which are carbohydrates, can be used to automatically assess whether there is enough information to determine whether a meal is consistent with a health goal.

To evaluate this system and its determinations, we used *crowdsourcing* to simulate conversations between a coach and a client discussing specific meals. In a pilot data set of 10 dialogs for each of 3 goals, we examined inter-rater agreement between registered dietitian labels of goal achievement and the rule-based system, and found high concordance.

Once the space of possible questions was defined, the next step was to consider how to choose the most informative follow-up question given a state of dialog. Here, I sought to compare multiple approaches for dialog management, with the following research question:

> *Research Question 3.3*: What are comparative benefits and limitations of different types of dialog management approaches for coaching chatbots, considering those that use reinforcement learning (RL), those that choose their questions randomly, rule-based, and fully-scripted. Specifically, how do these chatbots compare on their ability to reach their end goal, their conversational length, and their perceived coherence and user experience?

If the automated coach could ask one of many follow-up questions about a user's meal, Reinforcement Learning (RL) is a machine learning approach that can be used to prioritize among those choices. With RL, a system learns through trial-and-error, receiving different rewards for actions in different circumstances [240]. RL has shown tremendous success learning to play games from Atari to Go [180,233], and is also commonly used for dialog modeling, to help dialog systems achieve their intended outcomes more efficiently. For example RL can help a movie booking chatbot successfully book tickets by asking fewer questions [154]. However, RL is only applicable where there is an environment that can be simulated, or there are existing data sets of example dialogs to learn from. Such data sets are rare in health domains and do not exist for health coaching [146]. Without an existing corpus of coaching dialogs to learn from, new dialog data sets can be created with *crowdsourcing* [228,273], where crowd workers play the roles of multiple conversational parties to simulate conversations asynchronously.

Using a crowdsourced data set of 300 dialogs, 1 trained an RL algorithm, *q-learning*, to dynamically choose which question to ask in a given situation. Q-learning estimates the value of asking a particular question in a particular conversational state. I first validated the q-learning approach using simulated data, and then trained a model on the dialog data sets for each of the 3 goals in the crowdsourcing study.

In contrast with the data-driven approach, we also designed a rule-based system that takes advantage of the knowledge-engineered representation from the prior step.

To compare the rule-based and data-driven AI coaching systems, we compared 20 online dialogs per goal with dialogs created by two control conditions: 1) randomly generated dialogs, and 2) a simple, scripted, deterministic approach that always asked the same questions regardless of user responses.

The RL coach resulted in conversations that reached their objective with significantly fewer questions than both the random and rule-based conditions, suggesting promise of the RL approach to keep conversations brief and focused.

In addition, 36 participants reviewed complete dialogs generated from one of the 4 conditions and assessed the perceived user experience and quality of dialogs, and found no major differences in perceived quality or user experience across the conditions. Dialogs with the RL chatbot were rated as more coherent than scripted dialogs.

Together, these studies present initial steps towards designing more intelligent conversational coaching systems.

1.4 Contributions

This book makes a number of contributions to research in informatics, human-computer interaction (HCI), health coaching, and conversational interfaces.

In Aim 1, I contribute a method for translating ML insights into actionable recommendations with a rule-based expert system, which could be extended to other domains and data sets in health and wellbeing. In addition, the qualitative account of individuals' experiences receiving and using personalized goal recommendations from their own self-tracking data presents an important contribution area to the growing field of personal health tools that incorporate ML [117].

In Aim 2, I contribute a theory-driven chatbot for health coaching, t2.coach, designed through an iterative, user-centered process. Because t2.coach is adapted from an established protocol for goal setting, the dialog system could be adapted to other health domains. In the iterative design process, the approach for adapting the wizard-of-oz approach to deployment studies is a methodological contribution. Additionally, the qualitative comparison of human and automated approaches to health coaching via text messaging contributes to scholarly debate about the essentialness of human skills in coaching, and whether automated approaches can ever function as a health coach.

In Aim 3, I contributed a set of design needs for micro-coaching dialogs, which could offer scaffolding for future research in automated coaching interventions. In addition, the corpus of meal-related dialogs created as a part of this aim will be made openly available so that it can be used and extended by other researchers. Lastly the head-to-head comparison of data-driven and rule-based dialog management approach may provide insight to researchers who are considering multiple approaches to implement conversational tools.

Chapter 2: Background and related work

2.1   Chronic disease self-management

Chronic disease is a growing challenge for the healthcare system, where a focus on hospitals and fee-for-service reimbursement model is largely built for treatment of acute conditions. Patients spend very little of their time interacting directly with the healthcare system. instead spending time and energy to self-managing their health on their own. Living with a chronic condition involves hundreds of daily decisions that impact short-term and long-term health status [28,29]. Chronic disease care, therefore, is about supporting individuals in making those decisions, or self-managing their condition [29].

Self-management is challenging for a number of reasons. Knowing what changes to make to improve health status requires health literacy and knowledge, and it takes substantial motivation to succeed in achieving sustained change in behaviors. This is further exacerbated by individual differences in pathophysiology of different conditions. For example, individuals have different physiological responses to exercise and stress, and metabolism of different foods [10,33,167,181,221,234,268,272].

The burdens of chronic diseases are not shared equally. Low socio-economic status and communities of color have higher rates of chronic disease and worse outcomes [47,114,202]. In addition, individuals from these communities tend to have fewer resources and skills that enable self-management, like health literacy. Interventions that are not sensitive to the needs of underserved individuals and instead cater to well-off technology users have the potential to deepen existing disparities and even to create new intervention-generated inequality [52,254].

This book focuses on supporting self-management of type 2 diabetes mellitus (T2D). T2D is highly prevalent, currently affecting over 30 million Americans – almost 10% of the population – with 1.5 million new cases diagnosed each year [9]. Daily decisions about nutrition, physical activity, sleep, and stress all impact blood glucose control [10,81], and there are individual differences in these impacts [10,81,167,272]. The American Diabetes Association recommends individuals set personalized macronutrient targets with a diabetes educator, but does not provide explicit guidelines for how to determine these goals.

In-person education is shown to be effective in supporting self-management, and seeks to help patients develop requisite knowledge and skills [73]. Increasingly, self-management education includes aspects of coaching, seeking to establish a longitudinal relationship between the patient and the educator to not only increase knowledge but also cultivate motivation and patient empowerment. However, there are not enough educators to support the growing population with diabetes, and the most individuals with diabetes do not receive any diabetes education at all [81].

In contrast with in-person support, informatics tools can be deployed to offer a form of self-management support to a larger number of individuals. In the next sections, I review a selection of informatics interventions that take different approaches to support self-management. Some actively "push" content to users, while others rely on users to seek out and "pull" information from the application, and a combination of these approaches may be particularly effective to support self-management.

2.2   Informatics tools for self-management

2.2.1   Personal Informatics

Personal informatics includes a class of interactive technologies that allow their users to collect data about their behaviors and health, and explore those data for patterns and trends [52,152]. For example, data from sleep sensors can help users uncover the factors associated with a better night's sleep [51,157], and self-experimentation can help irritable bowel syndrome patients learn what foods trigger symptoms [131,132]. Because these technologies focus on individual self-monitoring data, they can support individuals in personal discoveries, which is especially useful for chronic conditions characterized by individual differences.

With some exceptions [117], PI tools focus on data collection, descriptive summarization, and visualization. With an emphasis on reflection [19,78,142,153,165], users must actively use the applications to explore their data – or "pull" from the application. Actionable implications for how to change behaviors do not come directly from the application, but through the user's thinking and reflection. The process of logging itself can also be quite challenging and burdensome [86,164]. Much of the PI literature focuses on individuals who identify as a part of the *Quantified-Self* (QS) movement, who are highly motivated to devote the time and mental energy necessary to make sense of their self-monitoring data [52,152,153]. Findings about the usefulness of these systems are unlikely to apply to the larger population with chronic disease, including individuals with lower literacy and numeracy from communities with a higher prevalence of chronic disease [46,145]. There is a need for solutions that take the burden off of individuals to analyze their data and help support actions.

2.2.2   Behavior Change Interventions

In contrast with PI interventions, which rely on users to actively and intentionally "pull" information, *targeted behavior change* interventions aim to help individuals adopt healthy behaviors by proactively "pushing" the right information and support to users at just the right time [147,186]. Often, these interventions use behavior theories to offer notifications and messages to "nudge" users towards a pre-specified behavior change goal [147,216]. Interventions can be as technically straightforward as targeted one-way text messages, for example sending messages to encourage smoking cessation that are tailored based on the user's motivation and willingness to change [215]. More technically complex examples use mobile phone sensor data and reinforcement learning to discover more optimal times to send tailored nudges that will be most successful in encouraging physical activity in the moment [98,150,193,246].

Tailored one-way messaging interventions can be effective in helping individuals adopt healthy behaviors to support weight loss, increase physical activity, and increase vaccination rates [110,115,198,236]. However, *targeted behavior change* interventions are limited because they rely on a predefined goal or target to nudge users towards. These interventions are useful when healthy behaviors are known a priori, perhaps from published clinical guidelines; increasing physical activity or quitting smoking will almost always be beneficial for an individual's health. In the case of T2D self-management, and other conditions with prominent individual differences, identifying target behaviors may not be as straightforward [10]. In addition, the approach of prespecifying target healthy behaviors does not empower patients to have input into the process, which could have a negative impact on autonomy and may not cultivate patient empowerment [130]. Along these lines, many studies find a diminishing "dose effect" of behavioral nudges over time, suggesting that these interventions may not be effective in cultivating long-term motivation to adopt healthy behaviors [138].

2.2.3   Combining push and pull with automated coaching

While some interventions primarily "push" information to users and others primarily allow users to proactively "pull" information, the two categories are not mutually exclusive. Many interventions combine both "push" and "pull" interactions, which can be more effective than either approach along. For example, two-way text messaging interventions are more effective than one-way messaging interventions in a number of domains [74,258]. Even the addition of simple yes or no questions to measure adherence can increase engagement over one-way messaging [27,35,111]. Some interventions take interactive messaging a step further to offer semi-automated coaching and feedback [88,133,206,256,257]. However, because they rely on human experts to provide feedback, these interventions face the similar scalability challenges to in-person education and coaching. Because coaching interactions can be initiated by either party, and because coaching is centered on back-and-forth exchange, conversational agents are a common option to deliver coaching support [83–85].

The theoretical components of health coaching are described in more detail in the review of theories, below.

2.3 Conversational agents

Conversational agents — sometimes referred to as chatbots, or intelligent assistants — are a class of applications driven by the exchange of natural language between a user and the system. One of the first conversational agents, ELIZA, was developed in the 1960's [264]. The first use case for ELIZA was to emulate a Rogerian psychotherapist with rule-based responses. Decades later, in the present day, more sophisticated conversational agents are nearly ubiquitous, from Siri in smartphones to Alexa in smart speakers [55].

Conversational agents have a number of potential advantages for supporting chronic disease self-management. First, natural language can provide an intuitive interaction method. A conversation is a very natural setting to both "push" and "pull" information to users in the same interface [201]. Speech entry is three times faster than typing [230], and may improve usability for low literacy populations [49,170,232]. Conversational interfaces may have usability advantages over graphical interfaces for individuals with poor vision and dexterity, for example in the case of complications due to T2D [23]. Finally, conversational agents have been shown to replicate some of the human, interpersonal aspects of the therapeutic relationship, for example expressing empathy or establishing rapport [22,159].

McTear [169] offered a useful categorization of conversational agents based on their functionality, distinguishing between three distinct categories: finite state-based, frame-based, and agent-based. Finite state-based systems follow a deterministic, structured dialog tree or use rule-based language processing to respond to user input. Frame-based systems are useful for task-based applications, where the designer can specify the types of tasks and pieces of information necessary to complete the task, or slots. Frame-based approaches then utilize natural language processing (NLP) to classify the user's intent, and fill the necessary slots in the frame to execute the task. For example, to schedule a medical appointment, a frame-based chatbot might need the date, timeslot, and chief complaint. Finally, agent-based or AI systems come closest to replicating human-human dialog, and rely on more complex logic to determine responses, often through data-drivel dialog models trained with machine learning (ML).

Many of the early examples of CAs were finite state-based [23,264], and rule-based agents continue to be developed [91]. Most of the CAs that are a part of the recent resurgence of conversational assistants in the consumer sphere, like Amazon's Alexa and Apple's Siri follow a frame-based architecture. While pitched as conversational experiences, these interactions are primarily task-based, and therefore researchers in human-computer interaction (HCI) have suggested that describing these interactions as "conversational" is inaccurate [207].

Recent approaches to designing more dynamic conversational AI agents rely on training statistical dialog models, for example deep neural networks, that learn from large corpora of example conversations [97]. Through thousands of examples, these models learn a mapping from input messages to output responses. This approach is made possible by many large, openly available corpora of dialogs in many domains like IT support and restaurant searching [161,227], and is usually centered on open domain chit-chat or task-based agents in a consumer setting. Extending these advances to other domains like health coaching would necessitate the creation and open availability of such corpora.

As shown in Figure 3, dialog corpora can be used to learn both *what* an agent should say in response to some user input (dialog management) as well as *how* to say it (dialog generation) [97]. Some modeling approaches seek to learn both dialog management and generation jointly, in *end-to-end* models that map directly from user input to the agent's output. This approach typically requires very large amounts of data, and may handle some tasks better than others depending on coverage in the data. An alternative approach is to combine multiple models that control different phases of the conversation (see Figure 4). For instance, a rule-based dialog management could delegate to one of many model-based agents depending on whether the user wants to discuss movies or music. This approach allows combining multiple specialized models, each of which may be better attuned to a specific task and require less data to train.

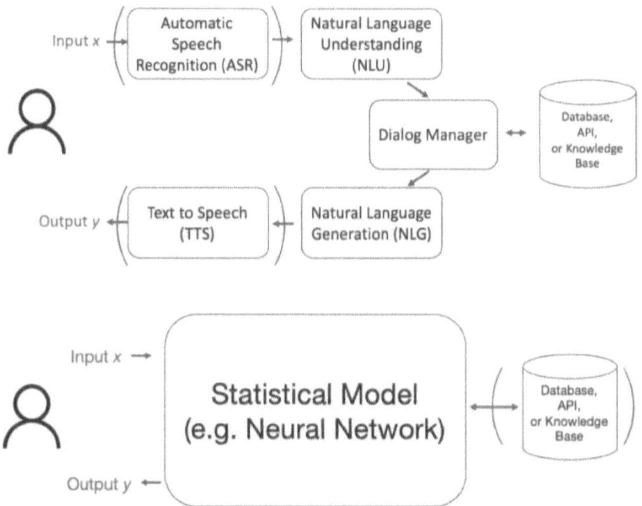

Figure 3. Two different architectures for dialog systems.
Top is a common setup for task-oriented and frame-based systems. Each component can be rule-based or data driven. Bottom represents more recent approaches to train end-to-end statistical models from dialog corpora. Figure adapted from Gao 2018 [97]

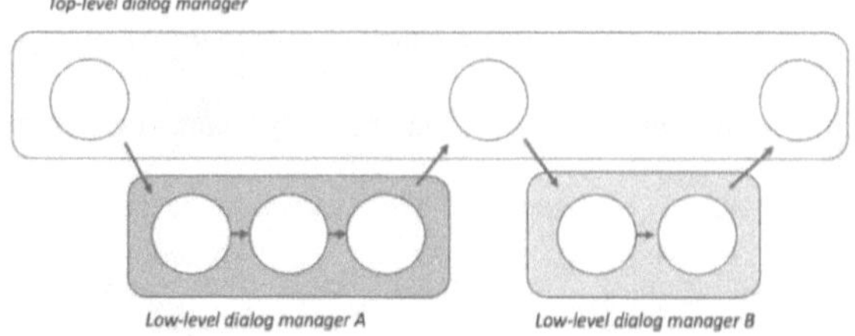

Figure 4. A representation of dialog systems with multi-level policy architectures.
A top-level dialog manager controls the overall dialog interactions, but delegates certain tasks or interactions to lower-level policies. Figure adapted from Gao 2018 [97]

2.4   Reinforcement learning for conversational agents

A common approach to improve the efficiency of dialog management is to apply

Reinforcement Learning (RL). RL is a distinct machine learning approach, and is separate from supervised learning — where the task is to predict a label or classification for instances in a data set — and unsupervised learning — where the task is to find hidden structures or relationships within a data set. The task for RL is to learn a policy for what actions to take in a given environment with a certain state. RL agents learn from trial-and-error, collecting rewards as they move through the environment, and keeping track of which actions in which situations bring about the highest long-term reward. In recent years, RL has shown strong performance in learning how to play many different games without any expert knowledge about the game's rules or strategy [233].

In addition to games, RL can be applied to data-driven dialog management for conversational agents. RL can help task-based agents accomplish their aim with fewer questions, or in a more natural way, depending on how the rewards are defined [154,156,238]. This can be accomplished as a part of end-to-end models, or dialog management alone [97].

A key distinction in RL is between online and offline learning. With online learning, the agent is able to interact with a simulated or actual environment to directly observe the impact of their actions on the state and reward collected by the agent [240]. This is partly attributable of the reason for the high-profile success of RL in playing many common games, where thousands upon thousands of iterations of the game can be simulated. In the case of dialog agents, this is not always possible, and learning in real time with actual users would take too long when the RL is in the early stages of training and makes many errors.

Many RL algorithms are able to learn offline from data generated by some other process. Offline learning with an existing data set can be used to train or pre-train RL models before deploying them into an actual environment, where they can continue learning over time [240,245]. When the generating policy for a data set is not known, it can introduce methodological challenges for offline learning, which is an open research area [127,245]. If the

generating process *is* known, it can simplify the RL approach substantially [245]

2.5   Conversational agents in health

A recent review by Laranjo and colleagues surveyed the use of conversational agents in

healthcare [146]. Their review identified 14 agents in a range of application areas. The majority

of the applications where to mental health, with a sampling of other health areas like asthma and

nutrition. Many agents implement some sort of clinical protocol like Cognitive Behavioral

Therapy [91] or Brief Motivational Interventions [159]. None of the agents identified were AI-

based; all were either rule-based or frame-based. The continued focus on rule-based and scripted

agents is partly because of a low tolerance for error in the health domain. With scripted agents,

the design knows exactly how the agent will respond to a given input from the user. With more

dynamic, data-driven approaches, the models are probabilistic, and because the responses can be

more variable the designer has much less control over what the agent my say to a user, which is

not a desirable risk if delivering health-related advice. In addition, because of HIPAA and other

data privacy protections, health-related data sets are rarely made openly available for researcher

use, and there is therefore a lack of publicly available dialog corpora in health domains

[146,227].

Unfortunately, many of the studies identified in the review did not include

implementation details [146]. In addition, most studies reported either technical outcomes, user

experience, or clinical outcomes, but rarely a combination [146]. Together, these shortcomings

make it difficult to replicate findings or build on prior work.

For studies that did report user experiences, common reactions to the agent included a

sense of accountability, feeling of empathy from and toward the agent, as well identifying a personality in the agent building a relationship with the agent [45,91,94]. These findings support the notion that conversational agents have the potential to support individuals in self-management by replicating parts of the health coaching process.

2.6   Review of relevant theories and frameworks

2.6.1   The Information–Motivation–Behavioral Skill (IMB) model

Many behavioral theories seek to characterize the predisposing factors and barriers for engaging in healthy behaviors [147]. The Information–Motivation–Behavioral Skill model (IMB; Figure 5) posits that these three concepts are primarily responsible for determining whether individuals engage in behaviors that help or harm their health status [89].

First, *information* and knowledge about a behavior and its likely impact on health are essential in determining whether a behavior will be helpful or harmful. Information includes both facts as well as heuristics and rules of thumb about how to act in a given situation. Second, *motivation* to perform health-related behaviors will also influence whether an individual's choices and decisions, and inform whether they take the sometimes more effortful option to improve their health. Together, knowledge and motivation help an individual develop *behavioral skills* to enact healthy behaviors in a variety of situations and circumstances. This concept encompasses both an individual's objective ability as well as their beliefs about their ability, or self-efficacy. As a whole, these three concepts influence an individual's likelihood to perform health improving or harming behaviors.

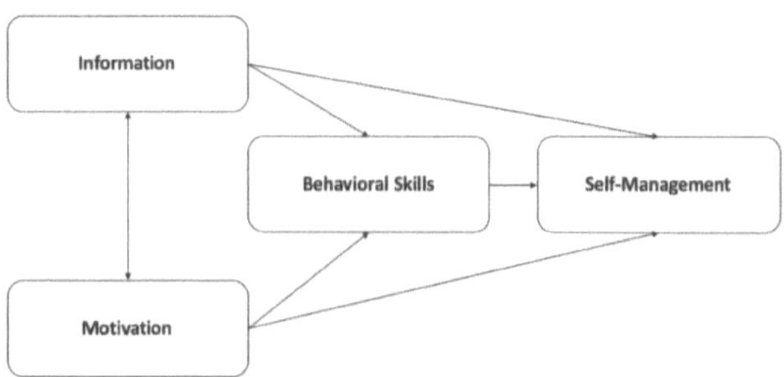

Figure 5. The Information-Motivation-Behavioral Skills model [89]

The IMB model was originally developed to understand engagement in HIV prevention behaviors [89], and has since been validated for a number of other health behaviors, including diabetes self-management [199]. The utility of the IMB model for understanding diabetes self-management is clear:

- *Information* is important, and not simply facts about the condition or healthy behaviors. Because of individual differences, knowledge about how a particular behavior will impact health requires self-knowledge

- While education-based interventions are important, they are not sufficient for individuals to adopt healthy changes. Coaching also emphasizes long term relationships and empowering patients to help cultivate their *motivation* over time.

- *Behavioral skills* and self-efficacy to perform them are emphasized in diabetes problem-solving [8]. This is especially important because of the many contextual and situational factors that influence self-management [209].

One limitation of the IMB model is that it does not directly represent the social support and environmental factors that have also been shown to be important in influencing self-management [147]. While not directly represented, social support is considered as a part of motivation in the IMB model, and the concept of behavioral skills includes consideration of environmental barriers and facilitators to self-management. Importantly, the interventions examined in this book focus primary on individual support for self-management, as opposed to intervening on social support structures, or public health interventions to living environments and communities, making the IMB model an appropriate choice as a guiding framework.

Throughout this book, the IMB model informs the approach and analysis. In Aim 1, the focus is primarily on information needs; the personalized goals generated by the GlucoGoalie system aim to help individuals better understand the relationship between their nutrition and blood sugar levels. Aim 2 takes a broader lens, considering not just information, but also motivation and behavioral skills, examining the ways that both human-powered and automated health coaching approaches impact individual's self-described motivation, as well as examples of users learning new skills by following the suggested plans from the chatbot's content base. In the third aim, the proposed structure of micro-coaching conversations supports information by offering individuals feedback on their goal attainment, supports motivation by offering positive reinforcement or establishing accountability, and supports behavioral skills my making suggestions to help individuals learn how to adjust their meals to be more in line with their goals.

In addition, the IMB model provides a theory-driven lens to understand the merits of health coaching, discussed below.

2.6.2 Health Coaching

While much attention has been paid to health coaching in recent years (see Figure 6), very little work has explicitly defined health coaching as a concept or framework. Many informatics interventions are described as "coaches," but these papers almost never reference a specific theory or background literature on coaching or health coaching [218].

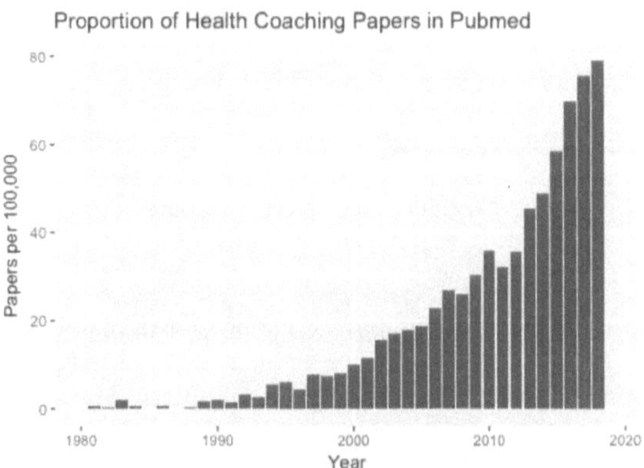

Figure 6. Proportion of papers published in PubMed and MEDLINE between 1980 and 2018 that use the keyword "health coaching"

Olsen [196] presented a concept analysis of health coaching which posited 7 attributes. Health coaching is *goal-oriented*, *client-centered*, a *partnership*, *health-focused*, *enlightening*, *empowering*, and takes place as a *process* through time.

1. The first central aspect of coaching is its goal-centric orientation, where the coach and client work together to set *health-related goals* and monitor success in achieving those goals over time. Goal-setting itself is an established and effective behavior change technique employed in many mobile health technologies [74,143,174,184,187]. Goal-setting serves as the foundation of health coaching, but there are many other essential components.

2. Coaching is *client-centered* because the coach seeks to personalize the experience based on the client's desires, respecting their autonomy.

3. Coaching requires a *partnership*, where both parties are actively engaged. In contrast to technologies that focus on "pushing" information to the user, or letting the user "pull"

information themselves, technology that facilitates partnerships lends itself to tools that push and pull information at the same time in an exchange or dialog.

4. Health coaching is definitionally *health-focused*, because its purpose and content is meant to improve the client's health, and contrasts with other forms of coaching like sports, executive, or voice coaching.

5. Successful coaching is *enlightening* for the client, delivering health education and also encouraging reflection, client identification of barriers and strategies to overcome them, and self-awareness. This relates to both *information* and *behavioral skills* from the IMB model.

6. Coaching is empowering for the client, and cultivates their autonomy, which connects to the concept of *motivation* in IMB.

7. Finally, coaching is not an isolated intervention, but a process that manifests over time, requiring action from the client and recurring sessions between the pair, and long-term engagement with the coaching process. This involves building a relationship and establishing report.

Recent work has emphasized the importance of personal and human skills to the perceived success of health coaching [218]. Based on interviews with self-described coaches, Rutjes argued that successful coaching goes beyond simply achieving goals, and also includes growing knowledge through the experience of coaching, building relationships, implicitly adapting to different contextual factors, and the importance of cultivating motivation. These aspects of coaching are consistent with Olsen's framework, but place additional emphasis on the human aspects of coaching that may be difficult to replicate with data-driven health technology. Self-monitoring data can reveal patient *behaviors* (like achieving or not achieving a health goal), but focuses less on the *experiences* of individuals in their daily lives [218]. Successful health coaching, Rutjes argues, must focus on individual experiences as well as behaviors. Self-monitoring data and technology, by capturing client behaviors, can help coaches to ask the right questions during the coaching encounter [218].

Considering the Information–Motivation–Behavioral Skills (IMB) model, coaching supports all three of the requisite components for adopting healthy behaviors. Coaching provides education to grow *knowledge*, establishes an interpersonal relationship the seeks to cultivate *motivation*, and helps patients build *behavioral skills* through a collaborative problem solving process [196,218].

In this book, health coaching is a central inspiration for the design of technology to support self-management. Aim 1 is focused on goal-setting, which is a central component of coaching. Aim 2 seeks to better understand the other essential components of health coaching through both a technological and human lens. Finally, in Aim 3, I implement and evaluate technology for automated coaching that builds on both health coaching theory and the findings from earlier aims.

Chapter 3: Aim I

Identify and evaluate approaches to translate machine learning inferences into recommendations for personalized nutrition goals

Self-managing chronic conditions like type 2 diabetes (T2D) presents continual burden because it impacts countless choices individuals make in their daily lives [29]. Making healthy choices requires literacy and sustained motivation [29]. Self-management is further complicated by the need for reflection and self-discovery due to high individual differences: for example, the same choices in diet and exercise can have profoundly different health impacts for different individuals [10,167,272]. These challenges contribute to growing health disparities; low income and minority communities have higher prevalence and worse outcomes from chronic diseases and lower access to critical resources like diabetes education [47,114,202].

The American Diabetes Association (ADA) recommends setting personalized nutrition goals and plans with a heath coaching professional like a Certified Diabetes Care and Education Specialist (CDCES) [10]. Coaches work with their clients to determine appropriate health goals, including macronutrient targets for different meals. However, this level of care and support is still out of reach for many individuals living with T2D. Technology-powered coaching interventions can provide personalized support at a bigger scale. Mobile health (mHealth) apps and sensors enable the collection of person-generated health data streams like meal logs and BG readings. These new data streams, coupled with tools to analyze those data, could enable personalized coaching support from mHealth apps.

Despite this potential, however, many data-driven health interventions suffer from high user burden and low adoption [58,148,152]. The majority of interventions that incorporate self-tracking focus on viewing, visualizing, or reflecting on personal data. These approaches place the burden on individuals to derive insights from their data and determine how to change their behavior [117,164]. As a consequence, individuals with low technology and health literacy, who are most impacted by chronic diseases, are least equipped to reap the benefits [253,254].

One approach to help individuals more easily derive insights from their data is to apply *machine learning* (ML) to find patterns and make predictions. Recent research initiatives have demonstrated high accuracy in broadly health-related tasks [105,211]. ML methods can be applied to personal health data to find patterns of association between multiple streams of self-tracking data [20] or forecast changes in blood sugar levels [70].

However, incorporating ML into personal health applications has its own challenges. Interpreting the output of an ML algorithm also requires knowledge and skills, and can be just as challenging as exploring self-tracking data. What's more, even if ML can identify insightful patterns, those patterns may not be sufficient to help an individual understand how to change their behaviors: they may not be *actionable* if there is no information about what an individual can do to change or mitigate the unwanted outcomes [20,117]. For example, an identified correlation between weather and physical activity may be less actionable without specific suggestions for how to stay active on rainy days [20]. Similarly, a prediction of high blood sugar may be less actionable without explaining what contributed to the forecast or how to mitigate it [70]. Generating suggestions that inform individual action is the heart of the field of *recommender systems* (RecSys) [214,241]. However, even for health-aware RecSys, ML is used to infer preferences, rather than the health impact of different choices; the health constraints for recommendations are assumed, not learned with ML [77,208]. Other recent work has sought to incorporate recommendations based on ML-derived insights from self-tracking data, but were limited to an individual's own past meals and therefore lacked variability [272], or relied on user's self-perceptions of what behaviors impact health and were therefore unsurprising and less useful to users [117]. Thus, there a need for new approaches to translating inferences achieved with ML into recommendations that can guide individuals' action.

To address these research gaps, I have developed an approach to couple ML inferences with a rule-based expert system in order to generate actionable recommendations. This approach underlies the design of a system called GlucoGoalie which makes personalized suggestions for nutritional goals for individuals with T2D. GlucoGoalie uses ML to identify patterns in self-tracking data—meals and BG levels captured with the GlucoGoalie smartphone app—regarding the relationship between nutrition and change in BG after meals. Furthermore, GlucoGoalie relies on a rule-based expert system to translate ML output into a direct support for action by generating natural language recommendations for nutrition goals in order to improve BG levels. Goal setting is a common approach to behavior change interventions, and a core part of health coaching [74,184,187]. These goals reflect both individual patterns identified with ML and expert knowledge regarding ways to improve BG management, thus uniquely combining the strengths of both. Each personalized goal is a suggestion to increase or decrease the amount of a macronutrient in meals, or to replace one macronutrient with another. Finally, GlucoGoalie helps individuals work towards achieving their goals by asking them to self-assess prospective meals on their consistency with selected goals during logging and to review a summary of goal achievement.

In the next sections of this chapter, I present the design and the multi-part evaluation of GlucoGoalie. Section 3.1 describes the design process and mechanics of GlucoGoalie in more detail. Next, I present three evaluation studies: 1) an intrinsic evaluation of the ML method underlying GlucoGoalie, 2) a controlled lab experiment that assessed whether the goals generated by GlucoGoalie were *understandable* and *actionable* for individuals with T2D , and 3) quantitative and qualitative results from a 4-week deployment study of GlucoGoalie including an analysis of behavior change outcomes and qualitative findings on the experience of receiving and following personalized goal suggestions from the app.

3.1   The GlucoGoalie system

We designed GlucoGoalie through a user-centered design process building on our prior research with individuals with T2D from a predominantly Black and Latino economically disadvantaged community [213]. Figure 7 presents an overview of the pipeline for generating personalized goals. GlucoGoalie's goal-generating engine includes two main components: a machine learning algorithm for detecting patterns of association between nutrition in meals and changes in BG levels, and an expert system that uses expert knowledge to generate recommendations for nutritional goals in order to improve BG levels. I describe these in more detail below.

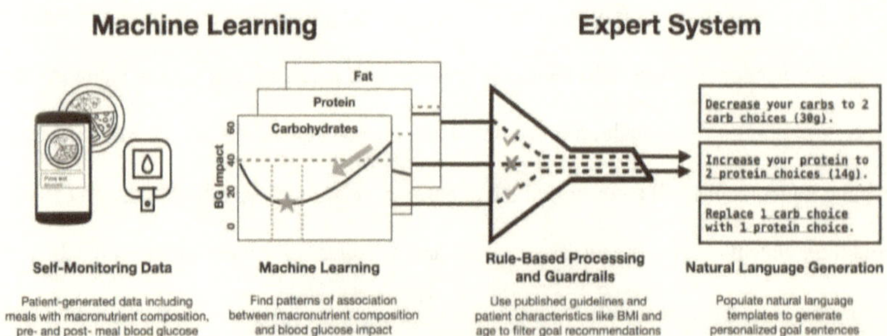

Figure 7. An overview of the pipeline for generating personalized goal recommendations in GlucoGoalie

3.1.1 Approach to goal setting

Our aim was to generate personalized recommendations for nutritional goals that can be actionable and easily understood by individuals with mixed levels of literacy. One of the key decisions in the design of GlucoGoalie was regarding the level of specificity in nutritional goals. We worked with a group of Certified Diabetes Care and Education Specialists (CDCES, n=3) to formulate goals that are consistent with the ones used in typical diabetes education and that focus on *changes to macronutrient composition of meals*. We made this choice for three main reasons. First, the macronutrient composition of a meal is directly related to its impact on BG, but the specifics of the relationship vary between individuals [81]. Second, nutrition education in diabetes emphasizes macronutrients to help individuals think flexibly about the nutritional composition of similar foods [265]. Third, using macronutrients as features has advantages for machine learning, offering a denser, low-dimensional feature representation compared to other representations like the specific food items in a meal. We worked with CDCES to create templates for goals that could be populated by an ML algorithm and identified three types of changes to meal composition that could impact post-meal BG: increase the amount of macronutrient, decrease the amount, or replace one macronutrient with another. Goals are meal-level because the balance of each meal has its own impact on BG, making day-level goals (e.g.,

daily calories) less appropriate. See Table 1 for a selection of goals.

Table 1. A selection of nutritional goals available in GlucoGoalie.

Generic goals are available for all users from when they first use the app. Personalized goals are recommended for an individual based on ML-based analysis of recorded meals and blood glucose readings. Underlined words are personalized for each user based on their data. Note: A food "choice" is a unit similar to a serving size that identifies servings of different foods with similar macronutrient compositions.

Type	Title	Description
Personalized	Decrease your carbs to 2½ carb choices	For high carb lunches, decrease your carbs to be about 2½ carb choices (38g). An example of 1 carb choice is 1 slice of whole wheat toast, ⅓ cup of plantains, or ⅓ cup of brown rice.
Personalized	Increase your protein to 3 protein choices	For low protein dinners, increase your protein to be about 3 lean protein choices (21g). An example of 1 lean protein choice is 1 ounce of lean ground beef, ½ cup of tofu, or 1 ounce of chicken breast.
Personalized	Replace 2 carb choices with 2 protein choices	For high carb dinners, replace 2 carb choices with 2 lean protein choices. For example, replace ⅔ cup of rice with 2 ounces of ground turkey or 2 ounces of tilapia.
Generic	Choose whole fruits	Choose whole fruits instead of fruit juices. For example, have a whole orange, an apple, or a cup of berries with your meals.
Generic	Choose plant proteins	Include proteins that come from plants, such as beans, nuts and seeds, and legumes. For example, choose a cup of beans, a handful of peanuts, or a cup of lentils to add protein to your meal.

3.1.2 Machine Learning

The high-level aim of the ML approach was to infer the relationship between an

individual's nutrition choices and changes in their BG levels after meals. The features in the ML

problem are the meals a user has logged, specifically the grams of carbohydrates, protein, and

fat. The outcome of interest—change in BG after a meal—is the difference between self-reported

BG before the meal, compared with 2 hours after, which is the clinical standard [13]. The ML

method to find patterns of association between nutrition and BG was based on Attributable

Components Analysis (ACA), a non-parametric method for estimating the conditional expectation of a quantity of interest based on a set of covariates [243]. Because self-monitoring data are manually entered by users, there are often a small number of data points that are prone to include errors and outliers. These characteristics pose challenges for ML, and, as I describe in more detail in the evaluation in Section 3.2, below, ACA has advantages over other methods like linear regression because it is able to capture non-linear relationships, is less sensitive to erroneous data points, and more effectively estimates uncertainty [179]. While ACA is a reasonable choice, any non-parametric regression could serve as the input for the expert system, described below.

3.1.3 Expert System interpretation and guardrails

While ML can identify patterns in the relationship between meals and BG, these patterns alone are not sufficient to inform behavior. In a series of 10 sessions, we worked with CDEs to establish rules for interpreting the ML output and translating it into goal recommendations. For example, GlucoGoalie suggests goals only if ML infers patterns with an expected increase in BG above a clinically significant threshold (40 mg/dl). In addition, CDEs pointed out that some automatically generated recommendations might be inappropriate irrespective of their impact on BG, for example a goal to eat 100g of fat in a single meal. To mitigate this concern, we added a set of guardrails to filter out extreme recommendations based on population-level nutrition guidelines.

In co-designing the goal templates with CDEs, we also sought to formulate goals such that they could be understood and acted upon by individuals, even those with low nutrition literacy. Because we could not assume nutrition knowledge, we embedded necessary information within the goals themselves. First, each goal includes three examples of concrete foods rich in a target macronutrient. Examples are drawn from a knowledge base created using an ADA resource [265]. To increase their relevance, examples were selected from meal logs captured by participants of a prior self-tracking study; these participants were recruited from a similar population and captured their regular meals for 2-5 weeks, thus creating a rich collection of meals. Second, we considered multiple approaches to describing target macronutrient amounts, including standard units like grams, heuristics like fists and thumbs, or even the proportions of a plate covered with different types of foods, an approach consistent with ChooseMyPlate [250]. However, we dismissed visualizing proportions on a plate due to their lack of precision (15g of rice could be gathered together in a ball or spread thinly over the entire plate). Instead, we opted for a the ADA-endorsed language of food "choices," a system meant to simplify nutrition education [265]. A food "choice" is a unit similar to a serving size; it identifies servings of different foods with similar macronutrient compositions. For example, 1 carbohydrate choice is 15 grams, which could be 1 slice of toast or ⅓ cup of rice. In addition, because "choices" are based on grams, the standard unit on food labels, each goal also includes the target amount in grams.

3.1.4   The GlucoGoalie App

To explore individuals' perceptions and experience receiving personalized goal suggestions in-the-wild, we included them in a custom smartphone application with logging and goal-setting functionality.

GlucoGoalie helps individuals set goals for improving their diet and work towards achieving these goals. Users begin by choosing one or more nutritional goals from a list in the app (see Table 1 for a selection of goals). To promote engagement with the application before users have tracked enough meals to receive personalized goal recommendations, all users choose from the same set of "generic" goals at the outset. Each generic goal describes a generally healthy behavior, and was developed by experts in nutrition and diabetes [61]. Twice per week, GlucoGoalie analyzes the data of each user with at least 8 meals to generate personalized nutrition goals, described above. If new goals are available, GlucoGoalie sends a push notification, and users can view the new, personalized recommendations and choose any they wish to follow (Figure 8d).

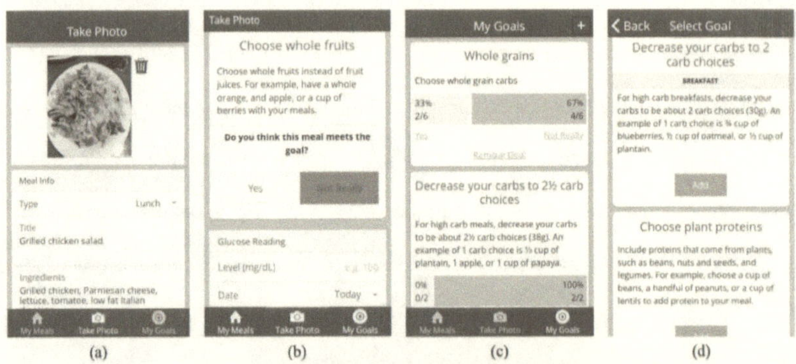

Figure 8. The GlucoGoalie mobile application.
(a) Logging a meal with a photo and free text description. (b) Users self-assess whether they met their chosen goals. (c) A summary of goal achievement. (d) Reviewing and choosing new personalized goals to work on after receiving a push notification.

Within the app, users can log their meals and enter their pre-meal BG. Two hours after the meal, GlucoGoalie sends a push notification reminder to enter a post-meal reading. To simplify the logging process, users log meals by taking a picture of the meal and typing a free text description (Figure 8a). Macronutrient data are entered by a team of Registered Dietitians (RDs) who assessed each meal following a standard protocol based on the USDA nutrition database [133], but similar results could be attained via crowdsourcing [194]. To keep goals as a central part of the experience and promote accountability, GlucoGoalie prompts users to assess whether their meal fits with each of their chosen goals while logging with either "Yes" or "Not

Really" (Figure 8b); "Not Really" was identified as a preferred and less judgmental option than "No" during user-centered design. Users can view their current goals, remove or choose new goals, and review a summary of goal attainment in the My Goals section of the app (Figure 8c).

Below, I describe a set of studies that evaluated different components of the GlucoGoalie system, including its ML engine, its expert system that generates nutritional goals, and the final GlucoGoalie app in a deployment study with individuals with T2D.

3.2   Study 1: Deriving insights from self-tracking data with attributable components

In the first study, I focused on evaluating the ML engine that drives GlucoGoalie. Because different individuals have different glycemic responses to different foods, there is a need for personalized approaches. Patient-generated data can help personalize support to each individual, but using patient-generated data for personalized analysis in the context of nutrition and BG poses challenges. BG measurements and meals need to be actively tracked by users, which requires effort. Fingers need to be pricked to record BG, and meal details need to be entered. Because of the burden of entry, these data points are incomplete and non-randomly missing [63]. In addition, glucometers can be miscalibrated, and users can mistype entries leading to both systematic bias and random errors. Glucose dynamics themselves are non-linear, oscillatory, noisy, and depend on individual characteristics [5,126]. Similar to the data quality concerns of electronic health records, the incompleteness, inaccuracy, complexity, and bias of patient-generated data create challenges for accurately representing a patient's state . Still, prior work has demonstrated that accurate inference can be possible with self-tracking data sets [5,6].

In addition to the challenges of the data, designing analysis for decision support tools brings its own substantial challenges. Algorithms need to be able to run as a part of an automated system, identifying complex relationships while being robust to outliers. In addition, it's important for the output to be interpretable. By interpretable, we mean that the relationships identified in the output of the model can be translated into useful and actionable support for decision-making. Notably, this definition diverges from "interpretable" as similar to "explainable" ML, which seeks to explain predictions achieved with deep learning and other black box models [107,118]. Interpretability is important because even the most accurate ML machinery is not useful if it cannot affect decision-making or be transformed into an understandable action. Quantifying uncertainty is an important part of interpretability, so that model output can be weighed appropriately in the decision-making process [43,44].

There is a need for methods that address these challenges. Optimal transport is a theory that offers tools to estimate and compare probability distributions [204,255]. In its original formulation, optimal transport sought to optimize the transportation of goods and resources, but has since been applied to many problems like computer vision and machine learning [204]. Optimal transport is particularly useful for data where values are highly individualized, as in medicine [4]. Blood pressure, for instance, may be related to many factors like age, exercise, diet, sex, prescribed drugs, and the device used to take the measurement. Here we adapt an optimal transport-based method invented by Tabak and Trigila [243] termed attributable components analysis (ACA). This method was created to explain variability in a quantity of interest based on a set of related or potentially confounding covariates, or "attributable components." Each component represents a contribution to the observed variability while simultaneously filtering out irrelevant effects to focus on a particular relationship.

In this section, I apply an adapted version of the ACA method to type 2 diabetes self-monitoring data, using ACA to estimate the mean glycemic impact of a meal—the difference between pre-meal and post-meal measurements—based on the meal's macronutrient composition. By estimating how each attributable component, in this case each macronutrient, contributes to the variability in BG after a meal, ACA can identify patterns of association between each macronutrient and expected BG impact. To better understand and convey how ACA performs for this task, we compare its output to linear regression.

3.2.1   Methods

Data Set

The data set used in this analysis originates from prior user studies of a smartphone application for diabetes self-monitoring very similar to the meal and BG logging functionality in the GlucoGoalie app, described above in Section 3.1.4. To log a meal, users captured a photograph of the meal, assigned a category of the meal (breakfast, lunch, dinner, or a snack) and entered a free-text description of the meal contents. Users entered pre-meal BG readings when logging the meal. Two hours after each meal, users received a notification to record and enter their post-meal BG reading. Later, each meal was evaluated by a registered dietitian (RD) who performed a nutrient assessment of the meal using a standard protocol and the USDA food composition database [3,252]. The RD recorded the carbohydrates, fat, protein, and fiber, in grams, as well as the total calories of the meal.

Data came from 40 users who used the smartphone application for 4 to 12 weeks in a separate IRB approved study. Each participant consented for their data to be re-used in future research. In this analysis, we included all participants with 30 or more total meals logged, and considered only the meals with both pre- and post- meal BG readings, for a total of 16 users.

The 16 users recorded a median of 67 meals over 4 to 12 weeks. As seen in Supplementary Figure A, most users logged close to the median number of meals, with a few users logging considerably more. As shown in Supplementary Figure B, users varied substantially in their BG levels before and after meals.

Two users, "A" and "B," were chosen for a detailed inspection of model performance because they were representative of the overall data set, but differed from each other in BG control and macronutrient consumption patterns. Users A and B logged a total of 58 and 88 meals over 4 and 12 weeks, respectively. See Supplementary Table A for a detailed breakdown by meal type. As seen in Supplementary Figure C, user A had less variability in BG impacts compared to B. Supplementary Figure D shows kernel density estimates of the macronutrient features for both users. Shown side by side, these densities show variability between and within each user. For example, user A ate 25 grams of carbohydrates at lunch most of the time, while user B had much more variability in their lunchtime carbohydrate intake. An important artifact and limitation is that nutrition evaluations only accommodated up to 100 grams of each macronutrient to be entered, yet user B regularly ate 100 grams or more of carbohydrates at dinner.

Feature Selection

We experimented with different representations of features to predict BG impact. We began with the three main macronutrients—carbohydrates, fat, and protein—represented as their weight in grams, or their proportion of each meal's calories. ACA performed slightly better when representing macronutrients as proportions than as grams, but we opted to use grams because we thought this would be more useful for decision support. In an effort to make decisions more straightforward, nutrition education in diabetes emphasizes the importance of macronutrients, and usually focuses on amounts of foods with units like grams, not their contribution to calories [265]. While some materials like the USDA's MyFoodPlate are based on the proportion of the plate filled with different foods, the proportion of calories is very different than the volume a food takes up on a plate. (Consider 1 stick of butter vs. 4 cups of raw spinach.) And finally, representing macronutrients as proportions means that the values sum to one, which introduces strong multicollinearity that creates challenges for inference with linear regression.

In addition, we also included fiber and pre-meal BG as features. We included fiber because increasing fiber is a common recommendation for individuals with diabetes [11]. We included pre-meal BG because of its relationship with post-meal BG. Glucose dynamics at their simplest consist of a glycemic response to nutrition. Because of this, to infer glycemic response to nutrition—to solve the equations uniquely—we need the initial state (pre-meal glucose), the kick (nutrition consumption), and the response (post-meal glucose).

A particular challenge of type 2 diabetes self-monitoring data is representing the impact of a particular meal on BG, or the glycemic impact. An optimal sampling rate for BG is on the order of minutes, not hours [37,100]. A single reading two hours after the meal is the clinical standard for postprandial measurement [13] but is not well suited to capture the fluctuations in BG after a meal. Even with appropriately sampled continuous glucose monitoring (CGM) data, it's not clear which features are most important to diabetes-related complications; the highest peak in blood glucose, the integral of the glycemic curve from the mean to sometime after the meal, the average value over time, or the speed of oscillations following a meal are different ways of representing BG impact, with different potential physiologic implications. While more frequent or continuous measurement would be preferred from a data standpoint, checking BG 6-10 times per day is recommended for those on insulin therapy, and there is no recommendation for those not on insulin [10]. Here, we follow the standard practice for postprandial BG measurement, and take the difference of post-meal BG minus pre-meal BG to represent the glycemic impact of a meal.

Attributable Components

Attributable component analysis (ACA; [243]) is a methodology for explaining the potentially nonlinear variability in a quantity of interest, x, in terms of covariates $z = (z_1, \dots, z_L)$. The method is highly motivated by theory and ideas from optimal transport [255]. In our application, x represents the glycemic impact, and z represents the macronutrient content of a meal. The covariates can be categorical (such as "meal," with values in "breakfast," "lunch," "dinner," real (such as "total amount of carbohydrates") or, in fact, of nearly any type. The output of attributable component analysis is $\bar{x}(z)$, the conditional expectation of x with respect to covariates z; this conditional mean is provided as a sum of components, which can be thought of as modes of variability. Each component is represented by the product of one-dimensional functions of each covariate z_l. A more detailed explanation of ACA is provided in [179], but a summary is provided here.

Given a set of m observations of the variable of interest x and L covariates, $\{\{z_l^{(i)}\}_{l=1}^L, x^{(i)}\}_{i=1}^m$, the ACA algorithm seeks to estimate the conditional mean $\bar{x}(z)$ with the following equation:

$$\bar{x}(z_1, \dots, z_L) = \sum_{k=1}^{d} \prod_{l \in L} \sum_{j} \alpha(l)^j (z_l) V(l)_j^k, \tag{1}$$

each k is a component of the variability in x, the V's are essentially basis functions that represent the variability, and can be represented by many classes of functions, e.g., as the sum of the product of sinusoidal functions in the case of Fourier decomposition (cf. Appendix (ACA; [243])), and $\alpha(l)_i^j = 1$ when $z_i^i = j$ and $\alpha(l)_i^j = 0$ otherwise.

The complete estimate of $\bar{x}$ based on all L features is useful, but being a probability distribution, is difficult to translate into useful recommendations because of the complexity dimensionality. To address this problem, we instead use the marginal dependence that translates $\bar{x}$ from an L-dimensional function into a one-dimensional function.

Interpretability through marginalization

We make the ACA output more interpretable for decision-making by "marginalizing" the ACA output function. To understand what this means, why this is necessary, and how this works, begin with the ACA estimated conditional mean that adopts the form in Equation 1 where the $V(l)_j^k$ are found by the algorithm, and the $\alpha(l)^j(z_l)$ are known via interpolation on grids or prototypal analysis. Even though this estimation allows us to make predictions for new values of z, its complexity makes it difficult to interpret. For example, if we limit the covariates to only binary forms, e.g., increases or decreases, then there are 2^L combinations of actions a person must interpret and choose among; this is too complex. Because the point of this intervention is to help people understand glycemic impacts of nutrition to make balanced choices that are sustainable behaviorally, we must translate ACA output into a simpler form, one where the impact of a single covariate is considered at a time, leading to only L different options. We can do this by asking simpler questions, such as: averaging over all other covariates, how does x depend on a specific z_l or small set thereof. Such questions ask us to marginalize the full estimated conditional mean and the separated form of the estimation makes it straightforward to perform this task. In order to find the marginal dependence of x on a group of covariates H denoted by $\{z_{h_t}\}_{t=1}^s$, with $h_t \in H$ and $s = |H|$, one has

$$\bar{x}(z_1, \ldots, z_L) = \sum_{k=1}^{d} \left[\frac{1}{m} \sum_{i=1}^{m} \prod_{h \notin H} \sum_j \alpha\,(h)_i^j V(h)_j^k \right] \prod_{h \in H} \sum_j \alpha\,(h)^j(z_h) V(h)_j^k. \qquad (2)$$

In this case, $\bar{x}(z_{h_1}, \ldots, z_{h_s})$ represents a function that captures the impact of a particular subset of features on x. For a single covariate of interest h, $\bar{x}(z_h)$ is a one-dimensional function that captures the impact that one covariate, for example fat, has on glycemic impact. In Figure 9, Figure 10, and Figure 11, where we compare the ACA to linear regression, the one-dimensional ACA output shown is $\bar{x}(z_h)$ as opposed to the full ACA model $\bar{x}(z_1, \ldots, z_L)$.

Other regression methods and ACA

There are other methods that can be used for similar tasks. ACA is a non-parametric density estimation method, and its task of explaining variability based on a set of covariates is similar to regression with clustering or principal components analysis (PCA). Importantly, ACA's output is more interpretable than these alternatives. If the goal is to identify patterns between an individual's nutrition and their glycemic control or to make recommendations to change diet, then it's important that the output can be translated for human understanding. With ACA, each attributable component is a covariate, meaning the relationships identified are in the same dimensions as the input data. PCA finds the uncorrelated components that explain the most variability in the dependent variable [129], but what exactly each component means could be difficult to explain in a clinical situation. Similarly, clusters can be difficult to convey to clinicians without extensive training, and require interpretation [86]. It's important that the model output aligns with cognitive models [200]; a complex, black box method with strong performance metrics is only useful if it can be translated into something clinically meaningful.

As ACA is operationalized here, its output is also similar to other regression methods like least-squares or support vector machine (SVM) regression. However, it's notable that the method by which ACA estimates this regression is by approximating a joint distribution and marginalizing over the features, which is different than how other methods fit the data.

In choosing a comparison method, we aim to identify and highlight qualitative and quantitative differences between ACA and another regression approach. We do not aim to argue for the hypothesis that ACA is the *best* method for this data and task, and an intrinsic evaluation of ACA has been reported elsewhere and is outside the scope of this work. As a baseline, therefore, we compare ACA against multiple linear regression [171]. While there are many potential choices for a regression comparator, including various non-linear variants, linear regression is a highly used model and is a reasonable choice for our data because its limited complexity means it has the potential to perform well on small, n-of-1 data sets in our experiments.

Comparator: Linear Regression

As a comparison method, we fit the data with multiple linear regression

$$\bar{x}(z_1,\ldots,z_L) = \beta_0 + \beta_1 z_1 + \beta_2 z_2 + \ldots + \beta_L z_L$$

where x is the quantity of interest and $z_1,\ldots,z_L$ are covariates and β_0 is the intercept term. More compactly

$$\bar{x}(z_1,\ldots,z_L) = \beta_0 + \sum_{l=1}^{L} \beta_l z_l$$

We then find the best fit using the ordinary least squares method [171].

As with ACA, to improve the interpretability of the output, we fit the model with all covariates, z, but marginalize to consider a specific z_l (or small subset) by averaging over the other covariates. To compute the marginal dependence of x on a group of covariates H denoted by $\{z_{h_t}\}_{t=1}^{s}$, with $h_t \in H$ and $s = |H|$, one has

$$\bar{x}(z_{h_1}, \dots, z_{h_s}) = \beta_0 + \sum_{h \notin H} \beta_h \left[\frac{1}{m} \sum_{i=1}^{m} z_h^{(i)}\right] + \sum_{h \in H} \beta_h\, z_h \tag{3}$$

The outcome of the marginalization calculation in Equation 2 and the linear regression in Equation 2 is a one-dimensional graph, e.g., Figure 9 where the macronutrient is given on the x-axis as the independent variable or covariate and the y-axis is the glycemic impact.

Uncertainty Estimates

We used several bootstrapping algorithms to estimate uncertainty of the regressions. Specifically, we used bootstrap to estimate distributions of regression coefficients, allowing us to quantify the variability of the estimate. Given this distribution we can calculate quantities that characterize the uncertainty; here we focus on confidence intervals over the range of input values. Often, bootstrapping is accomplished by drawing multiple samples with replacement from the data set and computing the estimate for that resampled data [69]. Empirical confidence intervals can be calculated from the distribution of estimates. In addition, ACA is stochastic, with a random initial state, so we can estimate the variability through repeated calculations with the same subset but different starting states. We experimented with both methods for bootstrapping ACA, and the results were nearly identical. We opted for the typical approach of bootstrapping via multiple subsamples so that we could apply the same bootstrapping procedure for both methods, because linear regression is not stochastic.

A second question is the size of the bootstrap samples. A common approach is for each bootstrap sample to have the same number of data points as the original data set. Because data sets for some of the users were quite small, there were advantages to using larger bootstrap samples. For example, bootstrap samples may have very few unique data points. This negatively impacts the performance of the model, and poses challenges for aggregating variance estimates across the complete range of feature values. Larger bootstrap samples can improve model performance, and help ensure that estimates cover the full range of independent variable values; of course, bootstrap ensembles cannot represent the tails of distributions that are not observed in the data, and can underestimate variance. We experimented with the original size of the dataset, 100, and 500 data points, and found that a bootstrap sample size of 500 performed well for both ACA and regression.

A third question is how many bootstrap iterations to run. 100 iterations has been suggested as a minimum for variance estimations, but it depends on the situation (Davison and Hinkley 1997). We inspected the change in variance across all iterations after each subsequent bootstrap iteration to look for convergence. We experimented with up to 200 iterations and found that 100 iterations were sufficient for variance to converge.

All analysis was performed in MATLAB 2016b (9.1). Additional plots and descriptive statistics were produced in R v3.3.2 with tidyverse v1.1.1.

Experimental Design

We estimated ACA and linear regression on the data sets for each user, as well as data subsets by meal type (breakfast, lunch, and dinner). To estimate confidence intervals, we performed a bootstrap with 100 iterations, based on the procedure described above. Each bootstrap sample had 500 data points, and the same samples were used to fit ACA and linear regression. 95% confidence intervals were determined empirically from the aggregated bootstrap output.

We then produced a series of plots for each user and closely inspected the plots for the two users introduced in the data set description. Each plot included an individual covariate (z_l) on the horizontal axis, with BG impact x on the vertical axis, the actual data points, and average fit of ACA and linear regression with confidence intervals. With each of the 5 features for the overall data sets and the 3 meal-type subsets across two users, there were a total of 40 plots. See Figure 9 in the Results for an example.

Evaluation

To compare the performance of the two models we calculated the root mean squared error (RMSE) of the data fit for both ACA and linear regression.

RMSE for the overall model:

$$\sqrt{\frac{1}{m}\sum_{i=1}^{m}\left|\bar{x}\left(z_1^{(i)},\dots,z_L^{(i)}\right)-x^{(i)}\right|^2}$$

RMSE for the marginals:

$$\sqrt{\frac{1}{m}\frac{1}{L}\sum_{l=1}^{L}\sum_{i=1}^{m}\left|\bar{x}\left(z_l^{(i)}\right)-x^{(i)}\right|^2}$$

In addition, we qualitatively inspected the plots for evidence of non-linear relationships, and examined the situations where the two models agreed and disagreed. To quantify non-linear relationships, we heuristically evaluated the plots to tally the number of data sets where the average fit line of ACA had more than a 10-degree bend.

To quantify differences in the uncertainty calculations between the two methods, and to assess the coherence and usefulness of the confidence intervals, we calculated the percentage of data points falling within the confidence interval across all data sets.

3.2.2 Results

As shown in Table 2, the RMSE for the full ACA model was significantly lower — by a

factor of ∼ 7 — than for linear regression with a standard deviation similarly lower by a factor

of ∼ 3.

**Table 2. Root mean squared error (RMSE) for ACA and linear regression,
for the full model with all covariates.**

ACA	Linear regression
4.36 ± 3.40	29.15 ± 10.02

However, as shown in Table 3, examining the marginal output that considers one feature

at a time, linear regression outperforms ACA in RMSE by 2 to 7 mg/dl for breakfast, lunch, and

dinner meals, while ACA slightly outperforms linear regression for analysis when all meals are

pooled together. The explanation: ACA, being a complex nonlinear regression, is more data-

hungry than linear regression, and because it underperforms linear regression for a single meal

but outperforms for three meals, it needs at most three times the data to have a lower RMSE than

linear regression.

**Table 3. Root mean squared error (RMSE) for ACA and linear regression, for the
marginal model considering one covariate at a time.**

Meal type	ACA	Linear regression
breakfast	28.81 ± 16.2	26.27 ± 14.3
lunch	35.06 ± 18.0	32.62 ± 16.0
dinner	40.21 ± 26.1	33.60 ± 20.3
overall	37.21 ± 21.3	37.44 ± 21.4

The difference between ACA and the marginalized ACA — that ACA itself produces

very accurate representations of the data while the marginalization is substantially less accurate

— has important implications. First, this difference shows that there is substantial correlation

between the covariates; this is not surprising because individual meals are combinations of food items, which in turn have combinations of macronutrients, suggesting that the macronutrients in a meal are not independent of each other. Second, it is clear that because of the systematic relationships between covariates, there is predictive information that we are not using to help people make decisions. The problem of course, is that the full portrait of how these covariates influence glycemic impact is a complex mathematical object. And to be useful in practice there is an imposed tradeoff that is not about algorithmic accuracy, but about human factors: we need the algorithm to be accurate but we must balance accuracy against the ability to use the output of the algorithm to make decisions. And this leads us to the third implication of the difference between the ACA and its marginalized form: we must find a way to exploit this yet-unused predictive information in a way that also allows for useful decision-making.

Non-linear relationships

In some situations, ACA did identify non-linear relationships between macronutrients and BG impact, as shown in Figure 9. Because of the regularization built into ACA, most of the identified trends were linear, but some were non-linear. Non-linear relationships may be expected in some situations because of the complexity of BG dynamics. Linear regression, of course, would by definition never be able to find a non-linear relationship.

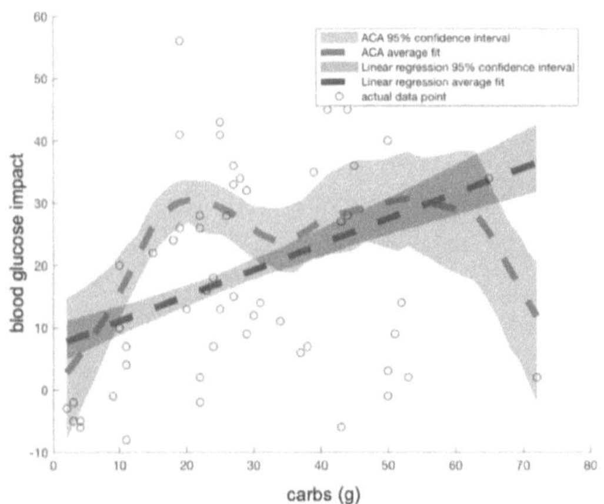

Figure 9. Comparison of ACA and linear regression for user A and the relationship between carbohydrates and BG impact, across all meals.
In this case, ACA identifies a non-linear relationship, while linear regression does not.

Outliers and errors

When inspecting the plots, we found that some data sets had outliers that were clearly

errors. For example, User A's data had two meals recorded with 50 grams of fiber. These data

points are clearly errors not only because they are visibly separated from the rest of the data, but

also because 50 grams was the default value for nutrient assessments by RDs, and 50 grams of

fiber is an infeasible amount to eat in one sitting. The recommended amount of fiber is 38 grams

per day for men, and 95% of adults don't manage to eat the recommended amount of fiber; 50

grams of fiber would be over 3 cups of lentils. As shown in Figure 10, linear regression is unable

to ignore the outliers, and continues the downward trend beyond what is reasonable. ACA, on the

other hand, also finds a slight downward trend in the non-outlier data, but evens out to be flat—

showing no relationship—over the sparsely populated region before the outliers. The ACA is a

more robust estimator (Huber 2011) than linear regression.

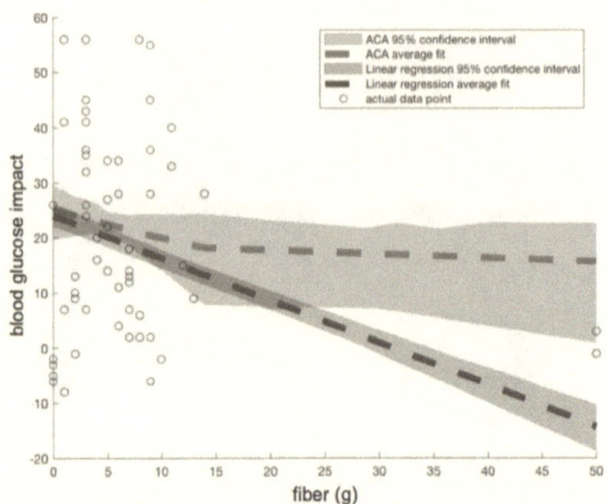

Figure 10. Comparison of ACA and linear regression for user A, and the relationship between fiber and BG impact, across all meals.
ACA shows no trend leading out to the outlier data points with 50 grams of fiber, while linear regression continues a downward trend beyond what is reasonable.

Uncertainty estimates

One of the most drastic differences between ACA and linear regression was in the size and variability of the confidence intervals. Confidence intervals for ACA were broad, and varied in their width across data sets. In some instances, ACA would have a relatively narrow confidence interval, suggesting a higher degree of certainty in the identified trend. In other situations, though, ACA has broad confidence intervals, encapsulating most of the data sets, suggesting a low degree of confidence in the identified trend. On the other hand, the less flexible linear regression typically had narrow confidence intervals, regardless of the plausibility of the trend identified. See Figure 11 for a comparison of uncertainty between two data subsets for the same user.

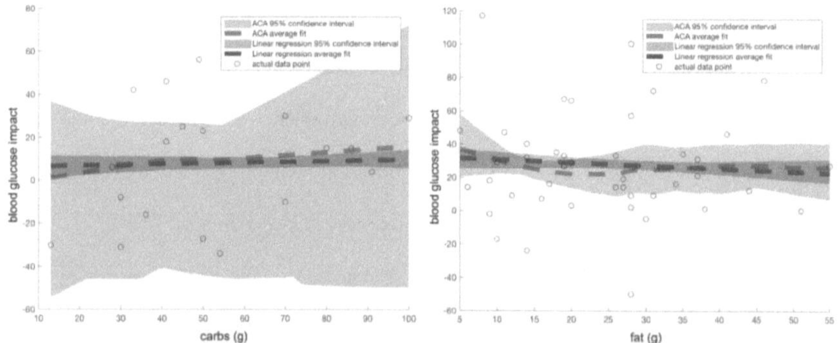

Figure 11. Comparison of ACA and linear regression for user B.
On the left is the relationship between carbohydrates and BG impact for lunch meals. On the right is the relationship between fat and BG impact at dinner for the same user. On the left, ACA has wide confidence intervals, indicating uncertainty about the true relationship, while confidence intervals are narrower on the right. In contrast, linear regression has narrow confidence intervals in both figures.

In general, the confidence intervals were much wider and more expressive with ACA. As shown in Table 4, more of the actual data points—by factors ranging from 2 to 16 with an average of 6—fell within the confidence intervals for ACA than with linear regression.

Table 4. Percent of data points within the 95% confidence interval for attributable components analysis (ACA) and linear regression.

	N	ACA	Linear Regression
User A			
Breakfast	13	84.62%	10.77%
Lunch	10	28.00%	2.00%
Dinner	23	58.26%	7.83%
All meals	58	15.17%	7.59%
User B			
Breakfast	16	96.25%	6.25%
Lunch	19	52.63%	8.42%
Dinner	44	32.27%	11.36%
All meals	88	22.05%	12.05%
All Users (Mean ± SD)			
Breakfast	23 ± 16	62% ± 21%	11% ± 8%
Lunch	21 ± 14	47% ± 21%	8% ± 6%
Dinner	24 ± 15	47% ± 22%	10% ± 7%
All meals	82 ± 63	25% ± 12%	12% ± 7%

3.2.3 Discussion

In this study, we explored the use of a method based on optimal transport theory to analyze patient-generated data. As compared to linear regression, we found that attributable components analysis (ACA) was able to identify non-linear relationships, was more robust to outliers, and offered more representative and accurate uncertainty estimates. These characteristics make ACA a good candidate to be used in the wild for decision support systems, for example smartphone applications like GlucoGoalie that delivers personalized nutritional recommendations directly to patients. In addition, the model output could be used in a tool to help clinicians deliver personalized coaching to patients with T2D, or to automatically generate meal plans.

Unlike post hoc data analysis, when datasets can be cleaned, curated, and processed, algorithms used in decision support systems need to run automatically without direct oversight using data with all their imperfections. Given the constraints of real self-monitoring data, the marginalized ACA performed well. But it is important to understand the modeling workflow we develop here, and its advantages and evaluation. We compared a simple regression, linear regression, to a complex nonlinear regression that was then simplified after the fact. It seems that, given enough data, it is more productive to begin with a model capable of representing the structures in the data and have the features *necessary for useful decision-making*, and then simplifying the model output as is required for practical decision support. Non-linear regressions are not always required or useful, and often a linear or logistic regression—as a sophisticated use of a simple tool—will be a better choice due to the needs of the application, e.g., [151]. Here we had substantial gains from basing the analysis in a more flexible tool, but also saw some drawbacks, all of which are noted below.

Nonlinear relationships in data and decision support

The ACA was able to identify non-linear relationships, which is important because of the complexity of BG dynamics and other systems in health. Importantly, ACA is also regularized to prevent overfitting, and the majority of relationships identified were linear. As discussed in the methods section (Section 3.2.1), one approach to make regression output useful for decision support is to use a clinically meaningful threshold for BG impact to identify ranges of values to expect higher or lower BG impacts. Because ACA is non-linear, it can identify multiple ranges, but with linear regression, this approach would only identify 1 high and 1 low impact range. Distinct ranges may be more clinically meaningful.

Robust estimation

ACA was more robust to outliers and erroneous data points than linear regression. Data accuracy is a central concern in assessing the quality of electronic health data [121,262], especially for patient-generated health data, when patients are directly entering data points [59]. While rule-based or statistical methods can be used to detect and remove outliers, analytic approaches that are robust to outliers, like ACA, are still advantageous.

Uncertainty quantification

ACA offered broader and more representative and accurate uncertainty estimates than linear regression. It's important to represent and consider the confidence of the model for a given patient's data set. Uncertainty is intrinsic to the practice of medicine. If a model is going to be used for clinical decision support, representing the uncertainty can help clinicians appropriately weight the information against everything else they know about the patient [43,44]. For patient-facing applications, the certainty can help prioritize what is and is not shared with users.

Reducing model flexibility for interpretability and decision-making

Linear regression is rather interpretable, especially in one dimension. A nonlinear regression like ACA, which models a distribution function that estimates glycemic response, is far less interpretable in its raw form; it often requires mathematical sophistication to interpret and is difficult to visualize due to the high-dimensional nature of the model. While the full ACA model with all covariates outperformed linear regression, the quality of the fit dropped substantially when considering one covariate at a time in the marginal model given the data constraints. We focused on the marginal relationship between each covariate and glycemic impact because interpretability and actionability for decision support was a key objective: simultaneously making changes to multiple macronutrients is challenging for individuals to implement because of the cognitive burden and because behavior change is often grounded on incremental, achievable adjustments.

The poorer performance of the marginal model points to a tradeoff between accuracy and interpretability in machine learning tasks [128]. In this context, there is substantial information shared between covariates that is lost through marginalization. While the full model may be too complex for tractable interpretation, future work could explore marginalizing out fewer covariates, to examine the relationship between two covariates H in relation to the quantity of interest $\bar{x}$, as opposed to a single covariate, as presented here. Three-dimensional surfaces can still be visualized and interpreted without adding unnecessary complexity, suggesting that this is a feasible direction for future work. In addition, such an approach could be employed alongside univariate marginalization when pre-hoc analysis suggests that two covariates share a great deal of information. At the same time, there is a need for richer and more detailed model outputs in clinical characterization [122], and future work could also explore ways to improve the interpretability of the full model with all covariates for use for decision support while still aligning with what clinician and patients need from a human factors standpoint.

3.3 Study 2: Assessing the understandability and actionability of personalized goals

In the second evaluation study, I move from examining the machine learning inferences underlying GlucoGoalie towards evaluating the output of the expert system: personalized nutrition goals. In particular, this controlled lab experiment examined whether the style of personalized goals generated by the system would be *understandable* and *actionable* for individuals living with T2D, with the following research question:

> *Research Question 1.1:* Would individuals with type 2 diabetes from medically underserved, low income communities be able to understand and act on computationally generated nutrition goals in a controlled setting?

3.3.1 Methods

Participants and procedure

Participants were recruited from two types of health centers in New York City: 1) a Federally Qualified Health Center (FQHC) in Brownsville Brooklyn, and 2) clinics affiliated with Columbia University Irving Medical Center. To be included, participants needed to be between 18- and 65-years-old with a self-reported diagnosis of type 2 diabetes (T2D) and proficient in English. After collecting consent, participants received a 10-minute, in-person nutrition training introducing the concept of food "choices" and reviewing macronutrients. Participants then completed the following three tasks:

Task 1: Goal Comprehension

To assess whether participants understood the content of the goals output by GlucoGoalie, participants were presented with an example goal "for a friend with diabetes," and asked to choose which of two meals were a better fit with the goal. Meals were presented as a free text description with a nutrition label in the style of Facts Up Front [276] (see Supplementary Figure E); nutritional labels were included to ensure that this task was testing *comprehension of goals*, rather than individuals' ability to assess nutritional composition of meals. This task was repeated twice.

Task 2: Goal/Image Matching

Because many meals are cooked at home, we included a second task to test comprehension of goal sentences using example meals *without* nutritional labels. Participants were again asked to choose which of two meals was a better fit with a presented, example goal, but could see only the meal image and description, with no macronutrient information (see Supplementary Figure F). Meal images were selected from a data set collected in ongoing research with individuals from a similar population. Meal pairs were chosen to include similar ingredients but vary in macronutrient content; the incorrect answer was at least 1 macronutrient "choice" different from the correct answer, and the difficulty varied across scenarios. To account for higher variability in meal images, this task was repeated for eight goal/meal-pair combinations.

Task 3. Meal Choice: The Virtual Buffet

To assess whether goals were actionable and participants could follow them, we simulated the process of choosing meals with a "virtual buffet" made up of food image cutouts (see Supplementary Figure G). Participants then received a tailored goal and were asked to choose additional meals with that goal in mind. Working 1-on-1, researchers asked participants to use the food cutouts to assemble a baseline meal for each type of meal (breakfast, lunch, and dinner) that was "closest to what you would normally eat." Importantly, there were multiple copies of each food item so participants could vary the amount of each food. Images were labeled with an amount in cups, tablespoons, or ounces, but never choices or grams (the units included in the goals themselves). We used images from a web-based resource [190] and our ongoing research and sought to include common staples like bacon and eggs as well as culturally relevant foods like fried plantains.

The baseline meals were used to identify goals that would require participants to vary from their typical macronutrient behavior by 1 to 1.5 macronutrient choices. For example, if a participant's baseline meal had 3.5 carb choices and 1 protein choice, they would receive two goals: one to decrease carbs to 2 choices and another to increase protein to 2 choices. Participants chose one of the two goals, and then assembled "breakfast," "lunch," and "dinner" for three days in a row, with the chosen goal in mind (9 total meals). Researchers tallied the chosen food items to calculate nutrient compositions. During the 1-on-1 activity, researchers made note of participant comments and feedback, for example, questions about missing or inappropriate food items.

Data Analysis

For the goal comprehension and goal/image matching tasks, we calculated binary accuracy as a percentage (#correct / [#correct + #incorrect]). For the "virtual buffet" experiment, we analyzed the data in two dimensions: direction and accuracy. First, we examined whether participants' meals were consistent with the *direction* of their chosen goal. For example, if the goal was to increase protein to 2 choices at lunch, we assessed whether subsequent lunches had more protein than baseline. A binomial test was used to determine whether performance was better than chance. Second, accuracy in meeting the goal target was measured with mean absolute error between participant choices and the goal target. For example, if the target was 2 choices, we assessed how close participant's meals were to the target, on average.

To synthesize participant's impressions from their unsolicited comments during the study, the research team met to debrief and aggregate notes in a series of meetings to inductively summarize key themes [36]. I collected and aggregated the handwritten notes taken during the study and created an initial coding scheme, which was discussed and refined with the full research team.

3.3.2 Results

Participants

We recruited and enrolled a total of 19 participants, including 10 from a Federally Qualified Health Center, and 9 from university-affiliated clinics. Four participants were excluded because of a data collection error for a total of 15 participants included in the analysis. As seen in Table 5, participants were predominantly female, and Black or Hispanic. Most were overweight or obese (body mass index $\geq$ 25).

Results

For the goal comprehension task, when choosing which of the two nutrition labels met a given goal participants were correct 89% (SD = 21%) of the time. When choosing which of two meal images was a better match with a goal, participants chose the correct meal 49% (SD = 25%) of the time. When composing meals at the virtual buffet, meals were consistent with the direction of chosen goals 67% (68 of 102) of the time, significantly more than chance per a binomial test ($p < 0.001$). There was no difference in the percentage of meals consistent with the direction of chosen goals by meal type, macronutrient, or direction of goal. At the same time, there was a high degree of variability in precisely meeting the goal target. Meals were an average of 0.83 (SD = 0.56) "choices" away from the goal target. For example, given the goal "reduce carbs to 2 choices (30g)," participants were an average of ⅘ carb choices (12g), from the target.

Table 5. Participant demographics for evaluation study 2

Demographics	Value
N Enrolled (Incl. in Analysis)	19 (15)
Sex	80% Female
Ethnicity	47% Hispanic
Race	17% White 42% Black 41% Other/Refused
Age	54 ± 9 years
Body Mass Index (BMI)	37.4 ± 13.9
Median Household Income	$20,000-$39,999
Median Education Level	Some College

We identified two key themes in the spontaneous comments made by participants during and after the virtual buffet activity. First, most participants commented on the limited selection of food items to choose from. Many recounted what they would normally eat, which was sometimes missing, for example oatmeal at breakfast. Usually, participants were able to select items they do eat from the available choices. Second, when choosing which goal to follow, participants often stated that they understood the goals. However, use of "choices" as a unit led to confusion, and some participants expressed uncertainty about how much food to take. Participants interpreted "2 choices" to mean two different food items, regardless of the amount (e.g., rice and bread) as opposed to a measurable quantity (e.g., ⅔ cup of rice), as intended.

3.3.3 Discussion

In this evaluation experiment, we found participants were largely able to understand and act on computationally derived goals in a controlled setting. Participants correctly chose meals that met a goal 89% of the time when these meals were accompanied by corresponding nutritional labels. When composing meals to meet a chosen goal at a "virtual buffet," participants assembled meals in the correct direction of the goal 67% of the time. This suggests that individuals were able to understand the personalized goals, and were moderately successful when composing meals to meet goals. At the same time, additional findings highlight the complexity of nutrition decisions. When choosing which of two meal images met a given goal without nutrition labels, participants were correct only 49% of the time. This aligns with prior research suggesting that individuals have difficulty comparing macronutrient quantities from photographs alone [40]. In addition, participant comments during the study indicated confusion about some of the nutrition terminology in goals, and there was considerable variability in meeting the exact goal target. This suggests that participants formed a general idea of how to achieve goals, but had difficulty precisely implementing the recommendations. These preliminary qualitative findings are built on with the analysis of a deployment study with GlucoGoalie, described in the next section.

3.4 Study 3: Quantitative and qualitative findings from GlucoGoalie in-the-wild

After evaluating the components of GlucoGoalie in a controlled setting, we sought to examine the feasibility of the approach and the GlucoGoalie smartphone application with a 4-week deployment study [34]. In particular, we sought to understand to what extent individuals with type 2 diabetes from communities that have been historically underserved by the medical establishment, particularly racial and ethnic minorities including black, brown, and indigenous people of color, as well as those from low income and low wealth communities would engage with the self-tracking and goal setting features of the app, as well as examine whether using the application had a positive impact on self-management behaviors. In addition, we sought to more fully understand participants' experience receiving and following personalized goal recommendations based on their own self-tracking data, and conducted a qualitative thematic analysis of interviews with a subset of the participants who completed the 4-week deployment study.

> *Research Question 1.2*: What is the experience of receiving and following recommendations for nutrition goals based on one's own self-tracking data in a smartphone app?

> *Research Question 1.3*: Will individuals with type 2 diabetes report a higher frequency of self-management behaviors after using the GlucoGoalie over 4 weeks?

> *Research Question 1.4*: For individuals who receive personalized goal recommendations, will they change their meal choices — specifically their macronutrient consumption — to more closely align with those goals?

3.4.1 Methods

Participants

Participants were recruited from two health centers in the New York City metro area: 1) a Federally Qualified Health Center (FQHC) in Brownsville Brooklyn, and 2) clinics affiliated with Columbia University Irving Medical Center. To be included, participants needed to be between 18- and 65-years-old with a self-reported diagnosis of type 2 diabetes (T2D) and proficient in English.

After collecting consent, participants completed a series of baseline survey measures and demographics. Participants' self-management practices were measured with the Summary of Diabetes Self-Care Activities (SDSCA; [247]), a 12-item measure with subscales examining the frequencies of diet, exercise, and blood sugar testing activities in the prior 7 days. During the training visit, participants received a 10-minute, in-person nutrition training introducing the concept of food "choices" and reviewing macronutrients, as a primer for the goal recommendations they might receive during the study period.

An investigator introduced participants to the GlucoGoalie application, helped them set an initial goal of their choice, and practiced recording a meal and blood sugar reading. We then asked each participant to use the app on their own at home to record meals and blood sugar readings (before and two-hours after each meal) over one month.

During training, we told participants that GlucoGoalie would recommend goals based on their own records, that these goals were made by a computer, not a human expert, and that available goals would change over time.

Each meal entered by participants was evaluated for its macronutrient composition and whether it was consistent with the user's nutrition goals by a Registered Dietitian (RD) from a pool of RDs following a standard protocol and the USDA food composition database [252].

When new personalized goals became available, the app sent a push notification. In addition, the study coordinator also contacted participants if they had not selected a new goal within 3 days of receiving the push notification to make sure there were no technical difficulties.

After the 4-week period, participants completed the SDSCA again as a post-measure, and were invited to participate in 1-hour semi-structured interviews.

To minimize barriers to participation, individuals without a smartphone received an Android phone and could keep it after completing the study (participants who had their own smartphones received its monetary equivalent, $150). All participants received $20 for each visit and a package of 50 blood glucose testing strips.

Data analysis

Quantitative analysis

We downloaded usage log data from the application server and calculated descriptive usage statistics including the numbers of meals logged, goals selected, and goals used.

To examine changes in self-reported self-management behaviors, we compared the difference in pre- and post-study scores for each of the subscales of the SDSCA. Given the small sample size of this feasibility study, we primarily estimate effect sizes and trends. We compared the difference in means to estimate effect sizes and a pair samples t-test to assess the strength of these trends.

To explore the extent to which users achieved the nutrition goals they had chosen in the app, we compared user-entered and RD-entered assessments of whether each meal was consistent with the user's chosen nutrition goals. We also viewed goal achievement across all participants as a time series, to see if goal achievement improved over the study time period. To account for participants with different numbers of goals, goal achievement was averaged within each participant, and we compared mean goal achievement between participants.

Time-series data were examined in two ways. First, was the straightforward way of considering the chronological time since the start of the study. Second, we also examined the time series as a sequence of meals records since first selecting a particular goal.

To examine whether adopting a personalized nutrition goal from GlucoGoalie may have impacted participants' behaviors, we examined the changes in the macronutrient composition of meals *before* and *after* selecting a particular personalized goal. Each goal suggestion referenced a specific macronutrient and included a *direction of change* from baseline as well as a *target amount*. We compared macronutrient consumption to see if it was consistent with the direction of change from the goal, and also examined whether users ate meals that were closer to the macronutrient target with the goal compared to baseline.

Qualitative analysis

Debrief interviews were audio recorded and transcribed verbatim. We analyzed interview transcripts and usage logs with inductive thematic analysis [36]. The lead author coded 2 transcripts (25%) collaboratively with a second author to create an initial codebook. Then the first and senior author independently coded an additional 2 transcripts (25%), and met in person to discuss coding schemes and resolve all discrepancies through discussion. The remaining interviews were coded independently by the first author with periodic discussion with the research team, followed by an affinity mapping session to group codes into primary themes and subthemes. Participant meal logs, usage, and goal attainment were considered throughout the coding process to contextualize user statements. After coding was complete, we examined data saturation and theme comprehensiveness across participants [95,104].

3.4.2 Quantitative Results

Participants

As shown in Table 6, the demographic breakdown was comparable with participants in the controlled evaluation (Study 2; Table 5). Participants were majority female, and Hispanic, and only 20% white, with an average body mass index (BMI) considered obese.

Table 6. Participant demographics for study 3

Demographics	Deployment Study Participants	Interviewed Subset
N	20	8
Sex	85% Female	71% Female
Ethnicity	60% Hispanic	86% Hispanic
Race	35% Black 20% White 45% Other/Not Reported	43% White 29% Black 29% Other/Refused
Age	52.90 ± 9.48 years	55.7 ± 9.5 years
Body Mass Index (BMI)	32.99 ± 6.86	41.8 ± 14.4

Self-management behaviors

To address the hypothesis that self-reported self-management behaviors would increase from before the study to after, we compared the SDSCA measure and found a statistically significant improvement in diet and blood glucose (BG) related subscales, but not exercise, food care, medication, or smoking (Table 7).

Table 7. Comparison of pre- and post-measurement for the Summary of Diabetes Self-Care Behaviors (SDSCA). Higher scores indicate a larger number of the last 7 days where self-reported care behaviors were completed.

SDSCA Subscale	Pre-Measure	Post-Measure	Difference
General diet	**3.58 ± 1.47**	**5.06 ± 1.62**	**1.48****
Specific diet	3.79 ± 1.77	4.41 ± 1.32	0.62
Combined diet	**3.68 ± 1.29**	**4.73 ± 1.23**	**1.05*****
Total exercise	2.94 ± 1.7	3.16 ± 1.9	0.21
BG testing	**4.06 ± 2.54**	**5.38 ± 2.39**	**1.32***
Foot care	5.44 ± 2.65	5.13 ± 2.83	-0.32
Smoking	0.39 ± 1.31	0.13 ± 0.5	-0.26
Medication	6.00 ± 2.35	6.56 ± 1.75	0.56

$*p < 0.05, **p < 0.01, ***p < 0.001$

Engagement

To characterize the extent to which participants engaged with the GlucoGoalie application during the 4-week study, we calculated descriptive usage statistics, presented in Table 8. Participants recorded a median of approximately one meal and 1.5 BG readings per day, though this varied significantly across participants, with one consistently recording more than 5 meals per day during the study period. Participants selected a median of 3 different nutrition goals in the app.

Table 8. Engagement statistics during the 4-week study period

Usage Statistic	Value
# Meals recorded	Median: 28 (Range: 0 to 158; IQR 13 to 51.75)
# Blood glucose readings	Median 43.5 (Range 0 to 314; IQR 19 to 77.25)
# Goals used	Median 3 (Range 0 to 9; IQR 1 to 4.25)
% who received a personalized goal suggestion	40% (8 of 20)
% who selected a personalized goal	75% (6 of 8)
# Personalized goals used (among those who received one)	Median 1.5 (Range 0 to 5; IQR 0.75 to 4)

12 of 20 participants did not receive personalized goals during the study period, for a handful of reasons, which are summarized in Table 9.

Table 9. Summary of reasons that participants did not receive personalized recommendations from GlucoGoalie during the study period

Reason for not receiving personalized goals	Count
Fewer than 8 meals recorded with pre- and post- meal blood glucose readings	7
Technical issue with macronutrient assessments	4
Blood glucose well controlled	1

Overall Goal Achievement

Examining participants' goal achievement over the study period (Figure 12), we found that mean goal achievement increased, as assessed by both the RD annotators and participants themselves. However, there was a substantial gap between user and expert assessments, suggesting that participants were consistently more confident that they were achieving a nutrition goal than the expert assessment.

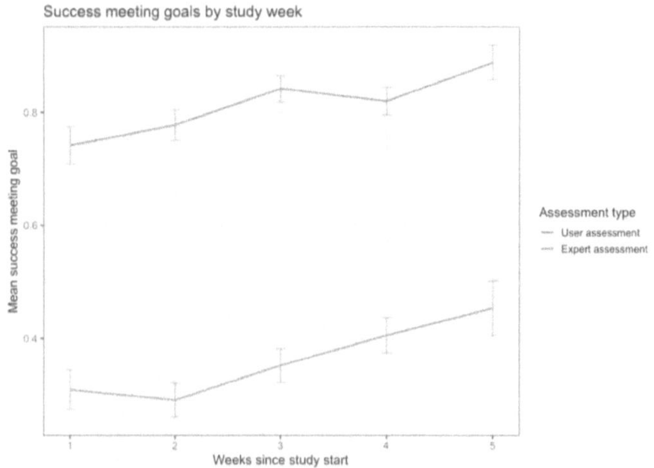

Figure 12. Success meeting nutrition goals by study week

Personalized Goal Achievement

When examining the achievement of personalized goals specifically, we found that participants improved in expert assessment of their goal achievement as they recorded more meals with a particular personalized goal.

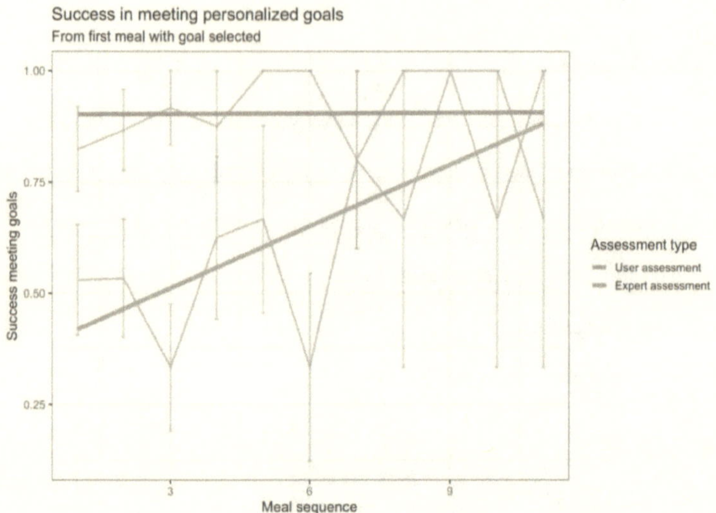

Figure 13. User- and Expert-assessments of success achieving personalized goals from GlucoGoalie, indexed by the sequence of meals recorded since selecting the goal.

The 6 of the 8 participants who received personalized suggestions selected a cumulative total of 17 personalized goals over the study period. In addition to the expert labeled assessments, we also examined changes macronutrient consumption for meals with and without a given personalized goal selected.

Three of the 6 participants selected only one or two personalized goals. These participants changed their macronutrient consumption consistently with the direction of the goal (e.g., reduced from baseline for "Decrease" goals) for all the goals they chose.

The other 3 of 6 participants tried 4 or more personalized goals, and were successful in adjusting their macronutrient consumption consisted with the goal for 40% to 75% of the goals they adopted. Due to the small sample, we did not test these differences for statistical significance.

In a second analysis of macronutrient consumption, we examined the target amount of macronutrient suggested in each goal, and measured the mean absolute distance from that target, in grams (Figure 14). We found that participant's meals trended towards being 20% closer to the goal target after selecting, compared with their own meals before selecting that goal.

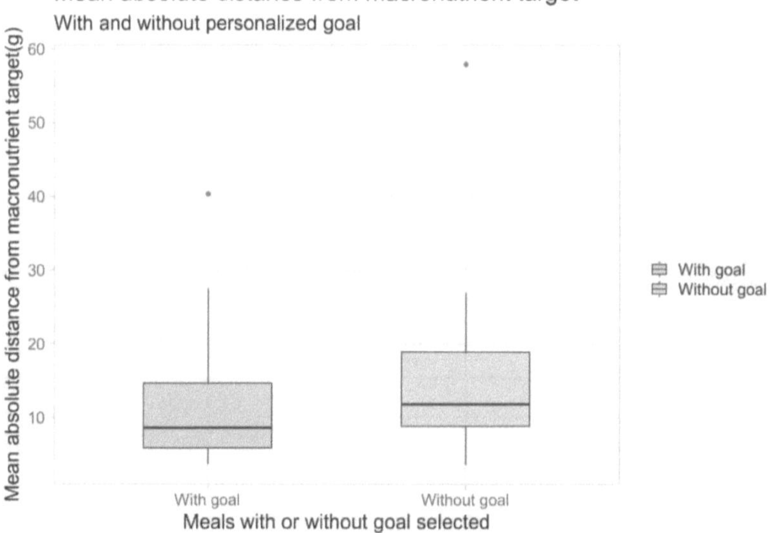

Figure 14. Box-and-whisker plot comparing the mean absolute distance from a goal's macronutrient target, in grams, for a user's meals with and without the goal selected.

3.4.3 Qualitative Results

Next, we describe the four main themes from the thematic analysis: 1) receiving goal suggestion informs self-discovery, 2) choosing goals highlights individual preferences, 3) following goals demonstrates the importance of feedback and context, and 4) challenges understanding and following goals in practice. As shown in Table 10, data saturation was reached and themes were prevalent across participants.

Table 10. Prevalence of themes across participant interviews. Each purple-shaded cell indicates that a theme was present for a participant. Theme 1 was prevalent in 100% of interviews, while Theme 4 was prevalent in 50% of interviews.

	P1	P2	P3	P4	P5	P6	P7	P8
Theme 1 - Receiving goal suggestion informs self-discovery	■	■	■	■	■	■	■	■
Theme 2 - Choosing goals highlights individual preferences	■	■	■	■	■	■	■	■
A checkpoint or a challenge	■	■	■	■	■			■
Importance of personal food preferences	■	■	■	■		■	■	■
Theme 3 - Following goals demonstrates the importance of feedback and context	■	■	■	■	■	■		■
Fitting goals with the context of daily life	■	■		■	■			■
Importance of feedback and seeing progress		■	■	■	■		■	■
Theme 4 - Challenges understanding and following goals in practice		■			■	■		■
Balancing abstract and concrete in nutrition goals		■			■	■		■
Imprecision of text for delivery of goal suggestions		■			■			■

Participants' background

Participants had mixed and often poor experiences with self-management prior to enrolling in the study. Many reported poor eating habits and being indiscriminate about their meals:

"... before that I eat whatever. Yeah, whatever. Dinner time, I eat whatever." P2

Others often skipped meals, which led to overeating later in the day:

"... I only skip breakfast. I wasn't always very good about lunch. So, then I'll be famished. I would eat crap because I was hungry." P5

Along with challenges with nutrition, participants described challenges keeping their BG within target ranges:

"Sometimes [my blood sugar] goes very high or goes very low." P4

"Yeah, a mess, my sugar level was high everyday 300, and the doctor was upset to me." P1

Some participants had tried prior bouts of focused self-management, with mixed success in the long run. Three participants had previously tracked their meals on paper, but none had tracked with an app.

Impressions of GlucoGoalie

Overall, participants reported that they enjoyed the experience of using GlucoGoalie, and found it fun, easy, and direct.

"It was fun. They laugh about me because every time I was going to eat — no, wait a minute. I can't start eating. I've got to take a picture of it... It was fun to play." P2

They also actively engaged with the main part of the app: setting and following goals.

"I try to follow the goals and instructions if I'm trying to improve my intake. That's what I'm trying to do most of the time. Because every day I try to follow a better diet and try to have more greens." P4

Participants in the deployment study showed high engagement with logging features: on average they recorded more than 1 meal per day, and all participants set at least one goal. However, only about 40% (3 of 8) of participants actively engaged with different features of the app, such as setting new goals and viewing progress towards goal achievement; these were savvy users of smartphones with previous experience using apps. In contrast, most of the participants in the study (5 of 8; about 60%) were more accustomed to using their smartphones exclusively to make phone calls and rarely used any apps. These individuals often took a minimalist approach to engaging with GlucoGoalie: they tracked their meals and assessed these meals on fit with chosen goals, but did not engage with any other features without prompts from investigators.

Regarding personalized goals, 88% of interviewed participants (7 of 8) received personalized goals while in the study; one participant did not receive any personalized goals because their BG levels were well-controlled. Of those who received a goal recommendation, 71% (5 of 7) selected at least one of these goals in the app. However, 3 participants did not notice a push notification informing them of a new goal suggestion, and only selected one after a call from the study coordinator.

As a result of following the goals they had chosen, many participants described developing new habits, suggesting they internalized parts of the personalized goal suggestions to the point that they became integrated with their daily practice:

"Even anything longer than two weeks will probably just make it into more of a habit for me. I'll probably eat two weeks to get comfortable with how much fat I'm taking, let's say the goal was on fat, so then after that it would just be more of a habit." P8

At the end of the study, many participants described seeing changes not just in their behaviors, but also in their actual blood glucose levels.

"I did notice because sometimes it was 200. When I see that it was 200, it was after I eat. Oh yeah. After I—but before, 250, 270—because I was eating a lot of food. Five or six in the night." P2

"And the sugar went down.... Today, I tested, it was 121." P6

Theme 1—Receiving goal suggestion informs self-discovery

To personalize goals, GlucoGoalie included features for tracking meals and BG levels. The study showed that even these requisite tracking features often led to discoveries and new insights. Furthermore, the experience of viewing both generic and personal goal suggestions helped individuals critically reflect on their behaviors, thus serving as an additional catalyst for learning.

Through tracking and reflecting on their meals, participants described some of the patterns and insights they observed between the foods they were eating and their BG levels.

"I did it for two days and I tested my sugar, oh, this is the rice… So, I stopped eating rice for two days, and then when I stopped eating rice, it got lower." P6

Beyond tracking, the goal setting features in GlucoGoalie scaffolded the self-discovery process. For example, P2 learned from their goal to "eat whole fruits instead of juice"

"When I drink the juice, I see that sugar is what was high. And I learned that that was the problem…. Now, when I eat, I don't drink juice." P2

In many cases, participants used the personalized goal recommendations they received to reflect on their behaviors and sought to reconcile these recommendations with what they had already knew or suspected about themselves.

"And I know that, my carbs like I said, are usually high. I think that, my first, what I gravitate to first in any meal is the carb and that's what I want more of... So, I'm not like surprised that it recommends reducing the carbs and trying to replace it with something else." P3

Participants sometimes noted that the goal they received was something they were already trying to work on. For example, P4 described their reaction to receiving a suggestion to reduce the amount of fat in their meals:

"I'm trying to decrease the amount of food and so that's why, I think it's important to decrease the amount of fat and that is one of the problems that I have with the fat." P4

Receiving personalized goal suggestions provided a reference point for participant's own views of their self-management pitfalls and needs, as well as a jumping off point to guide reflection on their behaviors.

Theme 2—Choosing goals highlights individual preferences

A checkpoint or a challenge

Most participants commented that some goals in the GlucoGoalie app seemed harder to achieve than others. However, when choosing which goals to follow, participants took a variety of different approaches. Some participants chose goals that seemed highly achievable, or were the sorts of behaviors they were already doing regularly; these participants viewed goals as a checkpoints or reminders to be more consistent.

"I like that it was a goal that it was more feasible to me. So, it was just a good like a checkpoint for me not sort of a reminder but kind of like, oh it's going with what I'm doing. So, it's just reminding me." P8

In contrast, other participants were interested in choosing goals that were more challenging as self-motivation to change their current habits.

"Yes, I go to the notification and started looking at the new one. That's why, when I first took the other substitute of water for over sodas. I realized, well that's not really a goal because I've been doing that already. So, I need to change to something more difficult because I was done with the other one." P4

Importance of personal food preferences

In addition to the perceived degree of challenge in a given goal, personal likes and dislikes regarding different foods factored in prominently to participants' decisions of which goal to choose. To illustrate personalized goals, GlucoGoalie included three examples with different foods at the end of each goal (see Table 1). For many participants, these examples were critical factors to deciding whether to try a goal or not. When asked to explain why they selected a particular personalized goal, participants often referenced the examples as their justification for selecting or eliminating a goal from consideration.

"That one is okay, because I used to eat the oatmeal, one slice of toast, yeah that one is okay." P1

Along with expressing their interest or distaste for certain foods, participants also mentioned the importance of variety, and opted for suggestions that incorporated new ideas to break what they perceived as the monotony of healthy eating. For example, P2 was looking for examples of vegetables they could eat other than broccoli:

"I don't know, like, if I want to eat like broccoli, I will be tired. And I'm not going to eat it every day." P2

Theme 3—Following goals demonstrates the importance of feedback and context

Fitting goals with the context of daily life

The need for greater personalization extended beyond choosing which goal to pursue and impacted participants' ability to successfully incorporate new goals within their daily lives. In some cases, participants had established patterns that they did not want to change, for example eating the same thing for breakfast every day because it worked for them, or skipping breakfast entirely because their morning routine did not allow for it. Furthermore, balancing meals within a day or week was just as important. What made sense for an upcoming meal depended in part on what happened earlier in the day.

"Since I'm a busy woman… it kind of just has to go back to like how my day is. So, I know that if I didn't meet it for one of my meals, I'll have to meet it for the next meal." P8

This balance extended to seasonal patterns as well, where different kinds of meals were appealing during different parts of the year.

"I don't want to have a hearty breakfast compared to like in the winter." P8

Many participants touted that it was easier to follow goals when preparing their own meals at home, but much harder when eating outside, at a restaurant or other gathering. Goals in GlucoGoalie lent themselves particularly to the home context, but different goals may be useful in other contexts.

"...well at least for me... it was very hard for me to manage using the app when I went out to eat." P3

When goals felt appropriate also depended on the context of other self-management and health goals, for example exercise. P5 noted that they often include more carbs in their meals after exercising, but less if they have not exercised that day:

"So, I know, if I have exercise, walking or an exercise routine after a meal that's going to be a little bit more high carbs. That has made an impact." P5

Importance of feedback and seeing progress

Participants were eager for feedback on their progress. This included whether they were successfully meeting the goals they had set in GlucoGoalie, for example, whether the amounts of specific macronutrients in their meals were more consistent with their chosen goals. Most participants found this challenging and had to come up with strategies. Some started measuring their foods to get a better sense for portion sizes and proportions:

" When I got after I started, I look for a [measuring] cup and I started to follow the instructions." P4

In general, participants were eager for feedback on their progress:

"Everybody would like to know how they're doing... Because if I'm eating less and it's not doing no good, what's the point of me doing it?" P2

In particular, many participants described not only the goals they had set with GlucoGoalie, but also their higher-level goals, motivations, and aspirations. These goals were not at the specific and achievable level of "drink more water," but reflected general desires for leading a healthy life. Importantly, different participants expressed different motivations. Some participants expressed a desire to lose weight, or to see that their blood glucose levels were lowering.

"Definitely in terms of weight loss but like also my actual numbers in terms of my blood sugar." P3

Other participants were also interested in improving their diabetes management, and had the goal of improving control of blood glucose levels, so that they could reduce their dosage of oral medications like metformin.

"Because I want to keep it as level as possible to try to stay off medications." P7

Theme 4—Challenges understanding and following goals in practice

Balancing abstract and concrete in nutritional goals

Nutritional goals in GlucoGoalie included references to both specific foods and food groups, such as "Drink more water" and also macronutrients, such as "replace 1 carb choice with 1 protein choice at lunch". Many participants' comments related to the interplay between abstract and concrete when thinking about nutrition.

In general, participants enjoyed goals that were concrete and easy to implement without additional knowledge. This was particularly the case for generic goals that typically targeted familiar foods or food groups.

"Those were right. Those were easy and I've been, I have been intentional to drink a bottle

of water at every main meal and then have a bottle or two in between." P5

However, personalized goals were more abstract with a focus on macronutrients rather than specific foods. These goals were typically described as harder to understand and meet.

"The replacement, it was, you know was dropping, half a carb replacing, half carb. That

was a little harder to figure out. So, it will require a little more thinking." P5

Furthermore, participants' attitudes towards more abstract, macronutrient-oriented goals were influenced by their apparent knowledge of nutrition. About half of participants were comfortable identifying macronutrients, estimating portion size, and discussing steps they could take to meet these goals with their meal choices.

"So, I still go by the basics even from when I went to the nutritionist of like using like my

palms, like the two fingers, index fingers. Actually, do work well for like teaspoons and

tablespoons." P8

The other half of participants described themselves as not being familiar with macronutrients and estimating portion sizes. For these participants, goals formulated using macronutrients and "choices" as units presented an impassable barrier and were often dismissed. These participants often referred to using visual proportions of different types of foods on their plate to gauge how healthy their meals were:

"I use my plate, but I try to go as they show me in the program, you see the plate then half

it's a vegetable or fruit, this is a protein and that one is a carbohydrate." P1

Imprecision of text for delivery of goal suggestions

Even for those with higher nutrition literacy, participants were not always consistent in how they interpreted personalized goals, and there were a number of misunderstandings. For example, some terminology, like "choices" as a unit of measure, was often interpreted as an option to choose two different food items, regardless of the amount. P2 described their effort to achieve a goal of eating 2 fat choice (10g) at breakfast by stating that they ate two high fat food, but not the amounts of either:

"Sometimes I put it together, the mozzarella on top of the egg which means I'm taking two fats." P2

While this meal may have been consistent with P2's goal, they are saying they believe they achieved their goal because they chose two fat-based ingredients, not because the amount of total fat in the meal is consistent with the goal.

In addition, participants sometimes struggled with the numerical content in goals, for example the combination of both "choices" and "grams" as units.

" 'Decrease your fat to about four fat choices.' That part is pretty clear. The only part that I say, kind of gets tricky where I guess you're adding numbers with words would be the '20 grams'." P8

In general, static text alone was limited in its ability to convey the more abstract nutrition goals. During the interviews, participants asked a number of clarifying questions, for example asking which foods count as which macronutrients. Some participants suggested that visual aids for portion size estimation would be a welcome addition.

3.4.4 Discussion

This results of this pilot study with 20 individuals with type 2 diabetes offers preliminary evidence for the feasibility of GlucoGoalie as an intervention. While usage varied, participants recorded a median of 1 meal per day over the 4-week study period. In examining changes to self-reported self-management behaviors, participants increased significantly in both diet and blood glucose subscales of the SDSCA [248]. GlucoGoalie intervened specifically on diet, but not on other components of self-management like physical activity, which did not show significant differences, suggesting that the improvement from pre- to post-measurement was not purely a result of social-desirability bias among participants. There was also a significant increase in the BG monitoring subscale of the SDSCA. While increased BG monitoring was not a direct target of the intervention, the use of GlucoGoalie provided scaffolding for participants to check their BG more regularly, and participants were provided with additional test strips, so the increase in self-reported monitoring is logical.

Alongside the features for goal setting and in-the-moment goal assessment, the primary innovative component of GlucoGoalie was the introduction of personalized goals, based on each user's self-tracking data. Only 8 of the 20 participants received these personalized suggestions, however. Of the 12 who did not, 7 did not record the minimum number of meals and BG readings for the personalized analysis to start (8 meals with both pre- and post- meal readings). This is in line with findings from many research studies in self-tracking and mHealth applications, that show great variability in usage, and step drop-offs in the number of users who use an app for extended periods of time [32,58,148].

In addition, user-entered data needed additional annotation to add macronutrient compositions to each meal. In this pilot, a team of registered dietitians (RDs) entered these macronutrient assessments, however, due to technical and personnel issues, 4 participant's meals were not evaluated within the study period, and therefore did not receive personalized recommendations. Other meal-logging approaches, like database lookup, could have enabled users to track their meals in a structured way with macronutrient amounts already estimated. However, due to the burden of such approaches and nutrition knowledge required to use them correctly, we opted for photo and text logging, to reduce the tracking burden for participants as much as possible. Researchers have also proposed crowdsourcing approaches for meal estimation, though these meal evaluations can also be costly [194].

The fact that some users did not record sufficient meals for personalization, while for others we encountered logistical challenges in completing timely macronutrient assessments, points to a limitation of data-driven approaches for personalization that rely on personal data. Lightweight logging approaches may encourage longer term engagement of a tracking application, but also offers a less detailed data representation for analysis with machine learning and other data-driven approaches [62].

Considering the participants who *did* receive personalized suggestion in the app, examination of changes in the macronutrient composition of their meals suggests that they were able to act on these goals, at least to some degree. Three participants tried 1 to 2 goals each, and they successfully adjusted their average macronutrient consumption following the recommendations from those goals. The three participants who selected 4 or more goals had mixed success, following some goals and not others. Overall, participants moved in the direction of their goals 65% of the time, which is consistent with the findings from the controlled experiment in Study 2 (Section 3.3), which found that participants assembled goal-consistent meal 66% of the time. These participants also ate meals that were on average 20% closer to the macronutrient target in their chosen goals, compared with their baseline consumption. These findings adds support to the feasibility of GlucoGoalie's approach to personalizing nutrition goals based on self-tracking data, and the potential of interventions like GlucoGoalie to have a positive impact on self-management behaviors.

The qualitative findings from the deployment study similarly build on the findings of the controlled evaluation. Participants reported similar successes and challenges to understanding and acting on goal recommendations. Specifically, participants described being generally able to understand goals, and at least attempted to follow them, but the results also reiterated challenges related to specific design choices, like the use of the word "choice" to describe macronutrient quantities.

In addition, the deployment study revealed a number of insights related to the experience of receiving and following goal suggestions in everyday life. Specifically, it highlighted the relationship between supporting reflection and direct support for action, the alignment between goals with individuals eating practices and larger aspirations, and the need for interactive approaches that enable feedback and negotiation. I discuss these point in more detail in the Discussion section for this chapter below.

3.5   Discussion

The goal of this research was to examine individuals' experiences with receiving, selecting, and following computationally generated nutritional goals for T2D. In designing GlucoGoalie, we took the approach of combining ML analysis of individuals' self-tracking data with an expert system to computationally generate recommendations for nutritional goals that are likely to lead to improvement in BG levels.

This approach has several important distinctions compared to previously proposed systems. First, the ML inference in GlucoGoalie directly examines the relationship between behavior and a health marker (BG) to inform recommendations; not by assuming which behaviors are healthy [208], or relying on user's self-perceptions of what behaviors impact health [117]. GlucoGoalie makes recommendations in the multidimensional space of nutritional composition, versus the unidimensional space of steps [143] or calories [208], which makes it more complex. Furthermore, unlike other recommendation approaches (e.g., MyBehavior [208]), integration of expert knowledge within the expert system enables GlucoGoalie to make suggestions that extend beyond individuals' past behaviors (previously captured meals).

In this aim, I completed three studies to design and evaluate GlucoGoalie, including an analysis of ML methods, a controlled experiment, and a deployment study. These studies helped generate a number of conclusions regarding the use of ML-driven coaching solutions.

3.5.1 Balancing support for reflection and action

Personal informatics aims to increase self-knowledge and, ultimately, inform future action through collection of and reflection on self-tracking data [152]. However, reflecting on data can be burdensome, and not everyone has the necessary time, mental energy, and literacy. In contrast, there is a long tradition of research in behavior change interventions that focus less on reflection and provide more direct support for action through a variety of behavior change techniques [174]. One limitation of traditional behavior change interventions is that they rely on predetermined behavior goals to nudge users towards, but in the case of chronic conditions like T2D, different goals may be appropriate for different individuals based on their physiology and response to diet. While a more direct approach may mitigate the burden of reflection, a potential concern is that it could lead to individuals following the system's recommendations without attaining the benefits of learning and self-discovery, which could have a negative impact on autonomy [130].

Our study suggested that it is possible to reach a middle ground between these extremes. Because GlucoGoalie used an expert system to generate concrete goal recommendations, it was able to provide direct support for action. At the same time, because goals were informed by ML analysis of self-tracking data, the participants often engaged in reflection similar to the one enabled by personal informatics solutions. The participants appreciated the more direct support for action through goal recommendations: those who selected personalized goals in the app described making changes and choosing meals that would be consistent with goals, for example taking increased care to measure the components of their meal. At the same time, the study showed that participants found tracking meals and BG levels to be informative, an experience similar to most personal informatics solutions [117,153]. Furthermore, we found that participants actively engaged with the recommendations they received and took them as an additional prompt and opportunity for reflection, beyond that provided by the personal data itself. Participants compared goal suggestions to their own self-perceptions of their eating habits and used them as a mirror to re-examine their past choices. In this way, we found a synergy between offering direct support for action as a part of an application that enables reflection via self-tracking.

These findings highlight the potential for solutions that balance support for both reflection and action. First, future work could more directly explore the relationship between actionable recommendations and reflection in self-tracking, for example comparing engagement in self-tracking with and without the addition of actionable recommendations. Second, in this work, the connection between one's behaviors and the recommendations they received were not explained or made explicit by the application, but relied on users to fill in those gaps. Future work could endeavor to make the connections between personal data and recommendations more salient for users, which may further support engagement and reflection. For example, actionable recommendations could be enhanced by presenting visual summaries of the self-tracking data that informed the specific goal recommendations [79,222]. This additional information can serve as a form of explanation for the recommendations, and prior work has demonstrated the importance of explanations in facilitating nutritional learning [40]. A growing body of research in explainable ML may offer potential avenues to make recommendations in support of action and ground them with an explanation to support reflection [259]. Future work could further incorporate advances in explainable ML to personal informatics applications.

3.5.2 Aligning goals with eating experiences and personal aspirations

Because GlucoGoalie relied on an expert system to generate recommendations as natural language sentences, one of our challenges was to find the right form to formulate these recommendations. Through the design process, we took the approach of formulating goals in terms of macronutrient amounts [81], which has the advantage of allowing individuals to flexibly apply their goal to different types of foods and meals, with the ability to freely incorporate their food preferences. However, this study demonstrated some limitations of this approach. While participants who expressed comfort with nutrition terminology were able to adopt goals, those with lower nutrition literacy and less comfort measuring or weighing their food had trouble understanding and following goals. Making meal choices ultimately comes down to what's on one's plate, and participants sometimes found it difficult to connect somewhat abstract goals to concrete meal choices.

An alternative and common form of nutrition suggestions are recipe or meal plan recommendations, which are much more concrete and consistent with how participants think about their meals and diet. However, as recommendations become more concrete, they need to take into account individual's food preferences, and there are more opportunities to miss the mark. We found this with the "examples" included with each personalized goal: idiosyncratic preferences for a single food item in the list was a major factor in whether a participant would choose a goal or not. Recommender systems (RecSys) excel at making concrete suggestions based on personal preferences, learned from users' past behavior or characteristics [214], and can incorporate additional constraints like food allergies [123]. While GlucoGoalie focused on personalizing recommendations based on health constraints, this approach could be complementary with growing research in health-aware RecSys [77]. Meal logs and macronutrient-centered goals from GlucoGoalie could be used as inputs to a preference-based RecSys to generate concrete suggestions that would help individuals connect their goals to what's on their plate.

In addition to food preferences, participants highlighted the importance of context in determining when a goal was appropriate, for example the time of year, how active one has been, and what other meals have been eaten recently. Making contextually-appropriate recommendations adds another dimension of complexity [209]. Mobile phones and sensors can offer clues to the user's current state, and there is a long history of research in context-aware computing within HCI and Ubiquitous Computing [71]. In health, location-based prompts have been used to help prevent relapse triggers [50], and step counts can inform adaptive fitness goals based on recent activity levels [143], but have not been widely used in nutrition [208].

A final tension was participants' desire for a greater connection between specific nutritional goals and their larger aspirations in life and health. Participants did not always see the connection between concrete, quantifiable self-tracking-related goals and larger, more abstract, qualitative motivations. Niess and Woźniak observed the relationship between tracking goals and qualitative health goals in the context of individuals setting goals with fitness trackers [192]. For example, a quantitative, self-tracking goal of walking 12k steps a day might be connected to a qualitative goal of losing weight, and a higher-level goal of feeling well. In the case of GlucoGoalie, because the algorithm suggests quantitative goals, it's even more important to draw a connection back to an individual's qualitative goals, like improving BG levels. Researchers have explored methods to elicit these values and motivations [21] and future work could explore how to connect them to quantitative tracking goal [192].

3.5.3   Interactivity, negotiation, and feedback

By taking the approach of using an expert system to interpret ML output, GlucoGoalie produced static, text-based recommendations. One of the limitations of this approach was that we were unable to resolve the misinterpretations and misunderstandings that are likely to arise in a complex domain like nutrition. In some cases, participants did not understand the nutrition terminology, and in other cases they understood the vocabulary, but misinterpreted the intended meaning. One approach to make nutrition goals more understandable is to incorporate illustrations. In health risk communication, illustrations and infographics have been used successfully to improve comprehension of complex information [12,102,274]. A similar visual approach has been applied to assist low literacy adults with portion size estimation [48], and could be used here to better convey numerical content in personalized goals.

A second approach is to offer the opportunity for questions and answers in a back-and-forth exchange. This more interactive approach could introduce concepts, answer users' questions, and more fully explain goal recommendations. Along these lines, conversational agents have been used to support interactive goal setting, health coaching, and motivational interviewing [26,149]. Generally, these approaches are based on a set list of goals, not personalized based on user self-tracking data. Combining conversational agents with computationally personalized goal setting is a potential direction for future work. A more interactive and conversational interaction style would also offer another approach to address the challenges of context, discussed above, to allow participants to have input on their goals and negotiate [141]. Finally, this approach might also address the lack of proactive engagement from some users, particularly those with less technology comfort, who did not explore app features and sometimes did not notice updates to their available goals. While many smartphone features rely on users accessing features to pull information or support, conversational approaches can proactively initiate interactions, which may lead to a higher level of engagement with these features [22,91,223]. Enabling negotiation within the space of possible goals expands on the complexity of recommendations, and may require more sophisticated and flexible methods than the rule-based expert system used in GlucoGoalie. Machine learning approaches like mechanistic, controller, or reinforcement learning models are a potential vein of future exploration [6,150,166].

In another opportunity for increased interactivity, participants expressed resounding interest in more feedback about their progress in achieving their goals, and the impact of this progress on their overall health. Feedback is an important component of learning in goal-setting [72], and while participants were able to self-assess each meal against their goal and view a summary of their goal attainment, they were interested in additional feedback from GlucoGoalie. One approach to providing feedback is to engage dietitians and other healthcare professionals. However, this increases reliance on human experts, thus limiting the scalability of the approach. Previous research in coaching interventions explored offering automated feedback, especially for physical activity [57,108,208]. Similar techniques could be applied to nutrition in future research.

3.6   Conclusion

In this aim, I described the design of a system called GlucoGoalie that combines machine learning with a rule-based expert system to translate insights from self-tracking data in to personalized goal suggestions. As a health coaching intervention, GlucoGoalie focuses primarily on goal setting, which, while essential, is only one component of health coaching practice. Suggesting a need for a more comprehensive coaching approach, participants in the deployment study who made use of GlucoGoalie expressed interest for more feedback on their progress, as well as connecting the very-specific goals with their higher-level goals and aspirations in health and life. Additional insight and approaches from health coaching could improve the framing of goals and delivery of feedback, which is further explored in Aim 2. Participants also wanted to see suggestions that were more relevant to the specific meals they had eaten and logged in the app, which will define the scope and focus of the coaching approach developed in Aim 3.

In the deployment study we observed a consistent discrepancy between user and expert assessment of goal achievement, which suggests individuals may not always be accurate in their self-assessment of goal achievement, with a bias towards being over optimistic. In addition, while many participants tracked enough data to receive personalized suggestions, not all individuals were able to track to this point, and described barriers to consistent data collection. Approaches that aim to minimize the burden of meal logging in the context of coaching are explored further in Aim 3.

Chapter 4: Aim II

Compare human-powered and automated health coaching via text messaging

While Aim 1 focused on goal setting as a foundational aspect of health coaching, there are many other important facets of coaching like establishing accountability, offering feedback, and building rapport through collaborative conversation [196,218].

In-person health coaching is a common and effective approach to promote self-management [73,197,229,267]. However, there are challenges to scaling in-person practice, particularly in low resource communities. Perhaps most significantly, there are not enough trained coaching practitioners to provide adequate education and support to the growing population of individuals with type 2 diabetes (T2D) [81,212]. In addition, there are barriers and disparities in access to in-person coaching, including transportation, community resources, and cost [81,205]. Individuals with low socio-economic status and ethnic minorities are disproportionately affected by chronic conditions, and the continued failure to identify effective interventions to reach these communities has the potential to deepen existing disparities [254]. Even for those with access, the quality of communication itself can be poorer for racial and ethnic minorities due to implicit bias as well as disparities in language and health literacy [14].

Technology has the potential to address these limitations and reach broader and more diverse individuals in their day-to-day lives. One approach is to introduce *technology-mediated coaching*, which seeks to connect clients with practitioners via telecommunication [212]; in recent years technology-mediated coaching has become increasingly common in practice

[30,173,212]. A complementary approach is to replicate the support provided by human coaches with computing technologies, for example *conversational agents*. Conversational agents have long been explored in many areas of health and healthcare [22,146,264]. Bickmore and colleagues have argued for the advantages of conversational agents to overcome some of the challenges and biases of interpersonal communication in health, while still being able to establish a form of social relationship between the agent and user [22]. There has been a recent increase in the number of conversational interventions in health, often taking the form of scripted, text-based chatbots, which have seen positive results in areas like telemonitoring, cognitive behavioral therapy, and medication management [91,146]. Furthermore, new advances in Artificial Intelligence (AI) pave the wave for more advanced conversational agents, capable of more fluid, human-like interactions [2,217]. However, in the context of health coaching, questions remain as to ***whether technology can ever truly replicate health coaching practice***. For example, Rutjes [218] argued that coaching's emphasis on building personal connections and adapting support to situation-specific contexts make coaching an essentially human activity that cannot be replicated by technology.

In this aim, I explored the space of automated, text-based coaching through the iterative design of a chatbot health coach for diabetes self-management. This chatbot relied on the same approach to generating personalized goals as described in Aim 1 and integrated these goals as part of the coaching experience. In addition, I sought to examine open questions and tensions regarding benefits and limitations of human versus fully automated conversational coaching by contrasting this chatbot coach with human text-message based coaching in a Wizard-of-Oz deployment study with individuals with T2D. I conclude with implications for the design of automated coaching interventions.

4.1 Iterative, user-centered design of *t2.coach*, a chatbot health coach for nutrition and physical activity goal setting

As described in related work (Section 2.5), a common approach to designing conversational agents in health is structuring dialogs to follow clinical protocols for specific coaching strategies, like Cognitive Behavioral Therapy [91]. In this approach, designers create a scripted dialog structure that anticipates the possible interactions between an individual and the agent and specifies appropriate responses. While less flexible than dynamic conversational agents, which are based on dialog models trained from a large corpus, fully-scripted agents have been successful in domains where corpora are not available or feasible to create, and also offer designers more precise control over how the agent will respond, which is important when delivering health-related information. Below I describe the initial design of T2 Coach that followed an established coaching protocol, and how I refined this design through a set of user-centered design activities.

4.1.1 Initial design of t2.coach

In the initial design of t2.coach, we followed an established protocol, Brief Action Planning (BAP; [109]) as the basis for the scripted dialog flows. BAP defines a set of steps for health practitioners to guide an individual towards choosing a health goal and making a specific plan to achieve it. The well-defined and discrete step, as well as example scripted dialogs, make BAP particularly well suited to be adapted as a scripted chatbot. More details about BAP in relation to health coaching can be found in Section 2.6.2. The content for goals and action plans in t2.coach were derived from a prior knowledge base of health goals for individuals with T2D [61], as well as the personalized goals based on computational analysis of individuals' self-monitoring data, as described in Section 3.1 [179].

Consistent with BAP, t2.coach included two primary dialogs: 1) a longer, weekly exchange to set a health goal, as well as 2) a shorter, daily, follow-up exchange to check in on goal progress, show in in Figure 15.

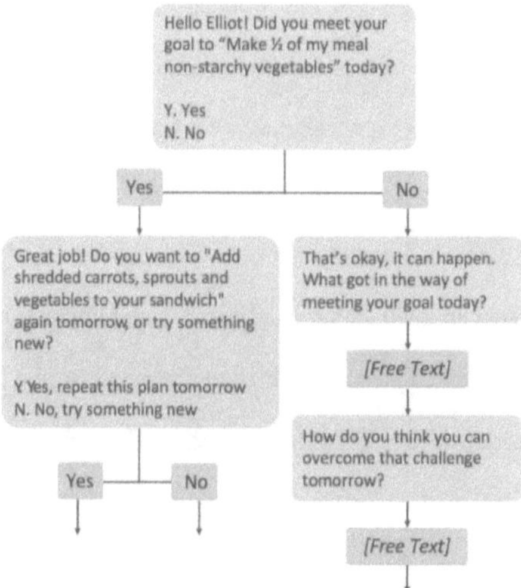

Figure 15. An example dialog tree from t2.coach for the daily check-in script

In addition to daily, system-initiated dialogs, meant to promote behavior change and account ability, early designs of t2.coach also promoted engagement by enabling users to initiate interactions. Users could ask questions and send messages to t2.coach throughout the day, and the chatbot would respond with answers similar to the types of question-answering offered by modern, commercially available agents (e.g. Siri, Alexa) [176], as well as tailored responses to certain requests, like diabetes-friendly recipes.

4.1.2 User-centered design methods

Participants

Individuals with T2D were recruited from two Federally Qualified Health Centers (FQHC) in the New York City metro area, one in Jersey City and the other in the Morris Heights neighborhood in the Bronx. To be included, participants needed to have self-reported diagnosis of T2D, be between 18 and 65 years old, and own a working smartphone.

User-Centered design workshops

Design workshops with 2-5 participants were held on site in conference rooms at the two FQHCs. Each session lasted up to 90 minutes and began with introductions and questions about participants' background with T2D and technology like smartphone and text messaging. Next, the research team presented a description of the envisioned t2.coach system and storyboards of interactions with the chatbot to elicit feedback. Attention was paid to participants' comprehension of and preference for different goals and action plans to further refine the content base, as well as different options in phrasing feedback and supportive messages. Each session also included a role-playing exercise to understand what questions participants might have for an always available virtual coach in various scenarios, like shopping in the grocery store, or choosing what to eat for breakfast after a high blood sugar reading in the morning. Each workshop was audio recorded, and researchers took contemporaneous notes.

Wizard-of-Oz Deployment Study

During the last 15-30 minutes of the user-centered design workshops, researchers set up participants' phones with a prototype of the t2.coach system. In order to collect participant feedback early in the design process, before the fully functioning system was implemented, we utilized a "Wizard-of-Oz" (WOz) approach. WOz is a common design approach where a research technician works behind the scenes to create the illusion of a fully functioning system, even if the system is only partially implemented [65,134]. While WOz methods have been used for many types of interactive systems, they particularly lend themselves to conversational interaction: the human wizard can easily recognize and interpret users' statements and requests and generate appropriate responses. However, the vast majority of WOz experiments reported thus far were carried out in a lab setting, rather than in deployment studies in-the-wild. Because t2.coach's dialogs rely on repeat interaction day-to-day in relation to an individual's goal attainment, interaction patterns with a WOz chatbot in a controlled lab setting may not be generalizable to in-the-wild interactions.

Implementation of Wizard-of-Oz in-the-Wild

Adapting the WOz technique to a real-world setting, however, posed multiple challenges, including the need for a lightweight system that works well outside the lab, an expectation of 24/7 availability of the agent, and the need to manage conversations with multiple users at once. Unfortunately, there are very few examples of WOz applied to longitudinal deployments or field studies in the HCI literature for researchers to leverage and build upon.

In designing and implementing the apparatus for WOz messaging I took advantage of existing available technologies to the extent possible. For simplicity, the wizard could use their own phone number for sending messages. However, to maintain privacy and allow severability after the close of the study, I implemented an SMS-forwarding proxy with Twilio Studio [277], illustrated in Figure 16.

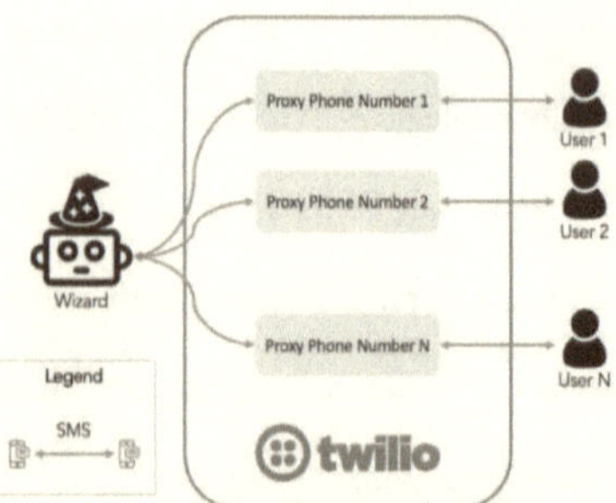

Figure 16. An illustration of the wizard-of-oz messaging proxy, implemented in Twilio Studio [277]

Because WOz methods are primarily focused on research in a lab setting, there were a number of challenges adapting WOz methods to a deployment study.

First, in order to create the illusion of an at least somewhat automated system, it would need to be functional at all hours of the day. This, however, would put undue burden on the wizard. The design of t2.coach included one chatbot-initiated conversation per day, and in an attempt to align the schedules of participants and the wizard, we scheduled a 1-hour long window to receive messages each day. This also allowed the wizard to be assigned to multiple participants at once. Importantly, to create a somewhat chatbot-like experience even when the wizard was not available, we configured Twilio to send a brief, automatic reply to let users know that t2.coach received their message and would respond within 24 hours. This type of automatic reply is uncommon when texting with a human conversational partner, and while not particularly informative, was meant to create the feeling of interacting with an automated system.

In addition to scheduling staggered conversation windows, to help the wizard manage conversations with multiple participants, we also made use of Trello [278], a project-management platform, which served as a central dashboard for the wizard to organize their work. The wizard used cards to schedule their needed outreach and outstanding items for each participant. In addition, we integrated Trello with the Twilio messaging. For example, we let the wizard update their availability on Trello in real time, which determined whether users would receive the automatic reply described above.

A third challenge was the expectation of relatively quick replies from a chatbot, in comparison to messaging with a human conversational partner. Instead of typing out responses, with wizard used keyboard shortcut apps to choose from the possible scripted responses [279].

Procedure

After the design workshop, the wizard initiated the first goal-setting conversation with each participant at the scheduled time of day. The wizard strictly followed the same rules and protocol that the fully implemented chatbot would use to respond, including the fallback response "I'm sorry, I didn't understand" and re-prompting the question for off-script replies.

To simulate question-answering, the wizard ran requests through a classifier built with AWS Lex [280] to categorize queries to different types of requests including recipe requests or diabetes knowledge questions. General informational questions were searched verbatim in Google, with the additional keyword "diabetes," and responses from Google snippets were sent with a link, after being approved by a CDE on the research team. If the question was unclassifiable, or the response was deemed inappropriate, the chatbot responded that it was unable to answer the question.

The wizard initiated messages each day at the scheduled time for two weeks, after which participants were invited to return for semi-structured interviews.

Analysis

After each workshop, we reviewed transcripts and researcher notes to iteratively update the behavioral goal and action-plan content base, as well as the t2.coach script, before the next session. In addition, as cohorts of participants began the WOz study, the research team met weekly to discuss participant responses to revise seemly confusing messages and discuss changes to the structure of the t2.coach script.

4.1.3 Results

Participants (n=23) participated in groups of 2-5 across 7 total design workshops from August to December 2019. Thirteen participants participated in the two-week WOz pilot study, of whom eleven returned for semi-structured debrief interviews.

Importantly, the WOz study surfaced a number of insights that may not have been uncovered with usability testing in a lab setting. Because we observed participants taking a considerable amount of time to respond to messages (Table 11) we made considerable changes to the BAP script as a part of this iterative design phase. While BAP was designed for human-to-human conversations in a single session, we found that the number of conversational steps was too long. Because of the delay and length of the scripted dialogs, many participants were not able to finish the initial goal setting conversation on the first day, let alone the scheduled hour overlapping with the wizard. To incorporate this feedback, we substantially reduced to the length of scripted dialogs to focus on the core steps of goal setting. For example, BAP includes a question to assess the client's confidence on a 1-10 scale before finalizing the plan, but this step was superfluous because all users replied they were highly confident (10/10). Importantly, the need to substantially shorten dialogs was an insight that would have been difficult to glean from a lab experiment, as users would have been more likely to complete the full conversation in a single setting under supervision of the researchers, without the distractions of daily life.

Table 11. Average delay in responses to incoming text messages, in minutes

	Wizard	User
Mean response delay *(p < 0.01)*	4.45 minutes	35.44 minutes
Median	0.92 minutes	2.41 minutes
Range	0 to 234.53 minutes	0.02 to 428.30 minutes

Second, the initial version of the script also included messages to remind users about the current active conversation if they were idle for more than an hour. Because users regularly took a long time to reply, these messages were unnecessary and also increased annoyance among early participants (one replied "please stop") and so we removed it from the script.

Third, while we expected participants to ask questions and initiate interactions with t2.coach, we found that users rarely initiated conversations or asked questions unprompted. Users initiated interaction with t2.coach only 16% of the time, and many of these were in the first session, when we asked each participant to send an initial question to t2.coach. It appeared that participants were willing to ask questions of t2.coach in the controlled setting during enrollment, but were less likely to follow through and ask additional questions in the wild. Based on this lack of utilization, we did not pursue adding additional question answering capabilities to the final implemented version of t2.coach.

Complete scripted dialogs from t2.coach after the completion of user-centered design are presented in the appendix in Supplementary Table B and Supplementary Table C.

4.1.4 Discussion

Through an iterative, user-centered design process we refined the design of t2.coach, a chatbot to support individuals with T2D. This design process relied on well-established approaches for conducting design workshops, as well as a novel adaptation of WOz methods to field and deployment studies.

The end result of this work was the protocol for scripted, text-based chatbot. t2.coach was ultimately implemented used the botkit framework with Twilio integration, and is currently being evaluated for its efficacy to support diabetes self-management as a part of a National Institute of Diabetes and Digestive and Kidney Diseases grant number R01DK113189.

In the remaining work of this aim, I present a study that zooms out the lens to examine how a scripted chatbot approach to health coaching compares and contrasts with its analogue of human-powered health coaching.

4.2   Experiences of automated vs. human health coaching

I have just presented the user-centered design of a chatbot intended to offer similar support to individuals with diabetes as a health coach would. However, previous researcher has questioned whether technology-based approaches can serve the role of health coaches [218]. To examine these tensions, I had the following research questions:

Research Question 2.1: Can a scripted, rule-based chatbot create a positive coaching experience, comparable to that created by a human coach using the same medium (text messaging)?

Research Question 2.2: What aspects of the coaching experience, if any, are uniquely human and do not lend themselves to automated approaches?

Research Question 2.3: What are the potential advantages, if any, of chatbots for virtual coaching?

4.2.1 Methods

Overview of the study design

In this study, we recruited participants with T2D from low-resource communities and assigned them to one of two groups. In the first group ("chatbot"), participants interacted with the wizard-of-oz version of the t2.coach chatbot described in Section 4.1, above. In the second group ("human coaching"), participants interacted with an actual human health coach. To reduce potential variability in approaches to coaching, both the chatbot and the human coaches followed the same BAP protocol for structuring the dialogs; however, human coaches were actively encouraged to deviate from the protocol to provide the best support for their clients.

Messaging with human coaches

The health coaches involved in this study exchanged text messages with participants from their own phones using the same SMS-forwarding proxy as the wizard (see Section 4.1.2). Human coaches were given a set of tools to make it easier for them to serve as coaches and follow the BAP protocol. First, to reduce the need for repetitive typing of prompts, coaches were provided with a mobile phone keyboard app with shortcuts to quickly send messages written following the protocol (Supplementary Figure H). In addition, coaches were given access to a dashboard with resources including the complete set of BAP messages, and all of the goals and action plans in the chatbot's knowledge base. Furthermore, coaches could use the dashboard to access pages with all of the meals and blood glucose readings recorded by each of their participants during the study. As a part of training, each coach practiced following the protocol with a member of the research team to help ensure that deviations from the protocol were intentional, and not due to lack of awareness of the steps or technical difficulties following it.

Personalization and self-tracking

Coaching support strives to be personalized to an individual's behaviors and preferences, and many virtual coaching interventions are employed alongside self-tracking apps [101,212]. In light of this, t2.coach included a progressive web application for logging meals and blood glucose (BG) readings (Figure 17). In the app, users capture a photo of their meal and enter a free-text description. Next, they enter a pre-meal BG. Two hours after the meal, users are prompted with a text message reminder to enter a post-meal BG. These data were made available to the human health coaches to help them personalize their support. While these data were not used directly by the chatbot, we included self-tracking with the app in both study groups for parity and to examine participants' attitudes towards self-tracking as part of the coaching experience.

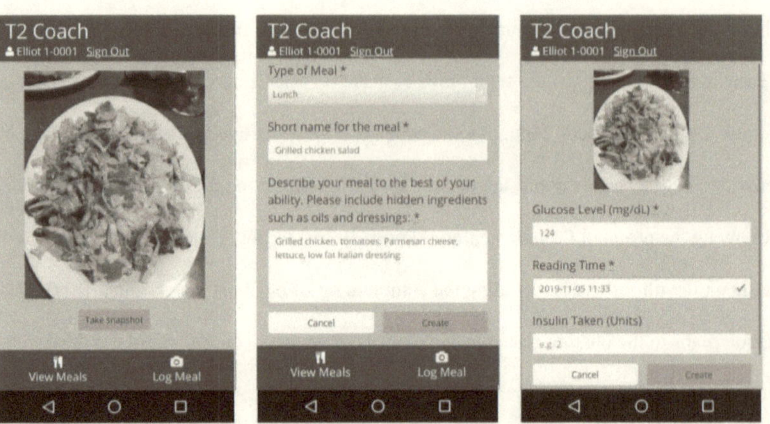

Figure 17. Screens from the progressive web application for recording meals and blood glucose readings.

Participants

Individuals with diabetes. Participants with T2D were recruited from two Federally

Qualified Health Centers (FQHC) in a major United States metropolitan area. Patients served by

these sites are predominantly minority (37% are African American and 60% are Latino) and low

income, with 64% being insured through Medicaid, and 16% are uninsured. To be included in

the study, participants needed to have self-reported diagnosis of T2D, be between 18 and 65

years old, and own a working smartphone.

Health coaches. We recruited practicing health coaches to serve as the virtual coaches in

this study. Coaches were recruited though researchers' professional networks including message

board postings. To be included, coaches had to be Certified Diabetes Educators (CDEs) and/or

be practicing health coach who works with diabetes patients at one of the community health

centers.

Procedure

After collecting informed consent, a study coordinator administered baseline

demographics and a measure of nutrition literacy [263]. Participants began the study in small

groups of 1-4 individuals with a 1.5-hour focus group on the design and content of t2.coach. All

participants in a given focus group were assigned to the same study condition.

During the initial session, researchers helped set up t2.coach on participants' phones, and

participants were asked to use t2.coach for two weeks. The intervention was described to

participants as a partially automated system, but an actual person would be reviewing their

messages to help t2.coach respond appropriately. In both groups, participants were encouraged to

respond to prompts from the coach and to ask free-form questions whenever they had them. In

the human coach group, participants were told that the person reviewing messages was a health coach, while in the chatbot group, participants were told that the person was not a healthcare provider, and therefore would not be able to answer all of their questions.

Because coaches and the wizard could not be available at all hours of the day, participants were asked to indicate a set of times they would be available to exchange messages. Participants and human coaches were paired based on how their available times aligned. Each participant was assigned to a single coach, while each coach was assigned multiple participants, which we refer to as their "clients".

Within 24 hours of enrollment, participants received a message to begin a goal-setting session. Each day at the agreed upon time, the coach initiated the daily check-in conversation. After the first week, the coach initiated another longer, goal setting conversation, giving participants the option to update their goal.

After two weeks, participants joined 30-60 minute debrief interviews over the phone. The interview guide included general questions about participants' background, their prior experience with health coaching and self-tracking apps, and their overall experience in the study. The second part of each interview was grounded in transcripts of individuals' exchanges with their coaches (human or chatbot); the interviewers asked questions based on transcript excerpts and asked participants to explain and contextualize their experiences within those exchanges. The interviewer also asked a targeted question about whether participants felt that they were working with a health coach. At the end of the interview, the researcher administered two post-measures, described below. Participants received $30 for their data plan, $20 for the initial visit, and 25 blood glucose test strips to use for testing during the study. The research protocol was approved by the Western Institutional Review Board (a single IRB for multi-center studies) and the local institutions' IRB.

At the close of the study, we invited the health coaches for 1-hour debrief interviews. We asked about their experiences in the study and how they compared to prior virtual and in-person coaching experiences. To better understand the coach's intention when they deviated from BAP, we reviewed transcripts of their exchanges with participants, to probe how they reacted to participant responses, why they responded the way they did, and if they would have done anything differently in retrospect.

Post-Measures

During the interview, we administered two adapted questionnaires. First, to assess the perceived usability of the text message interactions, we administered 10 items from the Subjective Assessment of Speech Systems Interfaces (SASSI), which has good coverage of broad usability domains [18,119]. Second, to assess the degree of collaboration and shared decision-making, we adapted a 9-item shared decision-making questionnaire (SDM-Q-9 [144]); instead of asking about shared decision-making in a clinical context, the adapted measure asked about shared decision-making related to choosing a health goal. See Supplementary Table D and D for the complete set of questions in the post-measures.

Data Analysis

For the quantitative analysis, we first calculated descriptive statistics of demographics and baseline measures. Our quantitative analysis aimed to answer the following questions: 1) Was there a difference in perceptions of usability or shared decision-making between human coaching experience and the chatbot? 2) Were there differences in conversational patterns between the two groups? and 3) Were there differences in goal attainment between participants in the two groups?

To answer these questions, we used the following methods: 1) To assess differences in perceived usability and shared decision-making, we compared differences in post-measures with an unpaired t-test. 2) To characterize differences in conversational patterns between the two group, we calculated the length of conversations as measured by the number of conversational turns (a switch from one speaker to the other) per day. 3) To explore how successful participants were in achieving their chosen goals, we did not directly measure changes in behavior [137]. Instead, we created a measure of self-reported goal attainment by analyzing text message transcripts to identify exchanges where the coach asked their client if they achieved their goal and the client replied with a clearly affirmative or negative response. Goal attainment was calculated for each week of the study and overall, and we compared attainment between the two groups using Fisher's exact test.

For qualitative analysis, participant and coach interviews were analyzed with inductive thematic analysis [36]. The lead author and senior author coded 10% of transcripts collaboratively, with the lead author continuing to code the remaining transcripts while keeping a detailed audit trail on the code book. The senior author independently coded an additional 20% of transcripts for periodic check-in sessions to compare codes and resolve discrepancies through discussion, followed by additional interpretation sessions for axial coding as themes emerged. After coding was complete, we examined data saturation and theme comprehensiveness across participants [95,104]. To compare the prevalence of themes between the two study groups, we tagged each transcript to the corresponding study condition and used the crosstabs features of NVivo to compare prevalence between groups. Themes were considered equally prevalent if the share of participants who reported that theme in one group was within 20% of the share in the second group.

4.2.2 Results

Participants

Individuals with diabetes. A total of 23 participants were enrolled in the two-week study,

of whom 18 participated in debrief interviews. As shown in Table 12, participants were

predominantly female and majority black or Hispanic, with a low median income for a major US

city. There were no differences in baseline demographics between groups.

Table 12. Demographics and baseline measures

N Enrolled	23
Age	54.92 ± 7.16
Gender	75% Female
Race	55% Black
	5% White
	5% Asian
	5% Native American
	30% Other/Refused
Ethnicity	30% Hispanic
Median Income	< $10k
Nutrition Literacy [263]	4.05 ± 1.61 (out of 6)
	20% possibly limited literacy

Health coaches. Four health coaches facilitated messaging in the Human Coaching

group. They had a range of 10 to 18 years working with diabetes patients, and 3 of 4 were

Certified Diabetes Educators (CDEs). All four self-identified as health coaches, worked for a

health system or in private practice, and felt that the coaching approach should be commonplace

in healthcare.

Post-measures and usage statistics

13 participants were assigned to the chatbot group and 10 to the Human Coaching (HC)

group. 5 participants (1 in the chatbot group and 4 in the human coaching group) were either lost

to follow-up or had to drop out of the study because of a family emergency. Dropout was disproportionately higher in the HC group such that only 6 of 10 participants in the HC completed the study and took part in the post-study interview.

Regarding possible *differences in perceived usability*, as shown in Table 13, there were no differences in reported usability, as measured by the Subjective Assessment of Speech System Interfaces (SASSI; [119]), or in shared decision-making of goal setting, as measured by the 9-item shared decision-making questionnaire (SDM-9 [144]).

Table 13. Comparison of post measures between the two study groups

	Human Coaching	Chatbot
N Enrolled (N Interviewed)	10 (6)	13 (12)
SASSI *(n.s. p = 0.94)*	4.20 (± 0.74)	4.23 (± 0.55)
Adapted SDM-Q-9 *(n.s. p = 0.73)*	86% (± 20%)	83% (± 17%)

Regarding possible *differences in conversational patterns*, daily conversations tended to be significantly longer in the human coach group (Table 14). The median conversation was 3 turns in the chatbot group (approximately the length of the daily check in script) compared to 5 turns in the HC group, with one conversation continuing for 51 turns.

Table 14. Length of conversations between participants and their coach in the two study groups

Conversational turns per day	Human Coaching	Chatbot
Mean (SD)* *(p < 0.001)*	7.89 (10.11)	4.22 (4.26)
Median (Range)* *(p < 0.01)*	5 (1 to 51)	3 (1 to 20)

Regarding *differences in goal attainment*, self-reported goal attainment was consistently higher in the chatbot group, averaging above 80%, while attainment was 36.4% on average in the human coaching group (Table 15), a difference that was statistically significant with Fisher's exact test. While attainment was relatively consistent in the chatbot group, attainment increased from 25% to over 40% in the human coaching group from the first week of the study to the second. While the increase was not statistically significant due to the small sample size, the difference between the chatbot and human coaching group was no longer statistically significant in the second week of the study.

Table 15. Self-reported goal attainment between the two study groups

	Human Coaching	Chatbot
Overall ($p < 0.01$)	36.4%	80.8%
First week ($p < 0.05$)	25.0%	80.4%
Second week (n.s. $p = 0.06$)	42.9%	81.4%

4.2.3 Qualitative Themes

In this section, we identify and describe the main qualitative findings from interviews with participants with diabetes and health coaches. After briefly describing participants and coaches in the study, we report 4 main themes, summarized in Table 16. As shown in Supplementary Table F & Supplementary Table G , themes 1 & 4 were prevalent across participants, while themes 2 and 3 were prevalent among either the human coaching or chatbot group, respectively.

Table 16. Summary of qualitative themes

Theme 1	Participants in both groups felt like they were working with a health coach
Theme 2	Human-powered coaching had the advantages of empathy and deeper engagement, but encountered multiple challenges with communication via text messaging
Theme 3	The consistency and predictability of the chatbot helped participants persevere in achieving their goals and promoted their autonomy
Theme 4	The directness and intimacy of text messaging created expectations for personalized and continuous support

Quotes from participants with diabetes are labeled with a participant number (e.g. P10), followed by their group in parentheses – Chatbot or HC (Human Coaching). Quotes from the 4 health coaches are labeled with Coach and a number (e.g. Coach #3). Excerpts from text message transcripts are included in `monospace font`.

Characterizing participants

During their interviews, many participants described challenges they had experienced in their prior efforts to self-manage their T2D. Many were in the habit of checking blood glucose (BG) at least once a day, but also described challenges in interpreting and acting on BG readings, especially unexpected or high readings. Participants also described a number of limiting circumstances that hindered their efforts towards self-management, for example inadequate food budgets, food allergies, disabilities, or other physical impediments.

Participants described a range of familiarity with and use of technology. Many were comfortable with text messaging; for example, P10 described regularly messaging with family and friends:

"All the time... I hit the messenger send my message, I message my daughter, my son, I have friends that I text with them too" P10 (Chatbot)

However, others were less familiar with texting, and in some cases adamantly disliked it, preferring to return texts with voice messages, or send voice memos:

"The only time I text to my children is this day at work and I have to tell them something... I don't like texting, I don't." P5 (Chatbot)

In terms of using technology to support their self-management, none had ever used an application on their phone for self-tracking before this study, though some tech-savvy users had set up medication reminders on their phone, or used YouTube to find exercise videos or recipes.

Characterizing health coaches

During interviews, each coach described their health coaching philosophy. Overall, the coaches' philosophy aligned very closely with BAP [109], used to guide both the chatbot and human coaches. Coaches described the importance of being **patient-centric**, respecting **autonomy**, and letting clients drive the process.

"I would say my general philosophy is very patient, participant driven, so I really am very much of a coach in the true sense of the word that I work with them on their goals, and I never really, at least at this point in my practice, tell a patient what to do. I just try to get it to come from them." Coach #2

With goal setting, coaches emphasized helping their clients arrive at **goals** that are **specific and actionable**, and advocated for working on only one or two goals at a time. Coaches felt that goals were meant to be cumulative, focusing on **small, incremental changes** to participant's current practices, to help them **build up healthy habits** over time. Lastly, coaches described the importance of **asking questions** to learn about participants current practices and help drive them towards practical goals.

Theme 1: Participants in both groups felt like they were working with a health coach

Notably, nearly all participants in both the human coach and chatbot groups stated that they felt they were working with a health coach and used words like "coach" or "teacher" to describe the system. When describing their experience in the study, participants mentioned a number of phenomena consistent with health coaching. For example, setting actionable goals was the focal point of conversations with t2.coach; participants in both groups chose goals to work on, and most recounted examples of behaviors they changed to meet their goals. Many participants described their experiences acting on specific suggestions from their coaches; for example, P8 followed the recommendation to find a friend to go on walks with.

"I did find a friend. She does walk with me... We did from here to ▮▮▮▮*, walking." P8 (Chatbot)*

In the process of working towards their goals, participants in both groups described how working with the coach ***increased their motivation*** to pursue healthy behavior changes.

"I like it's better than you know, you try to work on the key issue like motivate it for me. It gives me motivation and teach me" P15 (HC)

In addition to following goals and experiencing increased motivation, participants in both groups recounted other experiences related to different aspects of coaching. In both groups, participants commented that their exchanges with the coach felt like a ***conversation***, appreciating the communication and the back-and-forth exchange. It was perhaps unsurprising that participants in the human coach group described how they felt they were ***building a relationship*** with their coach over time. More notably, participants in the Chatbot group similarly described that they appreciated the relationship with their coach especially when they did not always feel that they were able to talk about their diabetes with others in their life.

"Yes, it was nice to talk to somebody, you know, about diabetes because I don't even want to talk to stuff like this to somebody else. Who wants to know what the goals were and what I would like to do and what I would like to accomplish?" P6 (Chatbot)

For many participants, the regular contact from their coach **helped promote mindfulness** of the goals they had chosen, and determine a plan to meet that goal. The regularity of communication with their coach also helped participants to feel that there was an entity keeping an eye on them. This feeling of someone looking out for them helped promote a sense of external

accountability to work towards meeting stated goals. Through the process of working with their coach, participants described *learning and gaining knowledge* of new approaches for their self-management, whether altogether new behaviors or new ways to accomplish longstanding goals. Participants in both groups described a number of other experiences consistent with health coaching, which we summarize with illustrative quotes across both groups in

Supplementary Table H. These themes were prevalent across participants in both study groups; while not every single participant experienced all positive aspects, each theme was found across both study groups approximately equally (within 20%).

The exchange between the chatbot and P5 in Table 17 exemplifies the manner in which even the fully-scripted chatbot created an opportunity for a conversation that promoted mindfulness and reflection over the participant's experience pursuing personal goals. P5 responded thoughtfully to open-ended prompts from the chatbot, to reflect on the barriers they encountered meeting their goal and formulate a plan to address those barriers.

Table 17. An exchange between P5 and the chatbot coach discussing strategies to overcome barriers in goal attainment.

Coach (Chatbot)	Good morning! How did it go with your plan yesterday? Did you meet your goal to "Make ½ my meal fruits and/or vegetables"? (Yes/No)
P5	Not well,I missed lunch and I ate dinner late. I forgot to take my metformin last night.
Coach (Chatbot)	I'm sorry, I didn't understand that. Please respond with "yes" or "no"
P5	No
Coach (Chatbot)	That's okay, it can happen. What got in the way of meeting your goal?
P5	I accompanied a relative to a doctor's appointment. Then we went to 2nd appointment and I skipped lunch. My glucose level started to drop so I ate 6 short bread cookies. I didn't get home until after 8:00pm from 10:30 am. There was no place I could eat in the area .
Coach (Chatbot)	How do you think you can overcome that challenge tomorrow?

P5	Packing sandwich in my bag just in case I'm out without access to the right kind of foids.
Coach (Chatbot)	Thank you for sharing that with me
Coach (Chatbot)	Would you like to choose a specific plan to meet your goal tomorrow? ...

The interview with P5 provided additional context for how communication with t2.coach helped participants in achieving their goals, including by promoting mindfulness and accountability.

"I think the questions made me pay attention to more of what was going on with myself, instead of being distracted because of what I was doing and what I was going through emotionally with situations with my relative and it made me concentrate on what I need to do for myself." P5 (Chatbot)

In this exchange, P5 describes how they were going through a challenging time caring for a relative, and not prioritizing their own health. The questions and messages from the chatbot were prompts for P5 to step back and reflect in-the-moment on their health goals and how to continue achieving them despite stressful daily circumstances, and maintaining accountability to meeting goals.

Theme 2: Human coaching had advantages, but encountered barriers with text messaging

While there were surprising similarities between the coaching experiences of participants in both groups, there were numerous ways in which the daily exchanges varied between groups. While human coaches started off following the BAP protocol, they ended up embellishing it, and eventually went completely off-script. There were several notable situations when coaches went off-script: to provide empathy and appear more human, or to respond to their clients' broader needs beyond the protocol. We discuss these below.

One of the prominent places where human coaches went off-script was to express

empathy and display their **humanness**. Table 18 shows an exchange between P17 and their

coach (#4) where P17 says that they have not been feeling well, and the coach responds

empathetically, in a way that might appear second nature for human conversation.

Table 18. A brief exchange between P17 and Coach #4, where the coach responds with empathy after the participant shares that they are still not feeling well.

Coach (Coach #4)	Hi ▮▮▮, how are you feeling? How has it been going with your meals?
P17	Still not feeling well and my eating is not good right now but I am working on getting better. Thank you for asking. Appetite is not good.
Coach (Coach #4)	Ok, I'm sorry to hear that. Feel better. I will check in with you again tomorrow at this time. Do you have any questions for me now?
P17	Not yet but waiting on feeling better and then I will have questions.
Coach (Coach #4)	Ok sounds good. Take care. Talk to you tomorrow

In their interview, P17 described the appreciation they felt for their coach, who they

believed was truly concerned about them and their wellbeing.

"Even though I don't know whether that person was human or was it, you know, automated,

I felt like is it like human and has to be concerned about my health. Because on those days I

wasn't feeling well... even though she didn't say I'm disappointed I felt like I can't let her

down." P17 (HC)

In addition to expressions of empathy, coaches were also able to follow their human

instincts and go off-script to ask questions that ***expanded the scope of their coaching support***.

Many participants were experiencing deeper challenges that were preventing them from fully

pursuing nutrition-related goals. This was the case, for example, with participants who experienced unstable housing. When one of these participants brought it up during an exchange, the coach pursued it with further questions and eventually shared additional information about a homelessness resource and also shared information about an upcoming job fair.

"There were a lot of barriers there… she is going through homelessness basically… And that's why you see… I try to give her some help with the housing and stuff like that which wasn't really like you know the normal track that we would do. You have to deal with some of that first." Coach #1

In a minority of cases, coaches' questioning led to very fruitful exchanges, enabling much more personalized suggestions and support. For example, in Table 19, we see an excerpt of a conversation between P13 and their coach (#2), where the coach learns about the participant's temporary housing status, and asks a series of questions to learn about their situation and preferences, and help them arrive at healthier breakfast options. This conversation was one of the longest, with 68 utterances and 32 conversational turns over 35 minutes.

This in-depth exchanged helped the participant to arrive at many reasonable options for healthier breakfasts, which they described trying and enjoying. This type of in-depth exchange was unique to the human coaching group and exemplifies the advantages of the human-driven approach.

Table 19. An in-depth exchange between P13 and Coach #2

Coach (Coach #2)	Hi ███ , first, great job adding the green beans
Coach (Coach #2)	I reviewed your food logs, as well as your blood glucose levels. I'd love to continue to help you to set goals.
Coach (Coach #2)	Let me know and we can chat about them
P13	I am at a disadvantage I am not home I'm in transitional housing
P13	this point. I try to work with what is offered to me. I'm not making
P13	excuses I'm trying to live on a budget that I am not always in

P13	I can eat because I have no way to cook here
Coach (Coach #2)	Thanks for sharing this with me, ███. That's totally understandable that you're limited in your choices. But not to worry, I have some ideas of what we can do
	. . .
Coach (Coach #2)	What other veggies did they serve, that you have tried?
P13	I like the protein idea yes I can do that
Coach (Coach #2)	Liked "I like the protein idea yes I can do that"
Coach (Coach #2)	Wonderful!
Coach (Coach #2)	Tell me about the veggies so I can help you with that part
Coach (Coach #2)	All these changes can help your blood sugars to get in better control.
P13	Today for breakfast I had two oatmeal cookies and that's all I ate
Coach (Coach #2)	Okay - let me help you with breakfast.
Coach (Coach #2)	I noticed on your logs that you sometimes eat a banana
Coach (Coach #2)	What is available at the housing for breakfast?

Text messaging created barriers to effective communication

Despite these successes, health coaches expressed overwhelming frustration with text messaging as a medium for coaching, and found it to be much more difficult than in-person or telephone coaching.

"Putting them in a hierarchy [in-person] would be the easiest and then more recently I've been doing a lot more phone calls which is harder in certain ways. Text messaging was even harder. There was no ability to pull out nuances." Coach #3

Participants often replied with short responses, which coaches had difficulty interpreting, and sometimes resulted in miscommunications.

"We're talking about do you want to keep the same plan tomorrow, "yes," but what does yes mean? Does that mean literally you're going to have the same dinner like yesterday?... There was no embellishment from her at any point" Coach #3

Furthermore, the lack of non-verbal cues made nuanced communication difficult, impeding the coaches' ability to build rapport with their clients, as they would in an in-person setting.

"I just find that difficult to establish a rapport... How can we ask you to establish a rapport with someone through just text message? It's pretty hard to convey who you are." Coach #2

Overall, text messaging as a medium limited coaches' ability to engage in the types of in-depth exchanges they were used to, and created barriers to effective communication that sometimes resulted in miscommunication and misunderstanding.

Coaching without nuance or context

In addition to challenges communicating via text message, coaches described difficulties developing a coaching relationship without any context about their client.

"I don't know if she likes apples, I don't know if she likes peanut butter and that she could be allergic to peanuts for all I know." Coach #3

In particular, coaches struggled to determine how engaged their clients were in the coaching process based on the short and ambiguous responses they often received, often after a considerable delay.

"I don't know if I should've taken it like, "I don't want to talk anymore," or "I'm tired right now," or it's you know, she wasn't welcoming to be pushed... the whole time I was getting mixed messages" Coach #4

When they perceived hesitation, coaches were uncertain about how to balance proactively pushing participants and continually messaging them, or to give their clients space.

Reflecting on their exchanges, coaches often viewed these interactions as missed opportunities to engage or push their clients further, and regretted it when they felt they were too hesitant.

Attempts for deeper engagement sometimes backfired

To try to combat the lack of context, coaches took up their tried-and-true strategy of **asking questions** to their clients. Coaches tried to probe participants to uncover more fundamental challenges they were encountering, or to find some jumping off point to drive the conversation forward.

"Sometimes you wait for that like little piece of information that's the entry into a bigger conversation. So maybe they would drop a little tidbit about money being tight, and now you have an opening to talk about budget and planning and frozen vegetables." Coach #3

As discussed in the beginning of this section there were a handful of circumstances where question-asking was fruitful in leading to in-depth coaching exchanges; however, there were many other situations when it was not as successful and, in occasionally even backfired. When participants were not as engaged, coaches continued to ask questions multiple times in multiple ways.

"So, I would ask the same question in different ways... you could see my maneuvering and trying to get her to focus." Coach #1

This repetitive questioning occasionally led to annoyance among participants, and a feeling that the coach was not actually listening. In one instance, Coach #3 included some additional clarifying questions to spur the conversation during a daily check-in with P14; P14, however, interpreted these questions to mean that the coach did not remember the goal they had set together the day before, a misunderstanding that put the participant off.

"I thought we were talking about it the other day what my goal was, we want to do it for the whole week... she has the same thing every day we talk it was like somebody was not listening" P14 (HC)

This example highlights the disconnect between coaches' and clients' perceptions of their exchanges, which sometimes led to dissatisfaction and frustration.

Coaches want a rewarding experience, too, but rarely received it

Overall, the health coaches in this study did their best to provide a positive coaching experience for participants, and took pride when their clients showed signs of success. In particular, coaches found satisfaction in the instances when participants engaged for more in-depth exchanges, like the exchange between Coach #2 and P13 in Table 19:

"He really opened up and was like very receptive to coaching. That was really cool. And it kind of worked out that like, the timing was good, too, like he and I were both online." Coach #2

While these were the highlight of the experience for coaches, they were also quite rare. The more common experience was frustration due to the challenges with text messaging and a lack of context, described above. Coaches disliked receiving short responses from their clients, and in response some coaches went out of their way to embellish their messages in an attempt to convey that there was a human on the other end.

"I tried to lighten the mood a little bit... One of the things that I wanted to avoid was it sounding like I was just a computer. I wanted her to build up there was an actual person on the other end." Coach #3

The disconnects that resulted from the challenges of text messaging, discussed above, led the coaches to feel frustrated and dissatisfied that their clients were not fully committed to the coaching process, and were not stretching or challenging themselves.

"At this point is when I realized that she [P14] chose the half a plate of vegetable goal because it was easy. This is like something that she did all the time." Coach #3

Ironically, however, Coach #3's dissatisfaction was the result of a fundamental miscommunication. In their interview, P14 discussed how they had completely changed their eating habits during the study, and were in uncharted territory with their nutrition goal.

"I am not normally eating salad, you know every day with my meals, I don't." P14

Because of the challenges of text messaging and difficulty perceiving how engaged their clients were, coaches received little direct feedback on how they were doing in their role as virtual coach. Even when participants were having highly positive experiences, coaches were not able to see this or share in this satisfaction until the very end of the study, if at all.

Theme 3: The consistency and predictability of the chatbot helped participants persevere in pursuing their goals and promoted their autonomy

While text messaging presented considerable barriers for human coaches, it also gave unique advantages to the chatbot. Specifically, its consistent, if annoying, behaviors helped individuals to persist in pursuing their goals. Furthermore, its strict adherence to the BAP script mandated consistency in including choices for goals and behaviors; these choices helped promote participants' autonomy and sense of agency.

Perseverance in pursuing goals

Many participants found the chatbot to demonstrated patience in its responses, always allowing users to make a choice, and re-prompting with the question if it did not understand the user's response.

"It always gave me an answer. It never cut me off like it gave me what you call feedback, computer talk or whatever… but it left it open so I could continue to think on it." P9 (Chatbot)

A common comment among participants in both groups was to describe their coaching experience as "annoying, but helpful." The "annoyance" was particularly salient for participants who were not frequent users of text messaging and who preferred talking on the phone. Part of the annoyance stemmed from the fact that text message notifications would sometimes arrive at inopportune times, for example during a doctor's appointment, at church, or when the participant was with friends. Poor timing of messages was compounded by the fact that participants felt obligated to respond to messages soon after they arrived.

"But it's just really annoying when it's just not giving the person a chance to think, understand. It's just fast, you have to answer fast… But when a patient or someone is doing something, we can stop what we are doing just because we need to answer this fast" P8 (Chatbot)

However, when discussing the aspects of the coach that they found annoying, participants in the Chatbot group often described them as a double-edged sword, acknowledging the pushiness of the Chatbot as a necessary evil in achieving desired changes in their self-management.

"There's a positive message and we have to believe each message that comes through is for a reason, is to keep us to maintain us healthy… even though it's from an automated service,

you know, so the power of positivity is there… Hey, you don't get rid of your mom because

she is annoying." P8 (Chatbot)

The features that contributed to annoyance, like the persistence and consistency of messaging, were also tied to participant's perceptions of what made the intervention helpful, by increasing motivation, and keeping behavior change intentions salient throughout the day to spur positive behaviors.

Choice and autonomy

One of the predominant themes unique to interviews of participants in the chatbot group was regarding their appreciation for **choices and options** presented to them by the coach. BAP provides an opportunity for participants to select a preferred option for setting goals. While human coaches followed this part of the protocol initially, they eventually wound up suggesting individual goals rather than sharing a menu of choices. One human coach participant (P13) said that the coach "gave" them goals "to be ascribed to."

```
Coach #4 to P17:  For this coming week, I want to make sure that you
make 1/2 of my plate fruits and/or vegetables. Is that something you
can do?
```

In contrast, the Chatbot was consistent in following the protocol and offering menus each step of the way. As a result, participants in the Chatbot group appreciated the freedom to pursue options that mattered to them.

"Not only did it give me the options. But then if I didn't appreciate those options it gave me

the chance to request another set of options, you know, I found that to be helpful as well."

P11 (Chatbot)

P6 poignantly contrasted their experience with the chatbot coach to receiving a prescription from a doctor's office. In the case of the doctor, it was an instructive, but with the chatbot, it was a choice.

"He gave you a variety of choices. It's not like if you go to a doctor he tells you, we have to put this medicine if you wanted to heal, you know, he gave you more choices… and see what works better for you, so I think that was better" P6 (Chatbot)

Theme 4: The directness and intimacy of text messaging created expectations for personalized and continuous support

While there were a number of differences in participants' experiences with human coaches in contrast to the chatbot, there were also a number of notable similarities, particularly in regards to their expectations from virtual coaching delivered through text messaging. Most notably, the participants saw the daily availability as a key advantage that also presented a stark contrast with their previous in-person coaching experiences.

"The thing that it kept track with you… it was constantly there for you almost every day. So, you're never really alone." P13 (HC)

However, daily engagement also raised expectations for a level of support that was connected to participants' daily activities. This heightened expectation was unrealized in both the Chatbot group as well as the Human Coaching group, with all participants wishing for suggestions that were more related to the specifics of the meals they were logging.

"I have salad with tomatoes, onions, and I put sunflower seeds, and I put dressing, you know, so was it okay or was it not okay, what should I not put in my salad?" P14 (HC)

The daily nature of virtual coaching combined with the fact that the study included meal and blood glucose logging may have contributed to expectations for more direct feedback on the meals they had entered. For example, P8 described that they felt the experience of logging was disconnected from their coaching experience, and wished to receive more feedback based on what they were eating, like what kinds of additions to oatmeal would be best for their BG.

"They are not connected because I took a picture of my food but you didn't say that is good. So its separate. Because if you eat a little bit of oatmeal and it raises your sugar 50% when it is supposed to be more healthy than there is something wrong, right? Is it the milk that I am using?" P8 (Chatbot)

This desire for more specific feedback and suggestions based on participants' meal logs was the most commonly expressed recommendation from participants in both groups. Along these lines, participants also asked for more actionable and varied suggestions like recipe ideas, workout videos, or lists of healthy food items to buy at the grocery store.

4.2.4 Discussion

In this research, we aimed to unpack tensions of humanness in virtual health coaching. While there has been an increased focus on conversational technologies in healthcare, some have argued that the human element is irreplaceable in health coaching [146,218]. We completed a two-week study with two versions of a virtual health coaching intervention. In one group, participants interacted with a scripted, wizard-of-oz chatbot based on Brief Action Planning (BAP; [109]). In the other group, participants interacted with an actual health coach, who started with the same protocol as the chatbot for consistency, but could embellish as necessary. We sought to compare and contrast the experience of coaching in these two groups, to explore 1) whether automated chatbots have the potential to serve as virtual health coaches, 2) whether there are any aspects of coaching that are uniquely human, as well as 3) potential advantages of automated conversational approaches for health coaching in a virtual setting. Below we discuss the main results of the study and their implications for future research in human-computer

interaction (HCI) and for the design of virtual coaching interventions in health.

A comparable coaching experience with a chatbot

One of the overarching questions in this study was whether fully automated coaching

systems are capable of creating positive coaching experiences. Overall, we found that

participants from both groups reported generally positive experiences, and described their time in

the study as working with a coach. Many of the themes observed in the accounts of their

coaching experience — like increased motivation, learning and education, and accountability —

align well with the description of positive coaching experiences by Olsen and others [196,267].

While it was not surprising that experienced health coaches were able to create a positive

coaching experience, it was notable how similar experiences were between the two groups,

despite divergent conversational patterns; human coaches had longer conversations that covered

broader topics than the chatbot. Moreover, there were no differences in post-test assessments of

usability or shared decision-making between the two groups. Interestingly, self-reported goal

attainment over the study period was higher in the Chatbot group (over 80%) than the Human

Coaching group (less than 50%). These results support the potential of even relatively simple

automated approaches to cultivate a coach-like experience to support self-management.

On one hand, these findings challenge previous arguments that coaching is a uniquely

human domain and that creating a positive coaching experience inevitably requires the

involvement of human coaches [218]. On the other hand, this finding is consistent with multiple

previous investigations that showed the efficacy of conversational agents in creating positive

experiences in many areas related to individuals' health [24,25,91,146,160]. Our study further

supports these previous observations and extends them into the context of health coaching.

However, our study also showed that while both human coaches and chatbots can create positive coaching experiences, they each have their unique advantages and limitations. We discuss these below.

Advantages and challenges of human-powered coaching via text message

Previous research argued that human coaches have characteristics that are uniquely human and cannot be replicated with automated systems [218]. Our study provided some support to this claim; human coaches were unmatched in their ability to express empathy and to flexibly expand the scope of support based on their understanding of individuals' needs. However, it also showed that text messaging as a medium for coaching had several important limitations, often leading to negative experiences for both coaches and participants. We discuss these below.

Empathy, expanded scope of support, and accountability.

In this study, coaches demonstrated several important characteristics that had a positive impact on coaching experiences. First, they were unmatched in their ability to express empathy and build a human connection with their clients. Many participants in the human coaching group felt that their coaches really cared about them, which was both motivational and encouraging. Second, coaches were able to use their intuition and experience to identify their clients' unmet needs, and used these cues to provide context-sensitive support for other aspects of participants' lives, including housing and employment. Both of these advantages in the Human Coaching group are consistent with Rutjes' account of health coaching, which emphasized interpersonal human connection and the ability for coaches to adapt support to situation-specific contexts [218]. In particular, the expanded scope of support and ability to adapt to multiple contextual factors is a substantial unsolved problem and area of ongoing work in conversational AI [97,146], but is incredibly important to support the complexity of self-care practices [195,209].

Similarly, while previous research has explored imbuing chatbots with empathy [159], other studies suggested that individuals can differentiate and prefer empathic responses from actual humans [182]. Pursuing automated approaches to empathy also has ethical implications, as there is potential for deceptive applications or unintended consequences on mental health and social interaction [182].

Another possible advantage of human coaching, less explored in the previous literature, is the sense of accountability inherent in relationships with human coaches. In the previous section we suggested that high self-reported goal attainment in the chatbot group indicated that individuals in this group met their goals more often. One explanation of this finding is that the chatbot was more effective than human coaches in helping participants achieve their chosen goals. More plausibly however, participants may have opted for goals that were easier to achieve with the chatbot, while human coaches encouraged them to take on more challenging goals. If that was indeed the case, chatbots could take concrete steps to encourage participants to set more challenging goals that are more likely to lead to improvements in health. For example, they could suggest incorporating a secondary, challenging goal alongside a primary, attainable goal [184], or setting adaptive goals that change over time based on the user's behaviors [143].

Furthermore, it is possible that the perception of social commitment and accountability varied between the two groups, which also contributed to the discrepancy in self-reported goal attainment. Many factors can influence goal choice and attainment, including social commitment and accountability [143,184]. It is possible that the perception of a human on the receiving end of messages in the human coaching group fostered accountability and honesty, while participants in the chatbot group felt less social accountability and were more comfortable over-reporting their accomplishments [183]. This explanation contrasts with findings in mental health treatment suggesting individuals may be more forthcoming with an agent than a human counselor [162].

However, a key difference here is that the health coach could view the participant's meal logs

and objectively assess goal attainment, which may have fostered accountability. Future work

could further explore perceptions of accountability with human and non-human conversational

partners in coaching.

Precariousness of in-depth conversations without common ground.

Despite these advantages, health coaches described significant challenges communicating

with clients via text messaging. Because text messaging has low information bandwidth [64] and

lacks nuance, coaches and clients described a number of disconnects and misunderstandings.

These at times led to frustration for both coaches and clients, thus negatively impacting the

coaching experience.

We relate these findings to the notion of *common ground* [56] common in HCI literature.

Common ground offers a way to describe the shared understanding between individuals

necessary to facilitate effective conversation. Common ground is built over time through

collaboration and discussion, for example between colleagues in a workplace. Coiera [60]

described how common ground can be relevant in understanding not just human-human but also

human-computer interaction. Common ground can be challenging even for more straightforward

tasks like scheduling, let alone complex tasks like health coaching [139]. Coaches in our study

had substantial difficulty establishing common ground with participants over text message,

despite their repeated attempts to engage in more in-depth conversations as they would in an in-

person setting. The lack of common ground in these conversations may have contributed to the

disconnect and dissatisfaction some participants reported. Furthermore, consistent with prior research [191], we found that delays in responses between coaches and participants further challenged understanding and satisfaction with conversations.

Notably, some of the successful in-depth conversations were proceeded by the coach reviewing the participant's meal logs, which Coiera describes as "pre-emptive grounding" [60]. While grounding may be more challenging via text message, clients' self-tracking data offers an avenue to build up common ground before coaching exchanges begin. Research in HCI has explored the use of self-tracking data artifacts and visualizations to improve common ground in patient-provider communication [54,221]. These approaches have so far been applied to in-person discussions, but the principles can apply to remote conversation as well, for example the need for both parties to view similar visualizations [116,165]. Self-tracking data also offers a path to grounding in automated systems, by incorporated user-tracked data to inform dialogs, for example offering feedback on specific meals, or tailoring suggestions based on the user's recent logs.

In addition to challenges in establishing common ground, our study highlighted multiple challenges related to coordinating and organizing conversations. Nardi et al showed that a significant portion of instant message (IM) exchanges in the workplace were focused on organizing the appropriate context for the information exchange; including negotiating availability and maintaining the sense of connectedness [189].This was also the case in our study, where coaches struggled to find appropriate times for engagement. Prior work has shown that some individuals can engage in in-depth exchanges with multiple threads in a single conversation thus covering both coordination and information exchange [125]; however, these exchanges were rare in our study. Furthermore, in a workplace setting, individuals who engage in simpler conversation instead addressed other communication needs like logistics and social ties outside of the IM conversation, which was not possible with text-only coaching [125]. Our results support the difficulty of establishing common ground and coordinating engagement via text message alone, and suggest that text-based coaching interventions ought to consider simpler exchanges with a lower cost of establishing common ground through conversation or provide other means for establishing common ground beyond brief text messages.

Difficulty assessing engagement without social translucence.

In addition to challenges establishing common ground via text message, there were also a number of important social cues missing. Challenges related to coordinating opportunities for engagement via text messaging, described in the prior section, were further exacerbated by the lack of cues that could help coaches and their clients to maintain awareness of each other's actions and context.

Previous research in HCI used the notion of *social translucence* [80] to identify important characteristics of digital systems for fluid social interactions, including *visibility* of the other party's status and availability. In our study, social translucence was lacking because coaches could not see when their clients were available to receive messages, or otherwise occupied, and had no additional information to interpret a lack of responsiveness or curt replies. Our attempts to impose external structure to promote coordination, for example allowing coaches and clients to list the times they would be available, were only partially successful. Previous research has explored conversational coaching via other text-based platforms that offer more visibility of a the user's status to better enable social translucence [168,242]; however, further research is required to support the fluid social interactions at heart of health coaching.

One potential direction is to utilize sensing capabilities of mobile platforms to infer a user's state and status [71]. Contemporary smartphones are able to capture considerable amounts of data about their users, and many contextual factors are relevant for chronic disease self-management [195,209]. In our study, this awareness of clients' context could have helped human coaches tailor their support, and offered more visibility into when they should persist with messaging or pull back. For automated coaching systems, contextual data could help to determine the times when clients will be most receptive to messaging [150,185]. However, prioritizing the visibility of a user's state is in tension with preserving their privacy [80]. Health coaching is deeply personal, and future work could explore this tradeoff in the context of health coaching, which may be different than in the workplace.

Heightened and unmet expectations for personalization.

Our study showed that text messaging as a coaching medium had several important limitations. At the same time, coaching over text messaging, combined with integration of self-tracking data, left participants with specific expectations for the type of support they would receive. In contrast with in-person coaching, participants appreciated that t2.coach was available every day to offer support and answer questions. Furthermore, by including self-tracking of meals and BG levels, participants expected the content of coaching to be highly specific to their own meals and behaviors, and wished for more specific suggestions about how to modify their common meals, or for other recipes to try. Yet this expectation for personalized support grounded in their self-tracking data was largely unmet in both groups. While half of the coaches attempted to review participants' records, they found this process inconsistent with their typical practice of relying on in-depth conversations with clients to obtain needed information. Furthermore, reviewing data collected by multiple clients would require considerable investment of time and efforts from the coaches [164].

In contrast with t2.coach, which focused on holistic coaching via goal setting and action planning, other prior coaching interventions have focused on feedback related to specific meals, images, or behaviors [57,120,165]. Given the positive coaching experience observed with t2.coach, it's possible that these approaches could be combined. In addition, data-driven systems can take advantage of machine learning to reduce the need for data analysis by human experts to personalize support. For example, many automated "coaching" interventions focus primarily on automatically generating targeted feedback on behaviors, captured with self-tracking and mobile sensing [57,130]. In addition, there is a growing body of research on nutrition-grounded and conversational recommendation systems, to make healthy recommendations based on what individuals have logged [53,220,239]. Indeed, because computational systems are able to process large amounts of data and make statistical inferences, automated systems may be especially well equipped to make certain kinds of recommendations, for example based on patterns in self-tracking data.

Unique advantages of chatbots as virtual coaches

While the virtual setting for coaching presented barriers for human coaches, it gave the chatbot a number of unique advantages. In particular, participants appreciated the "patience" and consistency of the chatbot, as well as the choice and autonomy it offered. While human coaches often went off-script to narrow their suggestion to a single goal, the chatbot consistently followed the protocol and always offered a menu of choices, which was highly appreciated by participants. Furthermore, the tone of its messages, carefully scripted by a team of experts in health behavior communication, was perceived as supportive and motivational. This is consistent with the argument by Bickmore and colleagues that automated conversational agents may not only be effective clinical communicators, but can be superior to human practitioners in some ways, because they can consistently follow clinical communication guidelines and best practices [22]. The chatbot's insistence to always offer a menu of options helped create a sense of autonomy for participants, who appreciated the freedom to find a goal that suited them. This emphasizes the importance of tone, style, and personality in chatbot design [66], and reaffirms for future interventions the common practice of designing conversational agents based on clinically validated protocols [91,146,159,223].

A second potential advantage was the chatbot's persistent nature, which allowed it to be "annoying but helpful," which many participants viewed as necessary in achieving desired behavior change. While human coaches were sometimes hesitant to appear too "pushy", the chatbot's insistence was appreciated by the participants, who admitted, however begrudgingly, that the persistence was necessary to help them go through with the changes and meet their goals. In some ways, this is consistent with research in text-messaging interventions for health promotion, suggesting that consistent messages at a regular cadence can effectively spur behavior change, even with little interactive engagement from participants [93,110,115]. This suggests that brevity and consistency may be important design goals for chatbots in health.

Future directions for virtual health coaching

While t2.coach was designed as a scripted chatbot, our results also have implications for the design of AI-based chatbots in health coaching. Often, the approach to building more realistically human chatbots in the AI community relies on learning from large data sets of example dialog between humans to train a dialog model [97,227]. Our results problematize this approach for virtual health coaching. In this study, both participants and coaches reported notable differences with their prior in-person experiences, and human coaches encountered substantial difficulties translating their expert approach to a text-based virtual setting. This suggests that a dialog model trained on in-person exchanges is unlikely to generalize to a virtual setting. Even a corpus of virtual coaching exchanges may be fraught, because of the messiness we observed as coaches adjusted to the text-based medium. Meanwhile, the chatbot was able to cultivate a similar experience without completely human-like dialog, suggesting multiple paths to effective conversational health coaching interventions. Together, these results suggest that pursuing more human-like coaching chatbots by learning from human-human exchanges may not be the right approach, and more research is necessary to first characterize what works for virtual coaching conversations, perhaps looking to the content of commercially successful coaching platforms [30,173].

In addition, our results suggest opportunities for systems that combine human health coaches with automated systems like chatbots. Notably, there was a synergy between areas where each excelled. The human coaches outperformed the chatbot in longer, more in-depth exchanges, while the chatbot was effective at daily, brief interactions. However, there are open questions about different ways to conceptualize this combination. On one hand, "humbots" described by Grudin and Jacues use humans quietly behind the scenes and often do not disclose human involvement to their users [103]. On the other hand, Seering and colleagues envisioned a way for chatbots to be embedded within social settings like forums or message threads [225]. In this vision, chatbots do not masquerade as humans, but exist within a conversational thread explicitly labeled as bots, and serving a supportive role for other humans in the interaction. In the case of coaching, the human might engage in less frequent, more in-depth conversations, while one or many chatbots engage in daily, automated check-ins. However, how to handle the handoff of information between bots and humans in the loop as well as how to balance the two are still open questions. Furthermore, the comparative benefits and limitations of these different approaches have not been studied directly and require further research, as well as unpacking the

ethical implications of how to label AI agents in human-AI collaboration [76,158]

4.3   Conclusion

Translating an intervention that works in an in-person setting to a virtual one is not

always straightforward. In a text-based virtual coaching setting, an automated chatbot was able

to cultivate an equivalently coach-like experience, and was advantaged by sticking to the script

to offer choices, and persistently checking in. Human coaches offered empathy and were able to

engage in deeper discussion, but encountered frustrations and barriers establishing common

ground and coordinating engagement with clients over text messaging. Future virtual coaching

interventions can incorporate more data driven personalization and consider novel ways to

combine automated and human expertise.

Chapter 5: Aim III

Explore artificial intelligence approaches to enable micro-coaching dialogs

The previous studies described in this book highlighted the potential of both conversational and machine learning powered coaching interventions. However, they also pointed to two major challenges. First, they showed that computational approaches that rely on complete and extensive self-tracking records (like meal logs with blood glucose records) will be limited in their ability to produce useful results because few individuals engage in self-monitoring consistently over time. Second, they showed the importance of short and to-the-point conversations to promote engagement. Recall that in Aim 1, participants found recording detailed meal and blood sugar logs to be burdensome; this need for extensive logging was an insurmountable barrier for many in the study. In Aim 2, we saw that lengthy dialog flows needed to be shortened substantially or users would disengage, suggesting that supportive coaching dialogs needs to accomplish their objective with as few conversational turns as possible.

The results of Aim 2 also outlined clear directions for automated coaching approaches that would be complementary to human coaching practice. First, they showed that users of the chatbot valued the brief, consistent, and focused interaction. In contrast, the human coaches were valued for more in-depth discussions, but these were rare because users' and coaches' schedules did not always align as they were going about their busy lives. Brief conversations with an automated coach could complement other interactions with coaching practitioners. Second, the participants of studies conducted in Aims 1 and 2 wished for more feedback on the specific meals they had eaten to know whether they were on track with their goals, and also wanted more suggestions and ideas for what to do differently that were personalized to their preferences and meal history.

Taken together, these findings point to a particular focus area and set of design needs for automated conversational health coaching interventions. Specifically, I propose a concept called *micro-coaching*; brief, targeted conversations about specific planned behaviors — in this case on nutrition, brief conversations about planned meals.

In contrast with the fully-automated approach described in Aim 1, micro-coaching is intended as a synergistic component within a larger coaching intervention. For example, individuals could work with a healthcare expert to identify an appropriate and meaningful health goal through in depth conversation. Alternatively, the individual's goal could derive from a set of recommendations based on automated analysis of self-tracking data. Once the goals are established, the aim of micro-coaching dialogs is to support individuals in achieving their goal when leading their daily lives.

The previous studies described in this book, together with review of literature on coaching (Section 2.6.2) helped to formulate several design needs for micro-coaching dialog systems (Figure 18). First, the system needs to be able to *automatically assess whether the user is on track to achieve their goal* with a planned meal. The assessment must be automatic in order to provide timely, in-the-moment support. Second, the system must *offer feedback* to the user based on the goal assessment. This could be positive reinforcement if the user is on track, or an acknowledgement and explanation if they are not. Third, if the user is not on track, the system must *offer suggestions* for how to modify their plan to better align with the goal. These suggestions should be personalized to an individual's preferences, and the context of the

alternatives available to them. Throughout all three phases of support, an overarching design
need is for conversations to be as ***brief and targeted*** as possible.

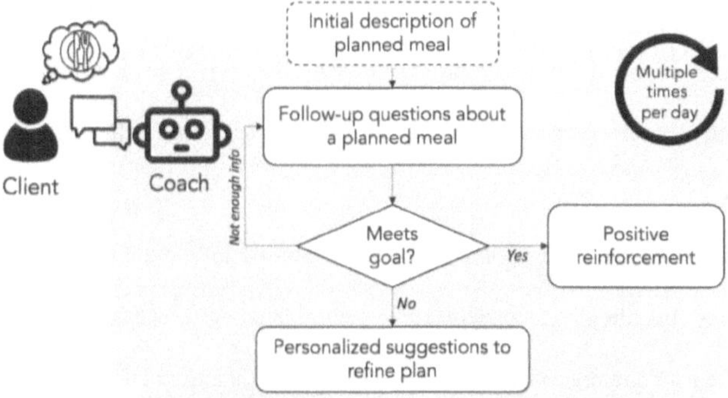

Figure 18. Proposed structure for micro-coaching dialogs.

The three design needs function as distinct phases of the conversation, each with their
own potential complexities and nuances. The remainder of the research presented in this book
focuses on the first need — the ability to automatically assess whether an individual's planned
meal is likely consistent with their nutrition goals. This step is a prerequisite to enable the
subsequent steps of offering feedback and suggestions, and itself presents considerable
complexity.

Achieving this vision requires a more intelligent approach than the scripted, finite state
agent t2.coach from Aim 2. To automatically assess if a meal is consistent with a goal, the
system needs an understanding of what the user is eating, how those foods relate to the goal, and
a strategy for asking follow-up questions.

5.1.1 Exploring the design space for micro-coaching systems

There are several approaches to develop more intelligent conversational agents. One such
approach to designing more intelligent conversational agents is primarily *data-driven*, where

machine learning (ML) models are trained with thousands of example dialogs from large corpora to learn how to respond to new, unseen inputs [97]. Such approaches have made tremendous strides in realistically human-like responses in in open-ended chit-chat conversation and many task-based applications [2]. However, these approaches rely on massive corpora from which to learn [227], and few such corpora exist for health-specific applications like health coaching [146].

An alternative approach is *knowledge-based*. Similar to frame-based conversational agents, these systems often include elements of natural language processing (NLP) to characterize the user's utterance and identify relevant entities in input text (named entity recognition; NER). These entities are then matched to a knowledge base to inform the chatbots next action and possible responses. These approaches build on a rich history of knowledge-driven and rule-based decision support systems [17,26,175,231]. For example, this approach has been used to create an interactive medication advisor, looking up queried medications in a medication knowledge base of contraindications [7].

The distinction between data-driven and knowledge-based approaches is in some ways a false dichotomy. Other than end-to-end dialog models, where inputs are mapped directly to output utterances, dialog systems are often created by combining multiple specialized sub-systems [97,169]. For example, a natural language understanding (NLU) system can process user utterances, while a separate component manages the dialog and decides why type of response to reply with (Figure 19). Some of these sub-components can be data-driven, employing ML, while others are rule-based.

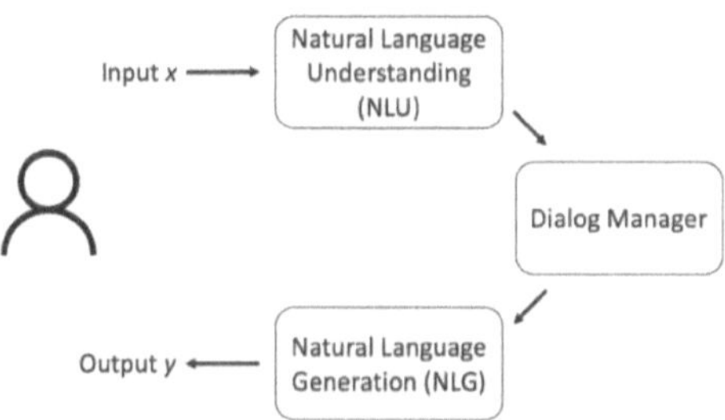

Figure 19. Common architectural diagram of frame-based conversational agents. Adapted from Gao 2018 [97]

With the aim of keeping conversations brief and efficient, reinforcement learning (RL) is an ML approach particularly well suited to dialog management [97,154,240]. With RL, a system learns through trial and error while interacting with an environment [240], and can be used to help dialog systems achieve their intended outcomes more efficiently, for example to help a chatbot that allows people to book movie tickets succeed with fewer questions [154].

While an RL approach has the potential to result in shorter conversations, it does require a corpus of data to learn from. Without an existing data set for health coaching dialogs, and because it's infeasible to learn directly from exchanges between coaches and clients, there is the possibility of creating new dialog data sets with *crowdsourcing* [228,273]. Researchers have used crowdsourcing to create new data sets for many chit-chat and task-based dialog use cases [227,228,273]. However, the coaching domain is unique because of the expert knowledge required, and differs from task-based and chit-chat application areas. Importantly, because the data set is for only one sub-component of the system, significantly less data is necessary than would be needed for an end-to-end model [97].

In this research aim, I explore multiple AI approaches to implement the first phase of micro-coaching dialogs — asking follow-up questions about meal to determine whether the user is on track to achieve their goal — with the following research questions:

Research Question 3.1: How do expert coaches formulate follow-up questions about meals their client is planning on eating to understand whether the client is likely to achieve their nutrition goal?

Research Question 3.2: How can existing, structured nutrition knowledge resources be utilized to design and implement a natural language understanding (NLU) system for dialogs about meals and generates a set of follow-up questions?

Research Question 3.3: What are comparative benefits and limitations of different types of dialog management approaches for coaching chatbots, considering those that use reinforcement learning (RL), those that choose their questions randomly, rule-based, and fully-scripted. Specifically, how do these chatbots compare on their ability to reach their end goal, their conversational length, and their perceived coherence and user experience?

5.2   Part 1: Characterize expert approaches to micro-coaching dialogs

To explore how expert coaches approach asking follow-up questions about meals, we conducted a small interview and structured survey study. In particular, we wanted to know *types of questions* health coaches would ask their clients about specific meals in order to assess whether a meal is consistent with a nutrition goal.

5.2.1   Methods

Health coaches, who were Certified Diabetes Care and Education Specialists (CDCES) were recruited from professional networks to participate in the study.

First, CDCESs joined for an interview where we asked coaches how they would interact with clients in the hypothetical scenario when they were always available in real time to discuss their clients' planned meals.

In addition, each coach completed a survey that prompted them to list the questions they would ask a hypothetical client about their meal if the only information the coach had available was a brief text description of the meal, and the nutrition goal the client is working on. In each survey, the prompt was repeated for 10 meals across 5 nutrition goals, and coaches were asked to list 3 to 5 questions per meal. We inductively categorized the yielded set of questions listed for each meal/goal pair in the survey to find patterns and groupings.

After completing the survey on their own time, participants returned for a second interview to discuss some of their specific responses, as well as to member-check the findings.

5.2.2 Results

Two CDCESs participated, competing surveys for a total of 20 meals covering 10 distinct nutrition goals and generating 60 questions.

We found that there was a very limited set of question types across all of the meal-goal pairs. At the highest level of distinction, some questions sought to *search* by asking individuals to list any additional food items not already mentioned, while other questions sought to *drill-down* on the details of food items that had already been mentioned. As shown in Table 20, the four main question types were "what else?", "what kind?", "how much?", and "how was it prepared?".

Within the question types, there are some variations. Some questions apply generically to the entire meal (e.g., "What else will you have with your meal?") while other question reference specific components of the meal (e.g., "What else will you put in your burrito?"). In addition, meal-specific questions sometimes referenced *sub-components* of a meal that were not explicitly stated in the meal description, for example asking about the amount of bread in "a ham sandwich."

Table 20. Types of meal-related questions asked my health coaches

Question Category	Question Type	Example
Search	What else?	"What else will you have with your meal?"
Drill-down	What kind?	"What kind of chicken will you have?"
	How much?	"What portion of rice will you eat?"
	How prepared?	"How was your spinach prepared?"

Considering which questions were applicable to which goals, we found that *search* questions were applicable across all goals. In contrast, *drill-down* questions were applicable to some goals and not others. For example, "How much?" questions were applicable to quantitative goals, while "What kind?" questions were more applicable to qualitative goals. In addition, some of the questions took different forms in the context of different goals. For example, "What kind?" questions might be asking about the fat content of yogurt (e.g., 0%, 2% or full fat) for a goal about lean proteins, while asking if the yogurt is plain or flavored for a goal about added sugars.

5.2.3 Discussion

Through this mixed methods study, we found that the space of possible questions is relatively small and well structured. The relevant questions depend on the content of the meal, so there is a need to not only identify the component elements of the meal, but also determine which foods would be applicable to which questions. In addition, we found that the relevant questions also depend on the goal in question, which implies a need to examine multiple goals, and consider each goal separately from a dialog management perspective.

5.3 Part 2: Designing a knowledge-based system for natural language understanding (NLU) and generating follow-up questions

5.3.1 Overview of the system

Based on the implications of the study in Part 1, we sought to take advantage of existing nutrition knowledge resources to design a pipeline for 1) processing user utterances describing a meal, 2) representing key goal-relevant attributes of those food items, 3) determining when, based on those attributes, there is enough information to determine if a meal is consistent with a goal, and 4) generating a set of possible follow-up questions. A visual overview of the pipeline is presented in Figure 20.

First, to parse food items from natural language descriptions of meals, we utilized Nutritionix, a commercial solution for named entity recognition (NER) of food items [275]. Nutritionix has been used as a component of other natural language food projects [188], and can handle common misspellings as well as brand name items. Each entry maps to the USDA Food Composition Database for nutrient estimates [252]. For many combination foods, Nutritionix includes a sub-recipe listing a food item's component ingredients. For example, "ham sandwich" has the components "ham," and "bread," which enables asking questions about meal sub-components not explicitly stated in the meal descriptions. In addition, to represent the amount of each food. We applied a rule-based NLP function to identify food quantities, extending open source code from the FoodKG project [113].

In order to both determine whether food items were consistent with a given goal, as well as to determine which questions would be applicable to which food items, we incorporated food types and categories from an existing and widely used food ontology, FoodOn [75]. For example, considering the question "What else will you put in your *<food_item>*?", some foods are likely to be containers for other foods, like sandwiches or burritos. In FoodOn, these types of foods are listed as "multi-component food items," which can be used as a heuristic to determine which food items the question is applicable to.

These attributes also help the system determine when a meal is or is not consistent with a goal. For example, for the goal "Choose lean proteins," attributes indicating which foods are proteins, and which proteins are lean or fatty, can be used to determine when all proteins have been clarified to be either fatty or lean, and the stop criteria are met.

In the last step, the system considers the question types relevant to the goal and the attributes present in the user's meal description to generate a set of possible follow questions, or "actions."

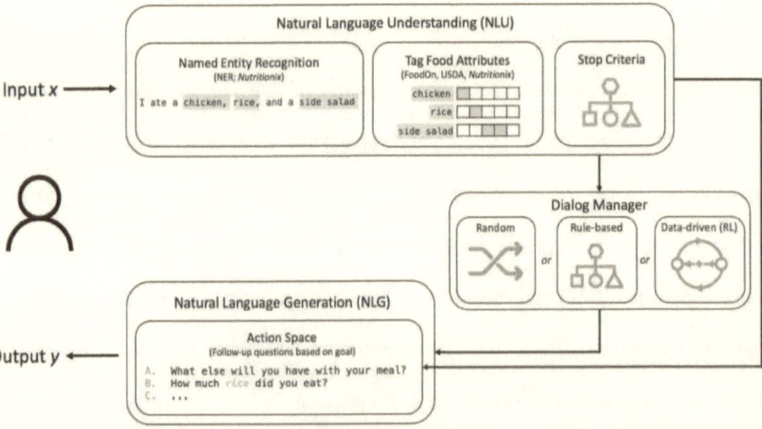

Figure 20. Outline of the process of parsing meal descriptions from input dialog utterances.

5.3.2 Choosing three goals as case studies

Because the applicable question types vary for different goals, it's important to consider multiple different nutrition goals when designing and evaluating the system. Specific nutrition goals can vary for different individuals, but there are many themes and similarities across them. We chose three nutrition goals to examine as case studies. Candidate goals were compiled from an existing knowledge base of diabetes-focused health goals [61], which were refined through the focus group in Aim 2, as well as the personalized goals from Aim 1. Some key dimensions of variance between goals are presented in Table 11.

Table 21. Dimensions of variance in common nutrition goals for individuals with type 2 diabetes

Dimension	Facet	Example
Qualitative vs. quantitative	Qualitative Quantitative (amounts) Quantitative (proportions)	Choose lean proteins Eat no more than 2 portions of carbs (30g) Make ½ my meal non-starchy vegetables
Presence vs. absence	Presence/increase Absence/decrease Both/replace	Choose whole fruits Choose foods without added sugar Replace 1 portion of carbs with protein

In addition, we sought to choose goals that were a reasonable level of difficulty for most individuals with diabetes, both in terms how often individuals achieve each goal, as well as how accurate individuals are in self-assessing goal attainment. If a goal is too easy to achieve, and individuals already understand whether they are achieving it, a dialog probing about details of the meal may not be necessary. Conversely, if a goal is too difficult, or users almost never agree with expert assessment of goal attainment, it may necessitate nutrition knowledge and education outside the scope of a brief micro-coaching dialog.

To examine the difficulty of each goal, we completed an analysis with an existing data set of meal logs with both user-assessed and expert-assessed goal attainment labels, which was collected as a part of the deployment study in Aim 1, Section 3.4, as well as prior self-tracking studies [41,70]. The data set included over 3,000 meals with assessments for over 30 nutrition goals. Because users could have multiple goals selected, there were nearly 9,000 goal evaluations for those 3,000 meals.

We calculated descriptive statistics summarizing the average goal attainment across all meals in the data set, as well as the average agreement between user-entered and expert-entered goal attainment labels. Based on these analyses, we arrived at a set of 3 goals to continue with for the crowdsourcing experiments, presented in Table 22. These goals varied to give coverage of all of the dimensions. Full results of this analysis are summarized in Supplementary Table I.

Table 22. Nutrition goals selected for crowdsourcing experiments

Nutrition Goal	Qualitative vs. quantitative	Presence vs. absence
Choose lean proteins	Qualitative	Presence/increase
Eat no more than 2 portions of carbs in each meal	Quantitative (amounts)	Absence/decrease
Make ½ my meal fruits and/or non-starchy vegetables	Quantitative (proportions)	Both/replace

For each of the three goals, we determined the action set — the set of potentially relevant follow-up question — based on the results of Study 1. See Table 23 for a summary of which actions apply to each goal.

Table 23. Summary of the action space for each nutrition goal, with examples.

Goal	Action set	Example
All goals	`What else?`	"What else will you have with your meal?"
	`What else in <container-food>?`	"What will you put in your burrito?"
	`Fallback`	"Could you please describe your meal using different words"
Choose lean proteins	`What kind <ambiguous_protein>?`	"What kind of chicken? (for example breast or thigh, with or without skin)"
	`How prepared <preparable_food>?`	"How will your chicken be prepared?"
Eat no more than 2 portions of carbs (30g)	`How much <goal_related>?`	"How much rice will you eat? (one fist is about the size of one cup)"
Make ½ my meal fruits and/or non-starchy vegetables	`How much <goal_consistent>?`	"How much broccoli will you eat? (one fist is about the size of one cup)"
	`How much <goal_inconsistent>?`	"How much rice will you eat? (one fist is about the size of one cup)"

In addition, we wrote a set of rule-based stop criteria based on the logic underlying each of the three goals and the attributes of foods in the meal. The initial version of all stop criteria are presented in Table 24.

Table 24. Summary of stop criteria logic for each of the three goals.

Goal	Stop criteria

Choose lean proteins	`[any(proteins) and none(ambiguously_fatty_protein)]`
	`or`
	`[none(proteins) and (n_food_items > 2) and asked_what_else]`

Eat no more than 2 portions of carbs (30g)	`[any(carbs) and all(has_amount(carbs))]`
	`or`
	`[none(carbs) and (n_food_items > 2) and asked_what_else]`

Make ½ my meal fruits and/or non-starchy vegetables	`[all(has_amount(fruit_veg)) and all(has_amount(non_fruit_veg))]`
	`or`
	`[none(fruit_veg) and (n_food_items > 2) and asked_what_else]`
	`or`
	`[none(non_fruit_veg) and (n_food_items > 2) and asked_what_else]`

5.3.3 Evaluation

In the prior section, we described a knowledge-based system to process user utterances describing meals, produce a set of possible follow-up questions, and determine when a meal is likely consisted with a goal or not. Because the stop criteria are the culmination of the prior steps in the pipeline (Figure 20), if the logic for the stop criteria result in accurate predictions, it suggests the components further up the pipeline are reasonably performant as well. Therefore, to evaluate the system, we created a set of dialogs with crowd workers describing meals, and examined the concordance between the system's determinations and the determinations of registered dietitians (RDs) who reviewed the dialogs.

Methods

Crowdsourced meal dialogs

We wanted to test the NLU system with dialogs about a diverse set of meals. Each dialog started with a "seed" meal to prompt crowd workers with content to describe. Meal images were drawn from prior self-tracking studies, like those described in Aims 1 and 2, as described in Section 5.3.2. For this evaluation, 10 meals were selected at random, balanced on the user, the type of meal (e.g., breakfast, lunch, or dinner) and the number of word tokens used to describe the meal. Each image was reviewed to ensure the food item(s) were clearly visible. Based on the image, and user-entered description, a member of the research team wrote an ingredient list, plainly listing the names of the food items in the photo.

To create the dialogs, we posted human intelligence tasks (HITs) to Amazon's Mechanical Turk (mTurk) platform. Each HIT included the seed meal image and ingredients, which were rendered as a photo to prevent copy-pasting verbatim, and a text-message conversation history between a fictious health coach and their client (Figure 21). Each crowd worker was asked to review the conversation history and the meal image/ingredients, and answer the question posed by the health coach. Each conversation started with the same opening question: "What are you thinking of having for *<meal_type>*?".

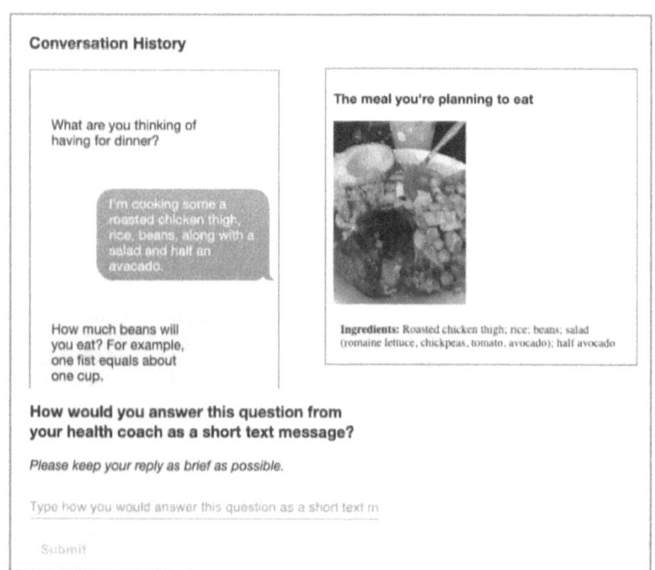

Figure 21. Example crowdsourcing task to create crowdsourced dialogs.

Completed HITs were reviewed manually to ensure they were sensical. After posting each batch of HITs, the responses were processed following the pipeline described in Section 5.3.1, and then the next response was chosen randomly from the available question types.

Each meal was used as a seed for 3 dialogs per goal, for a total of 90 dialogs (30 per goal). Each dialog continued until it was clear that there was enough information to determine whether the described meal achieved the goal, according to both the logic defined in Table 24 and manual review by member of the research team.

RD evaluation survey

For each of the 3 goals, we selected 5 dialogs where the stop criteria were met, indicating that here *was* enough information and the conversation could end, as well as 5 dialogs where the stop criteria had not been met (Figure 22). The dialogs were balanced on the number of turns to prevent any potential confounding effects of conversation length.

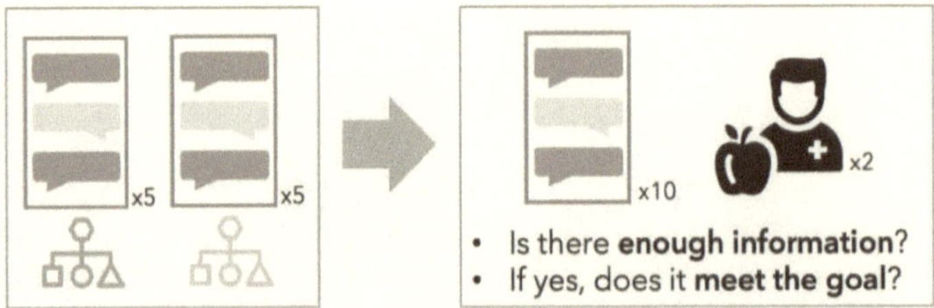

Figure 22. Study design for the evaluation of the natural language understanding (NLU) system, specifically the stop criteria

In a Qualtrics survey, RDs (n=2) assessed whether they thought there was enough information to determine whether the meal the individual was describing would likely meet their nutrition goal, or not for each of the 30 dialogs. If there was enough information, RDs also labeled whether the goal was met or not, and if there was not enough information, indicated what missing information was necessary for them to make the determination.

Inter-rater agreement was calculated with Cohen's Kappa statistic. After adding their initial labels, disagreeing items were discussed, and RDs had the option to change their labels. We calculated both the inter-rater agreement and accuracy of the systems determinations with those of the RDs.

In addition to inter-rater reliability and accuracy, I performed a qualitative *error analysis* to better understand the cause of situations where the system's predictions were incorrect. For each of the dialogs where one of the RDs disagreed with the prediction of the rule-based stop criteria, I categorized the reason for the disagreement and tabulated the frequency of each type of error.

Interrater agreement between the two RDs was initially only moderate $(\kappa = 0.46)$. Most of the disagreements were due to differing definitions of lean proteins between the two RDs. For the ½ fruit and vegetables goal, one of the RDs also made an assumption that if amounts for certain non-starchy vegetables (like carrots in soup) were not listed, they were likely small. After clarifying the rubric for the 3 goals, RDs adjusted some of their initial labels, resulting in a substantially improved inter-rater agreement score $(\kappa = 0.87)$.

Considering the agreement between the rule-based system and RDs, the average inter-rater agreement score indicated substantial agreement about whether there was enough information in the dialog to determine if the goal would be achieved $(\kappa = 0.67)$. Considering the overall accuracy of predictions of the rule-based system, the terminal states were accurate 83% of the time, and accuracy decreased as the goals increased in complexity (Table 25).

Table 25. Average accuracy of stop criteria from the rule-based system with expert registered dietitian (RD) annotations

Goal	Accuracy
All goals	83%
Choose lean proteins	95%
Eat no more than 2 portions of carbs (30g)	80%
Make ½ my meal fruits and/or non-starchy vegetables	75%

When there was enough information to for the system to make a prediction about whether the meal was consistent with the goal, those labels were 81.8% accurate with RD labels. These evaluation results suggest that the rule-based system is reasonably performant.

Results of the error analysis are presented in Table 26. The most common reason for error was that the dialog did not include a drill-down question asking about a food that likely contained a large quantity of other food items, like a smoothie. A handful of additional errors were due to disagreements about food item attributes with the labels from the FoodOn ontology, or errors with the Nutritionix named entity recognition system. The results suggest that there was not a single point of failure responsible for all of the errors.

Table 26. Error types, examples, and counts from the error analysis of the natural language understanding (NLU) system

Label type	Error type	Examples	Count
Enough information to assess meal/goal achievement	Unasked drill-down question	• Amount of fruit in a smoothie (Carb and Fruit/Veg goals)	4
	Disagreement about food item attribute	• Soy milk (Lean proteins) • Milk (Carbohydrate)	3
	Nutritionix missing sub-recipe	• System does not know that "Chicken noodle soup" contains "chicken" "noodles" or "vegetables"	1
	Assumed amount of food items	• Assumed quantity of carrots and onions would be less than the amount of shrimp, lima beans, and corn already stated (3 cups)	1
Meal/goal achievement	Differing amount estimates	• Is "1 cup of noodles" more or less than 30 grams?	3

Discussion

We designed a system for NLU of meal-related dialogs, incorporating expert knowledge to determine relevant food attributes, whether goals were achieved, and what follow-up questions could be asked. The results of the evaluation suggest that the system performs reasonably well in determining whether or not an individual is likely to achieve a given nutrition goal, though there is certainly room from improvement from 80% accuracy. Closer inspection of the performance of the individual components — the NER system and the food ontology — could indicate where additional improvements are necessary. In addition, the rule-based stop criteria could be improved upon, for example by treating the stop condition as a supervised learning problem, taking into account more features and the few considered by the rule-based criteria. However, the lingering disagreements between the two RDs suggests a subjective element to goal assessments that may introduce challenges in creating a gold standard.

5.4   Part 3: Comparing rule-based and data-driven dialog management

The knowledge-based system described in the prior section (5.3) can identify possible responses for the chatbot coach, but does not include any logic to indicate which response is likely to be most informative in a given situation. Instead, the *dialog manager* component of the overall system determines which question to ask next (Figure 23).

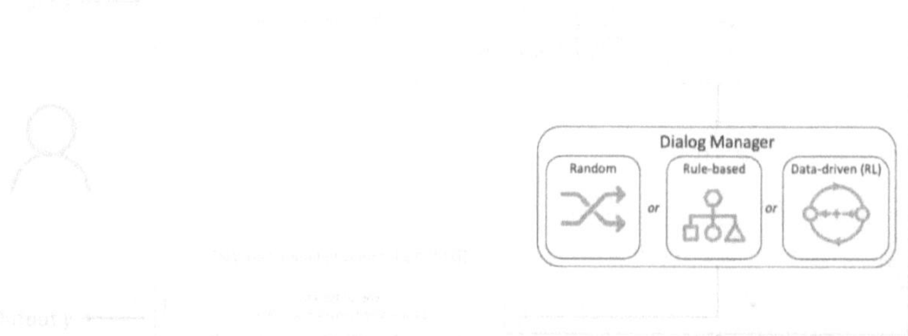

Figure 23. System overview highlighting the dialog management component.

Dialog management is a critical component of micro-coaching dialogs because of the design need to keep conversations concise. Certain questions are likely to be more informative than others, and choosing the right question is crucial to keeping conversations short. In this work, we explore two main approaches: rule-based and data-driven, and compare them with other approaches that may be used for dialog management (such as fully-scripted, and random).

5.4.1   Rule-based dialog management

The food items and attributes identified by the NLU system can be used as features to inform the selection of the next question to ask. For example, for the lean proteins goal, if one of the food items identified is an ambiguous protein then the system should ask "what kind" in an attempt to disambiguate whether the protein is lean or fatty.

Informed by the results of the study with health coaches in Section 5.2, we built on the infrastructure from Section 5.3 to design a simple, rule-base algorithm to choose the next action (Algorithm 1). To prevent premature closure of conversations, the rule-based system had a constraint to always ask one *search* question before the dialog was considered complete. For instance, for a goal about carbohydrate portions, if two high-carb food items were eaten, but only one was mentioned in the initial description, the conversation might end prematurely without searching for unmentioned or hidden food items. This constrained ensures at least some amount of *search* questions in each dialog.

Algorithm 1. Rule-based logic for dialog management

Repeat

   If there is a goal-related food item to ask a *drill-down* question about, **then** ask that question

    (e.g., if there is an ambiguously fatty protein for the lean proteins goal, then ask "what kind of <*ambiguously fatty protein*>?," or if there is a carbohydrate for the carbohydrate portions goal, then ask "how much <*carbohydrate*>?")

   Else if there is a *"container food"*, **then** ask "what else in <*container food*>?"
   Else ask "what else?"

until stop criteria is met **and** at least one *search* question has been asked

---

5.4.2 Data-driven dialog management

The same food items and attributes identified by the NLU system can also be used as features for an ML-based dialog management system. Reinforcement Learning (RL) is a machine learning approach that is well suited to the task of learning to choose the best action in a given circumstance [240]. However, data-driven approaches like RL require a corpus of examples to learn from.

A key consideration in training an RL model is the distinction between online and offline learning [240]. With *online* learning, an RL agent interacts with an environment following its own policy to explore and learning from trial-and-error. The online approach is common when the environment can be simulated or there is a low cost to exploring through the multiple iterations required for learning. In contrast, with *offline* learning, an RL agent learns from an existing data set of the actions, consequences, and rewards of another agent interacting with the environment. Offline RL is common when interacting with the environment is costly, or there is little margin for error, including many settings in the medical domain [245]. Often, a lack of knowledge about the policy that generated the training data adds additional complexity to offline reinforcement learning [127]. However, creating dialogs through a random search policy can sidestep much of this potential complexity and bias [245]. RL methods that learn from data generated with a different policy are referred to as *off-policy* methods [240,245].

Without an existing data set for micro-coaching dialogs, we used *crowdsourcing* to create a corpus of meal-related dialogs. Because of the potentially high costs and wasted resources of paying crowd workers for multiple iterations of *online* learning, we created a corpus of dialogs for *offline* learning.

In this section, I introduce the RL algorithm used in this analysis, q-learning, followed by a description of the state space and rewards. Then, I present two validation studies, first with simulated data, and then with a new, crowdsourced data set of meal dialogs.

RL algorithm: Q-learning

Q-learning [240,260,261] is an off-policy algorithm that aims to learn the action-value function $Q(s, a)$, which estimates the value of taking a particular action $a \in \mathcal{A}$ while in a discrete state $s \in \mathcal{S}$. The value is the reward $r \in \mathbb{R}$ gained from moving to the next state s' plus the sum of rewards that could be accumulated from s' onwards, reduced by a discount factor $\gamma \in [0,1]$. By observing the reward when moving from s to s', the q values are updated iteratively following a temporal distance learning algorithm (Algorithm 2). Through these iterations, the learned action-value function Q approximates q_*, which is the optimal action-value function.

Algorithm 2. Offline Q-learning adapted from Sutton & Barto [240]

Initialize $Q(s, a) = 0$ for all $s \in \mathcal{S}$ $a \in \mathcal{A}$
Repeat (for each dialog)
    Initialize S from the initial meal description
    Repeat (for each dialog turn)
        Choose A following a random policy
        Take action A, observe R and S'
        $Q(S, A) \leftarrow Q(S, A) + \alpha[R + \gamma max_a Q(S', a) - Q(S, A)]$
        $S \leftarrow S'$
        $\alpha \leftarrow \alpha - \omega$
    until S is terminal

The hyperparameters for the q-learning algorithm are the learning rate $\alpha \in [0,1]$, which controls the step size of each q-value update, the learning rate decay $\omega \in (0, 0.01]$, which gradually decreases the learning rate α over the course of training, and the discount-rate $\gamma \in [0,1]$, which discounts the value of future rewards thereby increasing the influence of immediate rewards.

Once q-values have been learned offline from an existing data set, the algorithm can be applied to prospectively collected dialogs, following a policy based on the pretrained Q-values. In a given state S, the best action according to the Q-values can be attained from $max_a Q(S, a)$. However, always greedily following the best action can pigeonhole the algorithm to following a particular path, and will not be able to continue learning about other paths. Therefore, the greedy algorithm can be modified so that at each turn a random action is taken with probability $\varepsilon \in [0,1]$. The algorithm of online Q-learning with an ε-greedy policy is described in Algorithm 3.

Algorithm 3. Online Q-learning, adapted from Sutton & Barto [240]

Initialize $Q(s, a)$ for all $s \in S$ $a \in \mathcal{A}$ with learned offline
Repeat (for each dialog)
    Initialize S from the initial meal description
    Repeat (for each dialog turn)
        Choose A following an ε-greedy policy
        Take action A, observe R and S'
        $Q(S, A) \leftarrow Q(S, A) + \alpha[R + \gamma max_a Q(S', a) - Q(S, A)]$
        $S \leftarrow S'$
        $\alpha \leftarrow \alpha - \omega$
    until S is terminal

State space and reward function

Two key considerations in applying q-learning to micro-coaching dialogs are representing the state space S and the reward function.

Considering S, the larger the state space is, the more observations that are necessary for the algorithm to converge. Therefore, smaller state spaces are desirable for a proof of concept. The nutrition knowledge applied to each dialog turn when creating the corpus presents a number of natural features to represent the state of the conversation. For instance, the number of food items identified by the NER system may be informative, as would the presence or absence of certain types of food items. For example, for the goal to "Choose lean proteins" the presence or absence of any proteins in the meal would be a relevant feature to determine which questions would be informative. Based on these features, we designed minimalist, discrete state spaces for each of the three nutrition goals used as case studies in this analysis (Table 27).

Table 27. State features and state space size for the three nutrition goals

Goal	State Space Feature	Values	N States
Choose lean proteins	Number of food items	(0, 5)	24
	Any proteins?	(0, 1)	
	All proteins non-ambiguous?	(0, 1)	
Eat no more than 2 portions of carbs (30g)	Number of food items	(0, 5)	24
	Any carbohydrates?	(0, 1)	
	All carbohydrates with amounts?	(0, 1)	
Make ½ my meal fruits and/or non-starchy vegetables	Number of food items	(0, 5)	96
	Any fruits and/or non-starchy vegetables?	(0, 1)	
	Any carbohydrates or proteins?	(0, 1)	
	All fruit and vegetables have amounts?	(0, 1)	
	All carbs and proteins have amounts?	(0, 1)	

Considering the reward function, it was of primary importance to reward reaching a terminal state, meaning a state where the stop criteria are fulfilled, with as few conversational turns as possible. The highest reward ($r = 10$) was given for reaching a terminal state. To reward questions that resulted in additional information, for example, finding additional food items or identifying a goal-relevant food item, a smaller reward was given ($r = 3$). To incentivize short conversations, a small penalty ($r = -1$) was given for questions that resulted in no changes to the state representation, suggesting that they were non-informative.

Creating a corpus for offline learning

In order to train a model with actual data, we needed data to learn from. To create a corpus for training the RL model, we used crowdsourcing following a similar process to section 5.3.3. For the crowdsourced corpus, the dialog management was handled by a *random* policy — the coaches' follow-up question was chosen at random from the possible question type.

We selected 25 meal images and ingredient lists to serve as seed meals for crowdsourced dialogs. Each meal was the seed for 4 dialogs per goal, for a total off 300 dialogs (100 per goal).

Each dialog continued for a total of 10 turns. The resulting corpus included 300 dialogs and 3,000 total conversational turns. The corpus is available for other researchers to use on GitHub in a JSON format similar to other open dialog data sets [228].[5] Descriptive statistics of the corpus are presented in Appendix for Chapter 5, Section B.

Validation experiments with simulated data

To validate this q-learning approach as a proof of concept, we first conducted an experiment with simulated data. The intention behind the simulation was to capture the logic for what *might* happen with actual dialogs after asking certain questions. In the simulated environment, each of the agent's dialog actions led to a change in state with a given probability. For example, the "what else" action led to the discovery of 1-3 new food items with a 90% probability. The simulation was also designed so that certain questions would indeed be more informative in certain states. For example, with the lean protein goal, asking "what kind of *<ambiguously lean or fatty protein>*?" would find a non-ambiguous lean or fatty protein and receive a high reward with an 80% probability if there were proteins present in the meal (i.e., any protein = 1), but would result in no change to the state and therefore 0 reward if there were no proteins to ask about.

Methods

We iteratively trained the q-learning model with the simulated data for hundreds of episodes. One training episode corresponded to observing all of the turns in a single dialog from beginning to end. We tuned the hyper parameters for the learning rate α, the learning rate decay ω, the discount-rate γ, and the number of training episodes by examining the changes in q value for convergence and the consistency in performance across multiple rounds of training.

To visualize changes in the q-values over the course of training, we plotted the change in q-values for each action in a given state over the training episodes.

To keep the simulation realistic to the planned offline learning use case, the training phase followed a random policy through the simulation.

To examine the performance of trained q-values, we then simulated the prospective, *online* collection of new dialogs between two policies: 1) a policy that greedily follows the action with the highest q-value, and 2) the same random policy that was used for training. We compared the average length of dialogs between the greedy-*q* and random policies, as well as the average reward attained per episode.

Results

As shown in Table 28, the tuned q-learning algorithm was able to learn a policy that resulted in shorter conversations, compared to a random policy.

Table 28. Average conversation lengths (number of turns) and reward earned per episode in the experiment with simulated data

	Greedy-*q* policy	Random policy
Conversation length (turns)*	2.36 (SD = 1.88)	3.34 (SD = 2.67)
Reward per episode*	9.99 (SD = 1.62)	9.41 (SD = 1.91)

*$p < 0.001$

Examining the change in q-values over the course of training suggested that the algorithm was correctly unpacking the signal in the simulated data, and finding different actions to be more valuable in different states. A side-by-side comparison of the q-value history for two different states and the "lean protein" goal is presented in Figure 24, which shows that the most valuable actions (the actions with the highest q-values) were correctly identified; in the situation where there are ambiguous proteins, the most valuable action is "what kind" to try to disambiguate that protein. In contrast, when no proteins have been identified, the most valuable action is "what

else," to continue searching for proteins in the meal.

In addition, the q-value histories in Figure 24 show that the q-values begin to find signal

and converge after 25 to 50 episodes, suggesting that a corpus of 100 dialogs or less should be

sufficient for training.

History of q-values for a state where the most valuable action is expected to be "what kind"

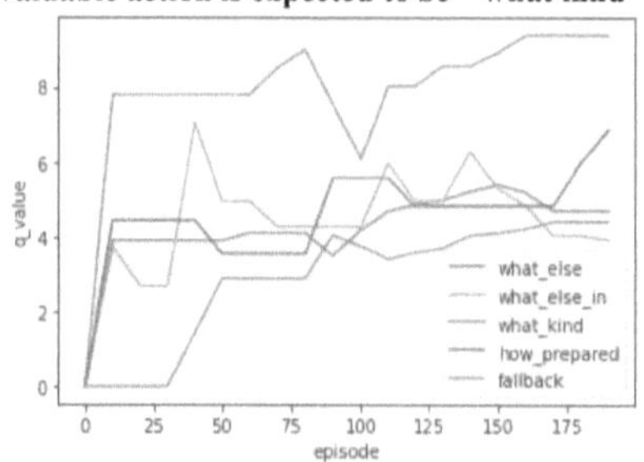

History of q-values for a state where the most valuable action is expected to be "what else"

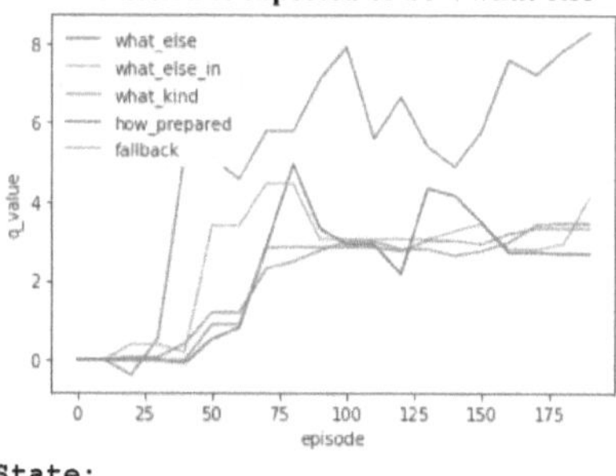

`State:`
`n_food_items = 2`
`any_protein = 1`
`all_protein_non_ambiguous = 0`

`State:`
`n_food_items = 2`
`any_protein = 0`
`all_protein_non_ambiguous = 0`

Figure 24. Comparison of change in q-values over training between two different states in offline learning with simulated data.

The only difference between the two states is whether any proteins have been mentioned by the user. If a protein has been mentioned, then the most valuable action is to ask "what kind" of protein it is to determine if it's fatty or lean. In contrast, that question is not as valuable when there are not proteins present, and instead asking "what else" to find addition food items that might be proteins is more valuable.

Validation experiments with crowdsourced data

After validating the q-learning approach with simulated data, we trained a q-learning

agent for each of the three goals using the crowdsourced dialogs.

Methods

The training data set was the corpus of 100 dialogs per goal, which was built using 25

meal images as seeds for the dialog. Following similar methods to the simulated data, we trained

3 separate q-learning models, one for each of the 3 goals. We inspected the changes in q-values over the course of training for convergence to tune the hyperparameters. Training for each goal ran for 150–200 episodes, randomly sampling the next dialog from the set of 100 dialogs.

In addition, I examined the dataset's coverage of the state space. For q-learning to converge, it needs to continue visiting each state-action pair [240,260], so if there are any states that do not appear in the data, then there may not be enough data to learn reliable q-values for those states.

Results

Examining the changes in q-values over the course of training demonstrated similar patterns to those found with simulated data. As seen in Figure 25, for the goal "Choose lean proteins," a policy based on q-values correctly learned to ask "what kind" questions when ambiguously fatty proteins are present and a number of other foods had been identified, but instead asked "what else" to continue searching if no proteins have been mentioned.

History of q-values when "what kind" is a logical action; multiple food items have been identified, and at least one is an ambiguously fatty protein

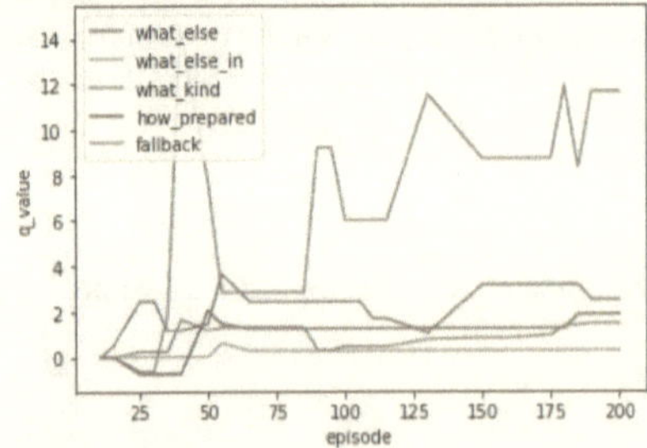

State:
`n_food_items = 4`
`any_protein = 1`
`all_protein_non_ambiguous = 0`

History of q-values when "what else" is a logical action; multiple food items have been identified, and no proteins have been mentioned

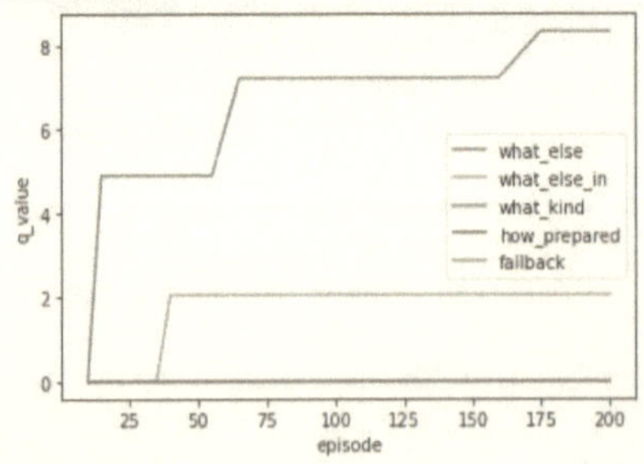

State:
`n_food_items = 4`
`any_protein = 0`
`all_protein_non_ambiguous = 0`

Figure 25. Change in q-values over 200 training episodes for two different states, for the goal "Choose lean proteins."

Interestingly, the RL agent did not always favor asking "what kind" questions when an ambiguously fatty protein was present. If there were few food items present (1 or 2) the agent would continue to *search* by valuing "what else" or "what else in" questions (Figure 26).

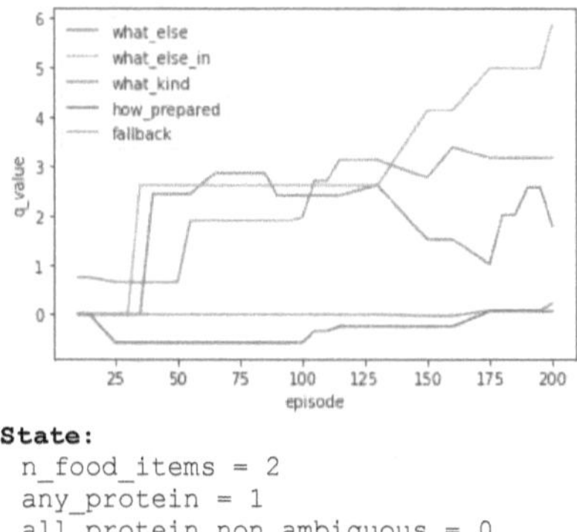

Figure 26. Change in q-values over 200 training episodes for the goal "Choose lean proteins," when only two foods are mentioned and one is a protein.
Higher q-values suggest an action will be more valuable in a given state.

For the second goal (Figure 27), "Eat no more than 2 portions of carbs in each meal (30g)", we similarly found that the RL agent would correctly favor asking "how much" questions to quantify the carbohydrate consent of the meal when at least one carbohydrate was present, but would instead search by asking "what else in" questions when no carbohydrates had been mentioned yet.

For the third goal (Figure 28), "Make ½ of my meal fruit and/or non-starchy vegetables", we found a similar pattern: the RL agent learned to prioritize asking for amounts of fruits and non-starchy vegetables when at least one had been mentioned without an amount. If amounts were present for all fruits and vegetables, it would instead prioritize asking about non-fruits and non-vegetables, like carbohydrates and proteins.

History of q-values when "how much" is a logical action; at least one carbohydrate has been mentioned with no quantity

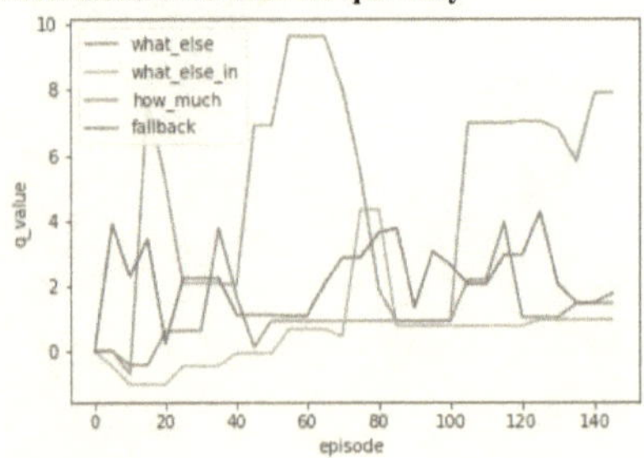

State:
```
n_food_items = 4
any_carbs = 1
amount_carbs_all = 0
```

History of q-values when "what else in" is a logical action; there is only one food item present and it is not a carbohydrate

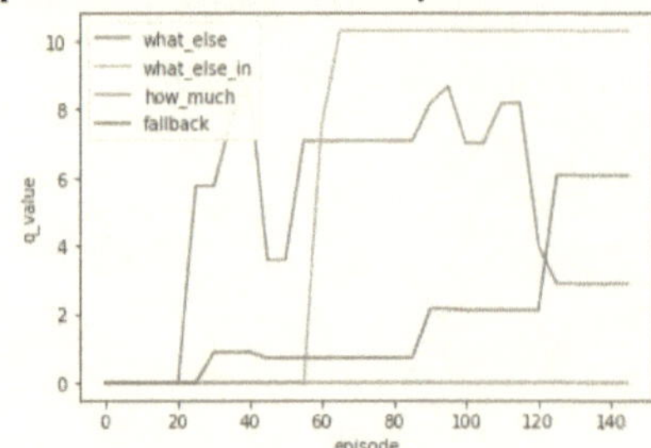

State:
```
n_food_items = 1
any_carbs = 0
amount_carbs_all = 0
```

Figure 27. Change in q-values over 150 training episodes for two different states, for the goal "Eat no more than 2 portions of carbs in each meal (30g)."
Higher q-values suggest an action will be more valuable in a given state

History of q-values when "how much consistent" is a logical action; at least one fruit or non-starchy vegetables is missing amounts and 4 food items have been identified

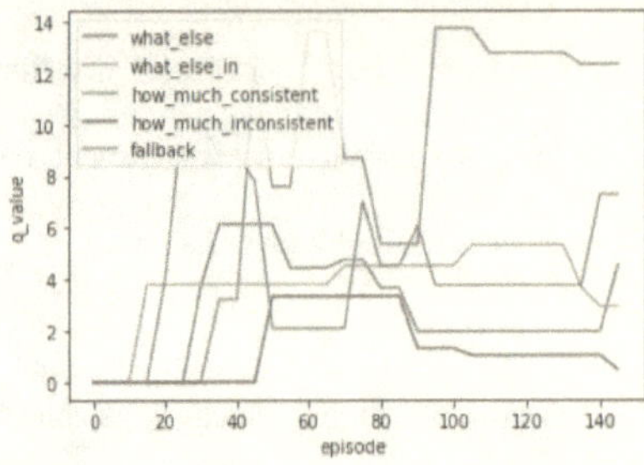

State:
```
n_food_items = 4
any_fruit_veg = 1
any_non_fruit_veg = 1
amt_fruit_veg_all = 0
amt_non_fruit_veg_all = 0
```

History of q-values when "how much inconsistent" is a logical action; amounts are present for all fruits/vegetables, and 4 food items have been identified

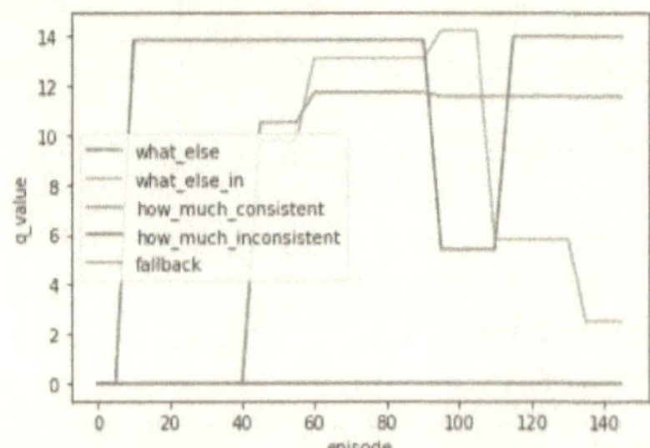

State:
```
n_food_items = 4
any_fruit_veg = 1
any_non_fruit_veg = 1
amt_fruit_veg_all = 1
amt_non_fruit_veg_all = 0
```

Figure 28. Change in q-values over 150 training episodes for two different states, for the goal "Make ½ of my meal fruit and/or non-starchy vegetables."

Considering the state-space coverage for the first goal, "Choose lean proteins" (Figure 29), all states are well represented except for one: when only one food item has been mentioned, and it is a protein, but it is ambiguous. For example, the user stating "I'm eating chicken" would result in this state.

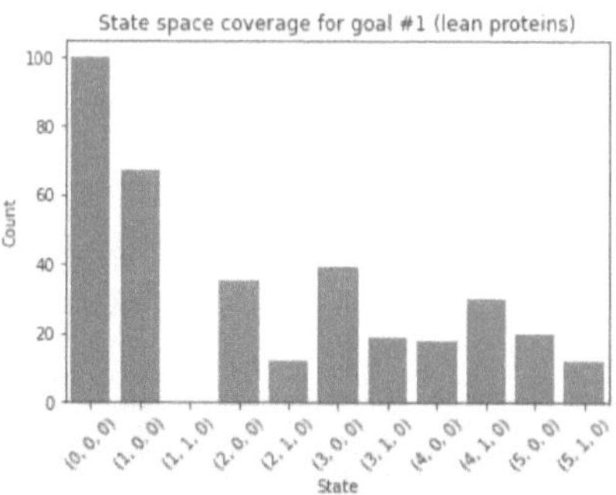

Figure 29. State space coverage for "Choose lean proteins"
The x-axis is labeled with the value tuples for the 3 state features:
(n_food_items, any_protein, all_protein_non_ambiguous)

For the second goal, "Eat no more than 2 portions of carbs" (Figure 30), there is relatively low coverage for states with a large number of food items (3 or more), but none of them are carbohydrates.

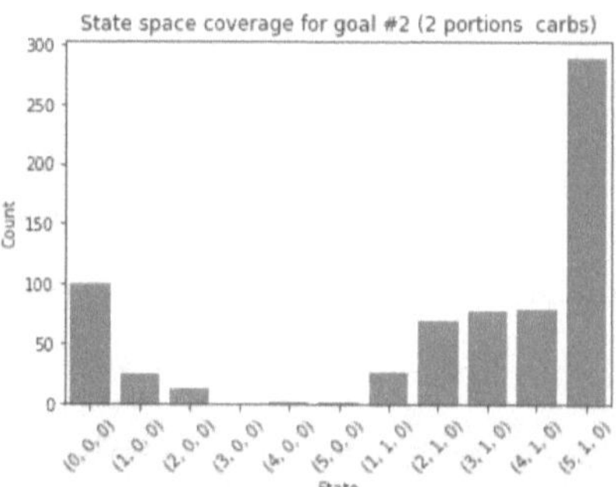

Figure 30. State space coverage for "Eat no more than 2 portions of carbs"
The x-axis is labeled with the value tuples for the 3 state features:
(n_food_items, any_carbs, amt_carbs_all)

The third goal "Make ½ my meal fruits and/or non-starchy vegetables" (Figure 31), has a considerably larger state space than the other two goals. Coverage was spotty when there were two food items identified, and exactly one was a fruit/vegetable and the other was non-fruit/vegetable. For example, "an apple and peanut butter," or "chicken and broccoli" would be examples of meal descriptions with low coverage in the corpus.

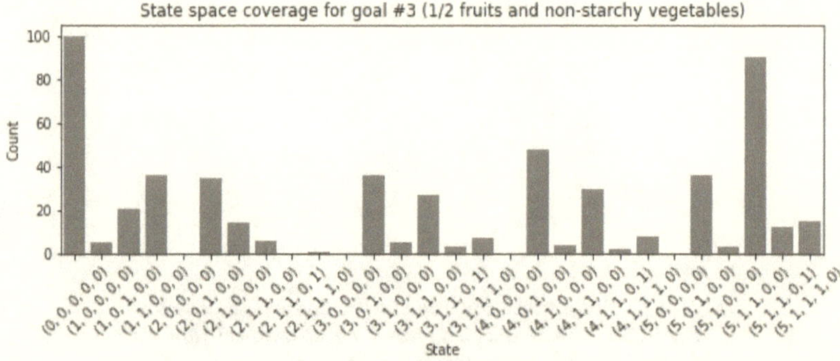

Figure 31. State space coverage for "Make ½ my meal fruits or non-starchy vegetables"
The x-axis is labeled with the value tuples for the 3 state features:
(n_food_items, any_fruit_veg, any_non_fruit_veg, amt_fruit_veg_all, amt_non_fruit_veg_all)

Overall, these results suggest reasonable coverage, with the caveat that if some states appear in the test set, q-learning may not have had the opportunity to learn reasonable q-values for that state.

Discussion

We applied q-learning to a specific use case within micro-coaching dialogs: to prioritize asking more informative questions within a given set of possible questions. With simulated data, we found that q-learning was able to uncover the patterns in the simulation, to correctly prioritize more informative questions based on a discrete state representation, and resulted in significantly shorter conversations within the parameters of the simulation.

To apply q-learning to actual dialogs, we used crowdsourcing to create a medium-scale corpus of 300 dialogs. When training the q-learning model, we found similar patterns in the changes to q-values as were observed in the simulation. In situations, were drill-down questions were expected to be the most informative, they had a higher expected value according the q-function. This suggests both that the simulation was likely a reasonably valid representation of what could happen in micro-coaching dialogs, and also that the q-values trained from the crowdsourced corpus are likely to result in shorter conversations. Evaluating the performance of the trained model for new meals requires the creation of additional dialogs. In the next section, we evaluate the trained q-learning model against the rule-based and random policies, to evaluate whether the RL-policy would result in shorter conversations.

5.5   Part 4: Evaluation

In the prior sections of this Aim, I have characterized the expert knowledge necessary for meal-related micro-coaching dialogs and explored multiple AI approaches to facilitate automated conversational micro-coaching. In Section 5.3, I introduced a knowledge-based system for natural language understanding (NLU). In Section 5.4, in introduced two approaches to dialog management, one rule-based, and the other data-driven, using reinforcement learning.

In this section, I seek to evaluate and compare these approaches by using them to generate new dialogs about unseen meals, with the following research questions.

Research Question 3.3: What are comparative benefits and limitations of different types of dialog management approaches for coaching chatbots, considering those that use reinforcement learning (RL), those that choose their questions randomly, rule-based, and fully-scripted. Specifically, how do these chatbots compare on their ability to reach their end goal, their conversational length, and their perceived coherence and user experience?

Methods

Four chatbot conditions

To address our research questions, we compared multiple versions of dialog management for a micro-coaching chatbot. Three of these approaches utilized the knowledge-based structure for NLU and generating possible responses, but differed in the approach to dialog management:

1) The *rule-based* chatbot utilized the rule-based algorithm introduced in section 5.4.1.

2) The *RL* chatbot utilized the trained q-learning models from section 5.4.2.

3) As a baseline comparison, we also included dialogs with the *random* policy that was used for creating the crowdsourced corpus in section 5.4.2.

In addition to these three conditions, we also included a fourth condition as an additional comparator. The *scripted* condition was a deterministic, finite state-based chatbot. The scripted condition differed from the other 3 because it did not include any of the NLP or knowledge-engineering approaches that were common among the other 3 chatbots. Instead, the scripted chatbot asked the same set of follow-up questions for each goal. The scripted questions were based on the same question types as the other conditions, but were rephrased to be appliable to the entire meal, and were not able to reference any specific components of the meal by name. The set of question in the scripted condition was longer for more complex goals, with the lean protein goal including just 2 follow-up questions, the carbohydrate goal including 2, and the non-starchy vegetable goal including 5. In addition, because the scripted condition did not include any logic for stop criteria, each dialog was exactly the length of the script, regardless of how the users replied. The complete scripted dialogs are included in Supplementary Table J.

Crowdsourced dialog test set

With 10 meal images that were not a part of the training set for RL, we crowdsourced 2 dialogs per meal, per goal for each of the 4 conditions, resulting in a total of 240 evaluation dialogs.

Dialog length

To examine the length of conversations, we compared the average number of dialog turns across each of the conditions, and tested for significance with pairwise Wilcoxon tests between the RL condition and three comparators, using a Bonferroni correction for multiple hypothesis tests.

Perceived dialog quality

For each of the four chatbots, we solicited crowd worker feedback on the quality of coaching dialogs with a *pairwise comparison* design. Pairwise comparison is commonly used to compare multiple entities on some subjective property, for example in preference elicitation and decision-making research [112,219]. Crowd workers were asked to consider the overall quality of the coach's *question-asking strategy* (following [155]), as well as the *naturalness* and *coherence* of messages from the coach (following [156]).

With 10 dialogs per goal and 4 conditions, there were a total of 60 unique comparisons per goal. Crowd workers completed surveys on mTurk with 30 randomly-selected comparisons. For each comparison, participants were shown two dialogs, and asked which of the two was superior in each of the 3 quality constructs (Figure 32).

Participants were recruited from mTurk, and needed to be United States residents with a 90% approval rate to be eligible. Participants were compensated $5 for completing the survey.

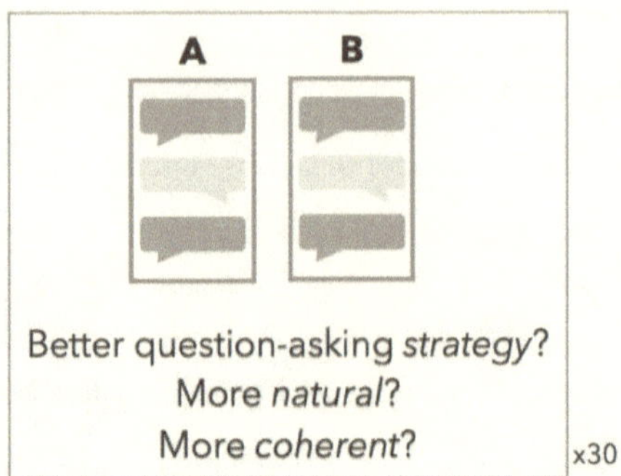

Figure 32. Illustration of the pairwise comparison task to evaluate dialog quality

For each of the four chatbots, I calculated how often that chatbot was chosen as higher in the quality constructs compared to the other three conditions. This resulted in an overall "win percentage" for each condition, for each of the 3 quality constructs, as well as a composite quality score from averaging the three constructs (strategy, naturalness, coherence) together.

In addition, to compare quality assessment based on the length of dialogs, I examined how often the winning dialog was longer (more turns), or shorter (fewer turns), or deemed it a tie if the dialogs were the same length.

Perceived user experience

A separate set of participants was recruited to evaluate the perceived user experience of interacting with the coach using the Subjective Assessment of Speech System Interfaces measure (SASSI; [119]), with a *between subjects* design. Participants reviewed 10 dialogs from the same chatbot, related to the same goal, and then were asked to consider the experience of the user and complete the full SASSI questionnaire. Each participant was compensated with $8 for completing the survey through the mTurk platform.

To test for differences in survey responses, scores were compared between the four chatbot conditions. Because survey measures are ordinal, values between the conditions were compared with the Kruskal-Wallis test, a non-parametric version of a one-way ANOVA.

Stop criteria for the scripted chatbot

Unlike the other 3 chatbots, which continued until reaching the stop criteria, the scripted chatbot always asked the same questions, regardless of the responses offered by the user. This meant that the scripted dialogs may not contain sufficient information to determine if the described meal is consistent with a goal. To quantify this discrepancy, I applied the same stop criteria to the scripted dialogs, to examine how often the scripted dialogs reach the stop criteria. If a dialog does not reach the stop criteria, there is likely insufficient information to determine if the meal is likely consistent with the goal.

Results

Dialog length

As shown in Figure 33, conversations with the RL chatbot were consistently shorter to meet their stop criteria. Conversations were an average of 3.56 turns long in the RL condition, compared with 4.18 turns in the rule-based condition, and 5.75 turns in the random condition. Scripted conversations were predictably an average of 4.33 turns long. A breakdown of conversation length across the 3 goals is presented in Table 29. The more complex goal "Make ½ my meal fruits and/or non-starchy vegetables" generally had much longer conversations on average than the other two goals. RL showed the most improvement over the random baseline for the goal "Eat no more than 2 portions of carbs (30g)"

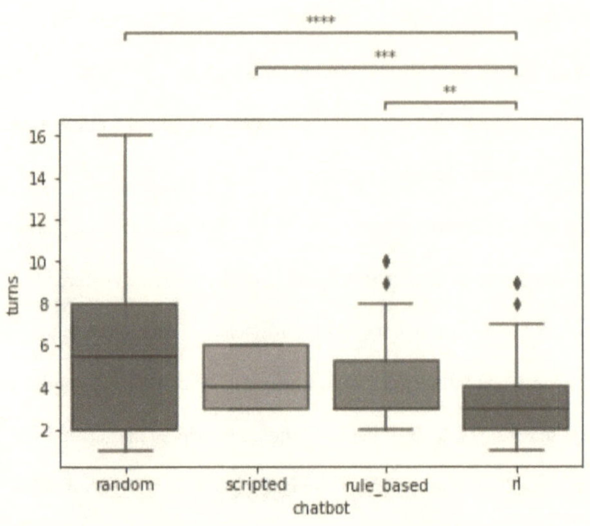

**p<0.01; ***p<0.001, ****p < 0.0001

Figure 33. Box-and-whisker plot comparing the number of conversational turns per dialog across the four chatbot conditions.

Table 29. Average turn length across the four conditions, by nutrition goal

	Random	Scripted	Rule-based	RL
Overall	5.75 (± 3.65)	4.33 (± 1.24)	4.18 (± 2.22)	3.56 (± 2.30)
Goal 1 "Choose lean proteins"	3.75 (± 2.59)	3.00 (± 0)	3.60 (± 2.20)	3.10 (± 2.41)
Goal 2 "Eat no more than 2 portions of carbs (30g)"	6.60 (± 4.07)	4.00 (± 0)	3.45 (± 1.35)	2.55 (± 1.02)
Goal 3 "Make ½ my meal fruits and/or non-starchy vegetables"	6.90 (± 3.28)	6.00 (± 0)	5.50 (± 2.44)	5.05 (± 2.36)

Perceived dialog quality

15 participants completed a pairwise quality comparison survey. The win percentage results are presented in Table 30. The higher quality condition varied by goal. The scripted

condition won most often in head-to-head quality comparisons, especially for goal #1, "choose

lean proteins," and goal #3 "1/2 fruits and non-starchy vegetables. For goal #2, "no more than 2

portions carbs," the RL chatbot was the most natural and coherent, while the rule-based chatbot

had the better question-asking strategy.

Considering the length of conversations (Table 31), shorter dialogs were considered

natural more often, while longer dialogs were considered to have a better question-asking

strategy.

Table 30. Quality construct "win percentage" for the four chatbots, by goal.

Goal	Condition	Win Percentage			
		Strategy	**Naturalness**	**Coherence**	**Composite**
Choose lean proteins	RL	34%	45%	34%	38%
	scripted	66%	49%	66%	61%
	rule-based	64%	57%	55%	59%
	random	36%	49%	44%	43%
No more than 2 portions carbs	RL	48%	62%	56%	55%
	scripted	47%	53%	51%	50%
	rule-based	58%	47%	53%	53%
	random	47%	36%	40%	41%
1/2 fruits and non-starchy vegetables	RL	35%	38%	37%	37%
	scripted	71%	66%	66%	68%
	Rule-based	42%	46%	46%	45%
	random	50%	49%	50%	50%

Table 31. Quality construct "win percentage" by dialog length
(excluding the scripted chatbot)

	Win Percentage			
	Strategy	**Naturalness**	**Coherence**	**Composite**
Shorter Dialog Wins	32%	46%	40%	39%
Longer Dialog Wins	48%	33%	39%	40%
Tie	21%	21%	21%	21%

Perceived user experience

When examining differences in perceived user experience through the SASSI, which has

a minimum score of 1 and a maximum of 5, 36 individuals completed the survey, and we found

no statistically significant differences were detected (Figure 34, $H = 0$.

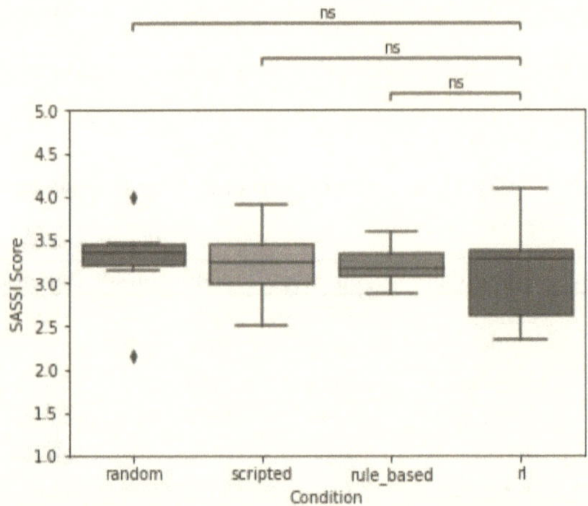

Figure 34. Average user experience scores across the four chatbot conditions, measured with the Subjective Assessment of Speech Systems Interfaces (SASSI; [119])

Stop criteria for the scripted chatbot

Dialogs from the scripted chatbot reached the stop criteria only 65% percent of the time.

5.6   Discussion

In this Aim, I explored multiple artificial intelligence approaches to design a

conversational coaching intervention. Informed by the results of prior aims, I proposed a set of

design needs for *micro-coaching* dialogs — brief conversations to provide support for planning

specific meals. Enabling such an approach required the ability to automatically determine whether an individual is likely to achieve their chosen goal, based on the description of their meal, which was the focus area of this research.

Specifically, I designed and evaluated a knowledge-based system that processes user utterances describing their meals and generates a set of possible follow-up questions. In addition, I compared multiple approaches to dialog management, including rule-based and data-driven approaches.

5.6.1 Alternatives to knowledge-based natural language understanding

In order to design a chatbot that can converse intelligently with users about their meals, we needed to integrate food-related knowledge. To this end, I designed and evaluated a knowledge-based system for natural language understanding (NLU) of meal-related conversations. The system incorporated existing tools for named entity recognition (NER) of food items, as well as a food ontology (FoodOn), to tag foods with relevant attributes like their primary macronutrient, and whether they likely contained sub-foods within them. This representation was used to inform both a set of possible follow-up questions about the meal, as well as for a rule-based criteria to assess whether the meal was likely consistent with a nutrition goal.

This system was able to assess when there was sufficient information to determine if a meal was consistent with a goal with more than 80% accuracy, and was also 80% accurate at making predictions about whether meals were consistent with a health goal. These results suggest the feasibility of such an approach. However, there are many potential directions to explore to improve the accuracy of this approach.

One approach would be to improve the underlying components of the overall system. As described in the error analysis, in some cases the NER system did not correctly identify the food items, for example parsing "rice crispy cereal" as "rice" and "cereal." Improvements to the accuracy of the system for complete and partial matches would improve the downstream analysis [226]. In addition, in some circumstances we found that the food ontology, FoodOn [75], was missing categorizations, for example, "grits" was only listed in its dry, unprepared form, not as a combination-food, prepared with multiple additions like butter or cheese. Updates to expand the ontology could improve performance as well.

In this work, the rule-based stop criteria were rigid, and limited to a discrete set of attributes to determine whether a meal likely met a goal. In a second direction to improve upon the system, these features could also be used, along with the full input text, as an ML classifier, treating the problem as a supervised learning task. This would require annotations added to a data set like the corpus of dialogs created in this aim. Such a gold standard would require expert resources to create, and the initial lack of agreement between expert labels suggests subjectivity and a challenge to creating a single set of gold standard labels, and may also place a ceiling on performance [99].

There are also alternative approaches to meal logging that are not text-based, for example food photo diaries. Researchers have examined photo-based food logs as a lightweight approach to logging, but photos by themselves do not contain the features necessary to assess goal achievement [62,78]. Considering the difference in performance across the three different goals, the results were not uniform — in particular the goal to "make 1/2 of my meal fruits and/or non-starchy vegetables" was less accurate than the other two. Since it is based on the visual plate proportions in the USDA MyPlate guidelines [250], a visual approach may be more successful for this goal. ML learning can be applied to food photos to detect component food items, or estimate nutrient values through comparison with other meal photos [135,136,172,270].

However, these systems are often inaccurate, or require additional database lookup and confirmation form users, which can increase the burden of logging. In addition, requiring a photo negates the ability to engage in meal *planning*, which the text-based micro-coaching approach facilitates. Once a meal is ready to eat, there's less that can be done to help support changes in-the-moment. In addition, text-based approaches can tie explanations and feedback back to the words people used to describe their own meals, which could facilitate more understanding and learning than the food items detected from a meal image. Future work could directly compare text- and photo-based approaches for lightweight logging as input to micro-coaching support.

5.6.2 Comparative advantages of rule-based vs. data-driven dialog management

In the culmination of this aim, we compared multiple approaches to dialog management for micro-coaching dialogs, including scripted, rule-based, and data-driven approaches. The scripted chatbot always asked the same goal-relevant questions, regardless of the meal and responses, The rule-based chatbot took advantage of the goal-relevant food features identified with the expert system to determine the next question with a small set of rules. The data-driven system used the same features as the rule-based system, but instead selected the next question based on a reinforcement learning (RL) algorithm. The RL algorithm, q-learning, was trained on a sample corpus of 300 dialogs created through *crowdsourcing* and learned which questions to ask to most quickly learn the goal-relevant aspects of the meal.

We tested the RL and rule-based chatbots by comparing the length of conversations with a random policy, as well as a scripted chatbot with none of the knowledge-based components of the other three chatbot. We also examined how individuals perceived the *strategy, coherence, naturalness,* and *usability* of the different chatbots, by asking crowd workers to rate the conversations and complete a usability assessment in a survey study.

The results of the evaluation study suggest that each chatbot approach had distinct strengths. Principally, the RL chatbot succeeded in its intended purpose of completing conversation with the fewest number of questions asked. The RL and rule-based chatbots, which both collected necessary information and reached the stop criteria 100% of the time, were generally perceived as less coherent and natural in pairwise comparisons. In contrast, the fully-scripted chatbot was rated as higher quality than the other chatbots; however, it only succeeded in collecting information needed to assess goal attainment 65% of the time. In addition, these pairwise comparisons considered each dialog in isolation, which may not have captured perceptions of the repetitiveness of the scripted chatbot overtime, as compared to the more dynamic chatbots.

These results are consistent with previous research on AI-driven conversational agents. For example, researchers of conversational symptom checkers have found that individuals dislike it when questions are asked in a seemingly random or nonsensical order [249], which may have been the case for the RL chatbot especially. This is also consistent with arguments in clinical decision support that models and explanations ought to align with the way humans think about a problem to be adopted and trusted [43].

These tensions also suggest a number of potential directions for future work. One approach could be to add additional inputs to the RL's reward function to consider not only the conversation length, but also the perceived user quality of resulting questions. Another approach could be to incorporate elements of explainable-AI to offer explanations for why a particular question is being asked [249].

Considering the length of dialogs, shorter exchanges were deemed more natural, but counterintuitively, longer dialogs were rated as having a better question-asking strategy. It's possible that this result was due to a disconnect between crowd workers' understanding of a high-quality coaching strategy, for example assuming that more questions implied a more through conversation. Future work could more directly examine the relationship between conversation length and user perceptions of the chatbot, as well as considering the quality ratings from those with more coaching expertise.

Considering the pros and cons of a data-driven approach, while RL resulted in shorter conversations, it did require the use of crowdsourcing to create a dialog corpus to learn from. While the resources for such a corpus were relatively modest (about $200 per 100 dialogs), the data set was not necessary for the rule-based approach. Still, both approaches were relatively simple, considering only a small number of features about the meal in question. To scale up either approach, either a more complex rule-based system to handle more cases, or a more sophisticated RL algorithm, would require additional resources. For the rule-based system, expert input would be needed to craft the additional rules and features in a more complex system. More complex rule-based systems, for example for motivational interviewing, can require hundreds or thousands of rules [224], and expert input to create a large number of rules could be more resource intensive than crowdsourcing. In contrast, scaling up the RL algorithm with more features in the state space, or a more sophisticated algorithm may require an incrementally larger corpus to learn from, but the other resource requirements of the approach remain the same. Because these results demonstrate the feasibility of using RL to manage follow-up question asking in dialogs, pursuing more complex RL approaches is a promising vein for future work. RL-based approaches also have the advantage of being able to continue to learn and adapt their approach once deployed [240], whereas a rule-based system would need to be explicitly redesigned and revised [175]. These results are consequential, in part, because little research has compared user perceptions of rule-based vs. data-driven dialog management systems side-by-side.

5.6.3 Future directions for micro-coaching

The research activities in this aim constitute initial steps towards enabling a larger proposed vision for micro-coaching dialogs. The results suggest feasibility of AI-based approaches for the first component, assessing the consistency of a planned meal with a nutrition goal. Additional proposed components of micro-coaching include offering feedback based on the goal assessment, as well as support in the form of personalized suggestions to modify the plan.

Feedback was something that participants in all of the prior studies of this book expressed a keen interest for. This applied to feedback on achieving particular goals, as well as overall improvements to self-management and health outcomes. Feedback and explanations are also important part of learning [39]. Considering the theoretical foundations of health coaching, feedback helps to establish accountability, as well as an opportunity for education and increasing an individual's nutrition knowledge [196,266]. Considering the information-motivation-behavioral skills (I-M-B) model of behavior change, feedback supports information needs related to eating goal-consistent meals, and positive feedback and accountability can also help to maintain an individual's motivation [89,199].

The rule-based approach to assessing meal dialogs against goals enables feedback with explanations as well, because the connection between each food item mentioned and the systems assessment is clear. Considering, for example, the goal to choose lean proteins, this would enable the system to explain to an individual that they did achieve their goal by eating "chicken breast without skin," or that they did not because they ate "bacon." Future work could explore additional ways of delivering feedback during micro-coaching conversations, and their impact on motivation and engagement.

The third proposed component of micro-coaching dialogs applies when a user's plan is inconsistent with their health goal — the coaching system can offer suggestions for how to adjust the plan to make it more consistent with the goal. Offering suggestions connects to the IMB model because it aims to cultivate behavioral skills — by receiving suggestions, users learn ways in which their commonly eaten meals can be more consistent with their self-management goals. In addition, personalizing suggestions to the preferences and context of the individual is deeply connected to the tenets of health coaching, by prioritizing personalize support and individual autonomy.

Such an approach would also require nutrition knowledge, but of a different form. Specifically, knowledge of what foods go well with each other, how meals could be adjusted to be more consistent with a goal, as well as similar, alternative meals would all be useful. In addition, personalizing suggestions would necessitate a representation of the user's preferences and context. Given these constraints, *conversational recommender systems* may offer a promising direction for future research. Conversational recommender systems are dialog systems that search among alternatives in a database (for example of restaurants or products) taking into account a user's preferences across multiple sessions. Such an approach could be applied to a database of recommendations, and research in meal similarity and ingredient substitution could also be applied in crafting suggestions [113,172,271].

5.7 Conclusion

This aim presents a human-centered vision for more intelligent, automated coaching interventions. Based on the results of prior studies with individuals with type 2 diabetes, I proposed a framework for micro-coaching dialogs to support individuals in achieving their nutrition goals. In this aim, I took a human-centered approach to integrating AI methods, like reinforcement learning, into the design of self-management support tools. Specifically, the user studies conducted as a part of prior aims informed the design needs, and the question-asking approach for the chatbots was built on findings from user studies. Principally, individuals wanted feedback and suggestions about their goals, with conversations that were as brief as possible. Together, these studies present initial steps towards developing intelligent micro-coaching dialogs, with implications and directions for future work.

Chapter 6: Conclusion

This book examined computational approaches and interaction styles, particularly conversational interaction styles, to enable automated health coaching systems. Specifically, the approaches focused on supporting self-management for individuals with type 2 diabetes.

In Aim 1, I extended computational analysis with self-tracking data — meals and blood glucose readings — to develop an approach to interpret patterns of association identified by machine learning and generate *actionable* suggestions in the form of personalized nutrition goals. A multi-part evaluation found evidence that individuals were able to understand and act on goal suggestions they received in both a controlled lab setting and a deployment study. Qualitative findings from interviews with users revealed a nuanced account of using the system, and point to future design directions for data-driven coaching interventions.

Aim 2 examined health coaching via text message by comparing human-powered and automated approaches. First, I designed a finite state-based chatbot t2.coach, through an iterative, user-centered design process. Then, in a Wizard-of-Oz study comparing the experience of interacting with a chatbot to the experience interacting with human coach via text messaging, I found that the chatbot was able to cultivate a coach-like experience that had many similarities to the experience of messaging with actual health coaches. In addition, the results identified unique areas of strength for both approaches. The automated chatbot was well suited to brief, daily exchanges; in contrast, human coaches excelled with more in-depth interactions, but there were many barriers to these conversations over text message, like a lack of expressiveness and delays in responses.

The results of the studies in Aim 1 and 2 culminated in defining the focus for Aim 3. In Aim 3, I defined design needs for automated coaching dialogs that focus on brief, targeted conversations about specific meals, an approach I defined as micro-coaching. I outlined micro-coaching as specifically focusing on supporting three design needs: 1) to automatically determine whether an individual's meal is consistent with their nutrition goal, 2) to offer feedback on goal achievement, with an explanation, and 3) to offer personalized, contextually relevant suggestions when an individual is not on track to achieve their goal. To address the first of these design needs, I explored multiple artificial intelligence approaches, including a knowledge-based system for natural language understanding, and a data-driven, reinforcement learning approach for dialog management. The results demonstrated feasibility of the knowledge-based system, and showed promise for RL-based dialog management to result in shorter coaching dialogs.

6.1   Contributions

This book makes a number of contributions to research in informatics, human-computer interaction (HCI), health coaching, and conversational interfaces.

A method for translating machine learning insights into actionable recommendations with a rule-based expert system. The approach to making personalized nutrition goal suggestions underlying the GlucoGoalie system in Aim 1 is innovative, and builds on both advances in machine learning with personal health data [5,251], as well as a rich history of research in rule-based decision support systems [203,231]. A similar approach could be applied to translate ML insights into actionable suggestions in other domains in and out of health and wellbeing.

A qualitative account of individuals' experiences receiving and using personalized goal recommendations from their own self-tracking data. The qualitative results of the 4-week deployment study in Aim 1 contribute to a growing research area of tools that integrate ML into personal informatics applications. Few such tools exist [117], therefore the qualitative themes and impressions represent a contribution to inform future research in this area..

A theory-driven chatbot for health coaching. In Aim 2, I presented the iterative, user-centered design of t2.coach, a scripted chatbot for goal setting and action planning. The design of t2.coach was adapted from Brief Action Planning [109], a protocol to guide practitioners through brief, supportive coaching interactions. While the content in t2.coach was specific to nutrition and exercise goals for type 2 diabetes self-management, the adapted dialogs and infrastructure could be extended to many other health domains by other researchers.

A design approach for wizard-of-oz prototyping with deployment studies. The design steps involved in the creation of t2.coach in Aim 2 included a user study with wizard-of-oz (WOz) prototyping. However, while WOz studies are usually conduced in a lab setting, t2.coach is designed to initiate daily conversations over a number of weeks, and user interactions in a lab may not have been generalizable. I adapted the WOz approach to a 3-week deployment study, which other chatbot researchers may borrow from and improve.

A qualitative comparison of human and automated approaches to health coaching via text messaging. The qualitative findings from the primary study in Aim 2 contribute to scholarly debate on the role of automated systems as health coaches. Some have argued that health coaching is innately human [218], while other researcher have pursued various approaches to automated conversational coaching interventions [57,84,212,235]. By directly comparing human-powered and automated coaching, the results of this study offer evidence for the potential efficacy of automated approaches, while still emphasizing the unique human advantages for coaching, and proposing a way in which the two can be complementary.

Proposed design needs for micro-coaching dialogs. Based on the results of the prior studies, in Aim 3 I introduce the concept of micro-coaching — brief discussions related to specific behaviors in the context of a health goal — and propose a set of design needs and structure for micro-coaching conversations. This could offer a framework for future directions of research in automated coaching interventions.

A corpus of dialogs discussing specific meals. In order to train the reinforcement learning (RL) model in Aim 3, I used crowdsourcing to create a corpus of 300 dialogs, and a total of 3,000 conversational turns. Currently, there are few examples of data sets in the health domain being made openly available [140,146,227]. Sharing this corpus with the research community would allow other researchers to build on the RL approach, or apply other ML methods.

A head-to-head comparison of data-driven and rule-based dialog management approaches. Despite rich research both rule-based [90,223] and data-driven [2,273] conversational agents, little research has directly compared the two for a particular objective. The comparison of multiple dialog management approaches and discussion of their relative advantages in Aim 3 therefore contributes valuable insight to researchers who are considering multiple approaches to implement conversational tools.

6.2   Limitations

The research described in this book has the following limitations:

Small sample sizes and generalizability. Across all three aims, the user studies included relatively small samples of participants. While participants were recruited from economically disadvantaged communities, they were not representative: participants were skewed female, and predominantly black or Latino. The samples for Aim 1 and 2 were recruited from a single United States metro area, which may not account for important cultural differences nationally or globally [237]. Together, these factors may impact the generalizability of the qualitative findings.

Short study timeframes. The user studies in Aims 1 and 2 ran for 4 and 3 weeks, respectively, and usage patterns and engagement may change with extended use, which could have impacted the findings and implications of these studies. Because of the short timeframe, we were only able to examine mediating factors, like self-management behaviors, and not actual changes to health that would manifest over a longer observation period.

Implications drawn from wizard-of-oz chatbot. In Aim 2, we examined automated chatbots in comparison with text messages from human coaches, however, the chatbot was a wizard-of-oz prototype, not a fully automated system, which meant that responses from the chatbot were delayed. This created a parity in experience between the two study groups, because messages from human coaches would necessarily be delayed, but may limit the generalizability of some of our findings to fully automated systems.

Limited sample of nutrition goals. The implementation of the first phase of micro-coaching dialogs in Aim 3 focuses on three particular nutrition goals as a case study. While these goals were chosen to be representative of a diverse set of nutrition goals, it's possible that the findings and approach may not generalize to other nutrition goals we did not examine.

User experience based on perceptions, not use. In Aim 3, the assessments of quality and user experience come from lay-individuals reviewing complete dialogs from one of four chatbots. However, the perceived user experience from reading a completed dialog may not capture the perceived user experience of directly interacting with a chatbot, and may have limited the ability

of the evaluation to detect meaningful differences in user experience. In addition, these studies

did not allow evaluating other important aspects of individuals' engagement with coaching

chatbots, such as trust. Finally, this study only focused on perceptions of the coaching chatbot,

and not on their impact on individuals' behaviors and health.

6.3   Future work

The results of this book point to a number of areas for future work:

Incorporate explanations alongside personalized recommendations. Future work could build

on the approach for personalized goal recommendation from Aim 1 to not only offer

recommendations but also *explanations*. In particular individuals may value not only a

recommendation, but also why they received such a recommendation, grounded in their data.

This additional information can serve as a form of explanation for the recommendations, and

prior work has demonstrated the importance of explanations in facilitating nutritional learning

[40]. For example, actionable recommendations could be enhanced by presenting visual

summaries of the self-tracking data that informed the specific goal recommendations [79,222].

This direction connects to the growing field of explainable ML and AI [1,106,259]. Future work

could further incorporate advances in explainable ML to personal informatics applications.

Human-chatbot symbiosis for health coaching. The results of Aim 2 pointed to

complementary application areas for human-powered and automated approaches to health

coaching. In Aim 3, I pursued a particular vision of micro-coaching, but future work could also

explore ways to better connect human coaches and clients with digital coaching interventions

[212]. Pursuing a hybrid approach would also necessitate researching ways for a team of human

coaches to hand off care to a chatbot, and pick up again with a summary. Important research questions remain unanswered in the area of summarizing self-tracking interactions for use by clinicians as a part of their care [86], and this is another promising vein for future work.

More sophisticated RL-based dialog management approaches. The RL approach employed in Aim 3, tabular q-learning, was relatively basic [240]. In addition, the features for the state space were limited to what the rule-based system needed. Future work could explore using additional meal-related features in the state space representation, as well as more complex RL-approaches. These would potentially necessitate more training data, but would also potentially be able to find more interesting patterns, and learn a policy that behaves differently for meals with different kinds of foods. Broadly, this approach could also be applied to dialog management for other coaching related domains like physical activity, or with a larger set of possible actions.

Complete micro-coaching dialogs. The research in Aim 3 considered only the first component of the proposed micro-coaching dialog structure, focusing on asking questions about meals to determine if they are consistent with a nutrition goal. The other design needs — offering feedback and suggestions based on the outcome of step one — present a different set of challenges, and would be a promising candidate for future work. Delivering feedback, for instance, connects to research in what kind of personality individuals prefer to feedback, some preferring a cheerleader while others preferring a realist [67]. Offering suggestions would also require nutrition knowledge, but a different type of knowledge about what foods go well with others, and how to modify meals to make them more consistent with a health goal. These knowledge sources may not be as readily available as the food item attributes from a food ontology were for Aim 3, but research in meal similarity and ingredient substitution may offer a

fruitful start [113,172,271].

6.4   Conclusion

As attention on the potential of AI to revolutionize healthcare has grown in recent years,

so too have critiques, pointing out unintended consequences and ethical ramifications of

improperly or naively applying AI to healthcare challenges. In this book, I aimed to take human-

centered approach to the design of technology-based interventions to support individuals with

self-management [269]. From an ethical perspective, I sought to design technology for those

who lack access to many current supportive resources, not those who are already avid

technology users [253,254]. In addition, I did not seek to design AI systems that would replace

human practitioners, but instead augment and extend human strengths and expertise. In doing so,

this work builds on findings and insights from human-centered research studies to inform the

application of computational and data-centric methods. This book may serve a contribution to

evolving and emerging models in informatics of how the computational might of AI can be

applied to tangible healthcare challenges in a human-centric and ethically considered way.

References

1. Amina Adadi and Mohammed Berrada. 2018. Peeking Inside the Black-Box: A Survey on Explainable Artificial Intelligence (XAI). *IEEE Access* 6: 52138–52160. https://doi.org/10.1109/ACCESS.2018.2870052

2. Daniel Adiwardana, Minh-Thang Luong, David R So, Jamie Hall, Noah Fiedel, Romal Thoppilan, Zi Yang, Apoorv Kulshreshtha, Gaurav Nemade, Yifeng Lu, and Quoc V. Le. 2020. Towards a Human-like Open-Domain Chatbot. Retrieved February 6, 2020 from http://arxiv.org/abs/2001.09977

3. Jaspreet K.C. Ahuja, Alanna J. Moshfegh, Joanne M. Holden, and Ellen Harris. 2013. USDA Food and Nutrient Databases Provide the Infrastructure for Food and Nutrition Research, Policy, and Practice. *The Journal of Nutrition* 143, 2: 241S-249S. https://doi.org/10.3945/jn.112.170043

4. David J. Albers, Noémie Elhadad, Esteban G. Tabak, Adler J. Perotte, and George Hripcsak. 2014. Dynamical phenotyping: Using temporal analysis of clinically collected physiologic data to stratify populations. *PLoS ONE* 9, 6: e96443. https://doi.org/10.1371/journal.pone.0096443

5. David J. Albers, Matthew Levine, Bruce Gluckman, Henry Ginsberg, George Hripcsak, and Lena Mamykina. 2017. Personalized glucose forecasting for type 2 diabetes using data assimilation. *PLoS Computational Biology* 13, 4: e1005232. https://doi.org/10.1371/journal.pcbi.1005232

6. David J Albers, Matthew E Levine, Andrew Stuart, Lena Mamykina, Bruce Gluckman, and George Hripcsak. 2018. Mechanistic machine learning: how data assimilation leverages physiologic knowledge using Bayesian inference to forecast the future, infer the present, and phenotype. *Journal of the American Medical Informatics Association* 25, 10: 1392–1401. https://doi.org/10.1093/jamia/ocy106

7. James Allen, George Ferguson, Nate Blaylock, Donna Byron, Nathanael Chambers, Myroslava Dzikovska, Lucian Galescu, and Mary Swift. 2006. Chester: Towards a personal medication advisor. *Journal of Biomedical Informatics* 39, 5: 500–513. https://doi.org/10.1016/J.JBI.2006.02.004

8. American Association of Diabetes Educators. AADE7 Self-Care Behaviors for Managing

Diabetes Effectively. Retrieved March 5, 2018 from
https://www.diabeteseducator.org/living-with-diabetes/aade7-self-care-behaviors

9.   American Diabetes Association. 2018. Statistics About Diabetes. Retrieved August 23, 2018 from http://www.diabetes.org/diabetes-basics/statistics/

10.   American Diabetes Association. 2018. 4. Lifestyle Management:Standards of Medical Care in Diabetes-2018. *Diabetes care* 41, Suppl 1: S38–S50. https://doi.org/10.2337/dc18-S004

11.   James W. Anderson, Kim M. Randles, Cyril W. C. Kendall, and David J. A. Jenkins. 2004. Carbohydrate and Fiber Recommendations for Individuals with Diabetes: A Quantitative Assessment and Meta-Analysis of the Evidence. *Journal of the American College of Nutrition* 23, 1: 5–17. https://doi.org/10.1080/07315724.2004.10719338

12.   Adriana Arcia, Niurka Suero-Tejeda, Michael E. Bales, Jacqueline A. Merrill, Sunmoo Yoon, Janet Woollen, and Suzanne Bakken. 2016. Sometimes more is more: Iterative participatory design of infographics for engagement of community members with varying levels of health literacy. *Journal of the American Medical Informatics Association* 23, 1: 174–183. https://doi.org/10.1093/jamia/ocv079

13.   Pablo Aschner. 2017. New IDF clinical practice recommendations for managing type 2 diabetes in primary care. *Diabetes Research and Clinical Practice* 132: 169–170. https://doi.org/10.1016/J.DIABRES.2017.09.002

14.   Carol M. Ashton, Paul Haidet, Debora A. Paterniti, Tracie C. Collins, Howard S. Gordon, Kimberly O'Malley, Laura A. Petersen, Barbara F. Sharf, Maria E. Suarez-Almazor, Nelda P. Wray, and Richard L. Street. 2003. Racial and ethnic disparities in the use of health services. *Journal of General Internal Medicine* 18, 2: 146–152. https://doi.org/10.1046/j.1525-1497.2003.20532.x

15.   American Diabetes Association. 2021. Diabetes technology: Standards of medical care in diabetes−2021. *Diabetes Care* 44, Supplement 1: S85–S99. https://doi.org/10.2337/dc21-S007

16.   Makkar B.M., Shaikh M., Shah A., Joshi S., Saboo B.D., Sosale A.R., Madhu S.V., Kovil R., Shah T., Chawla M.S., Chhawla R., and Kesavadev J. 2018. Conversational artificial intelligence for achieving activity targets through routine physical activity-longitudinal observational study among people with type 2 diabetes. *Diabetes* 67: A196. Retrieved

from

http://www.embase.com/search/results?subaction=viewrecord&from=export&id=L62356
6634

17. Harish C. Bahl and Raymond G. Hunt. 1984. Decision-making theory and DSS design. *ACM SIGMIS Database* 15, 4: 10–14. https://doi.org/10.1145/1017726.1017728

18. A Baki Kocaballi, Liliana Laranjo, and Enrico Coiera. 2018. Measuring User Experience in Conversational Interfaces : A Comparison of Six Questionnaires. *Proc. of British Computer Society Human Computer Interaction Conference (BCS HCI '18)*: 1–12. Retrieved July 24, 2018 from https://www.researchgate.net/publication/326188575

19. Eric P.S. Baumer, Vera Khovanskaya, Mark Matthews, Lindsay Reynolds, Victoria Schwanda Sosik, and Geri Gay. 2014. Reviewing reflection. In *Proceedings of the 2014 conference on Designing interactive systems - DIS '14*, 93–102. https://doi.org/10.1145/2598510.2598598

20. Frank Bentley, Konrad Tollmar, Peter Stephenson, Laura Levy, Brian Jones, Scott Robertson, Ed Price, Richard Catrambone, and Jeff Wilson. 2013. Health Mashups: Presenting Statistical Patterns betweenWellbeing Data and Context in Natural Language to Promote Behavior Change. *ACM Transactions on Computer-Human Interaction* 20, 5: 1–27. https://doi.org/10.1145/2503823

21. Andrew B.L. Berry, Catherine Lim, Andrea L. Hartzler, Tad Hirsch, Evette Ludman, Edward H. Wagner, and James D. Ralston. 2017. Eliciting Values of Patients with Multiple Chronic Conditions: Evaluation of a Patient-centered Framework. *AMIA ... Annual Symposium proceedings. AMIA Symposium* 2017: 430–439. Retrieved September 15, 2020 from /pmc/articles/PMC5977727/?report=abstract

22. Timothy Bickmore, Amanda Gruber, and Rosalind Picard. 2005. Establishing the computer–patient working alliance in automated health behavior change interventions. *Patient Education and Counseling* 59, 1: 21–30. https://doi.org/10.1016/J.PEC.2004.09.008

23. Timothy W. Bickmore, Laura M. Pfeifer, Donna Byron, Shaula Forsythe, Lori E. Henault, Brian W. Jack, Rebecca Silliman, and Michael K. Paasche-Orlow. 2010. Usability of Conversational Agents by Patients with Inadequate Health Literacy: Evidence from Two Clinical Trials. *Journal of Health Communication* 15, sup2: 197–210.

https://doi.org/10.1080/10810730.2010.499991

24. Timothy W. Bickmore, Laura M. Pfeifer, and Brian W. Jack. 2009. Taking the time to care: empowering low health literacy hospital patients with virtual nurse agents. *Proceedings of the 27th international conference on Human factors in computing systems*: 1265–1274. https://doi.org/10.1145/1518701.1518891

25. Timothy W. Bickmore, Rebecca A. Silliman, Kerrie Nelson, Debbie M. Cheng, Michael Winter, Lori Henault, and Michael K. Paasche-Orlow. 2013. A Randomized Controlled Trial of an Automated Exercise Coach for Older Adults. *Journal of the American Geriatrics Society* 61, 10: 1676–1683. https://doi.org/10.1111/jgs.12449

26. Timothy W Bickmore, Daniel Schulman, and Candace L Sidner. 2011. A reusable framework for health counseling dialogue systems based on a behavioral medicine ontology. *Journal of Biomedical Informatics* 44, 2: 183–197. https://doi.org/10.1016/j.jbi.2010.12.006

27. Kirsten Bobrow, Andrew J. Farmer, David Springer, Milensu Shanyinde, Ly Mee Yu, Thomas Brennan, Brian Rayner, Mosedi Namane, Krisela Steyn, Lionel Tarassenko, and Naomi Levitt. 2016. Mobile Phone Text Messages to Support Treatment Adherence in Adults with High Blood Pressure (SMS-Text Adherence Support [StAR]): A Single-Blind, Randomized Trial. *Circulation* 133, 6: 592–600. https://doi.org/10.1161/CIRCULATIONAHA.115.017530

28. Thomas Bodenheimer, Connie Davis, and Halsted Holman. 2007. Helping patients adopt healthier behaviors. *Clinical Diabetes 25*, 66–70. https://doi.org/10.2337/diaclin.25.2.66

29. Thomas Bodenheimer, Kate Lorig, Halsted Holman, and Kevin Grumbach. 2002. Patient Self-management of Chronic Disease in Primary Care. *JAMA* 288, 19: 2469. https://doi.org/10.1001/jama.288.19.2469

30. Jennifer B. Bollyky, Dena Bravata, Jason Yang, Mark Williamson, and Jennifer Schneider. 2018. Remote Lifestyle Coaching Plus a Connected Glucose Meter with Certified Diabetes Educator Support Improves Glucose and Weight Loss for People with Type 2 Diabetes. *Journal of Diabetes Research* 2018. https://doi.org/10.1155/2018/3961730

31. Christian Bommer, Vera Sagalova, Esther Heesemann, Jennifer Manne-Goehler, Rifat Atun, Till Bärnighausen, Justine Davies, and Sebastian Vollmer. 2018. Global economic

burden of diabetes in adults: Projections from 2015 to 2030. *Diabetes Care* 41, 5: 963–970. https://doi.org/10.2337/dc17-1962/-/DC1

32. Brian M. Bot, Christine Suver, Elias Chaibub Neto, Michael Kellen, Arno Klein, Christopher Bare, Megan Doerr, Abhishek Pratap, John Wilbanks, E. Ray Dorsey, Stephen H. Friend, and Andrew D. Trister. 2016. The mPower study, Parkinson disease mobile data collected using ResearchKit. *Scientific Data* 3: 160011. https://doi.org/10.1038/sdata.2016.11

33. C Bouchard and T Rankinen. 2001. Individual differences in response to regular physical activity. *Medicine and science in sports and exercise* 33, 6 Suppl: S446-51; discussion S452-3. https://doi.org/10.1097/00005768-200106001-00013

34. Deborah J. Bowen, Matthew Kreuter, Bonnie Spring, Ludmila Cofta-Woerpel, Laura Linnan, Diane Weiner, Suzanne Bakken, Cecilia Patrick Kaplan, Linda Squiers, Cecilia Fabrizio, and Maria Fernandez. 2009. How We Design Feasibility Studies. *American journal of preventive medicine* 36, 5: 452. https://doi.org/10.1016/J.AMEPRE.2009.02.002

35. Rena Brar Prayaga, Erwin W Jeong, Erin Feger, Harmony K Noble, Magdalen Kmiec, and Ram S Prayaga. 2018. Improving Refill Adherence in Medicare Patients With Tailored and Interactive Mobile Text Messaging: Pilot Study. *JMIR mHealth and uHealth* 6, 1: e30. https://doi.org/10.2196/mhealth.8930

36. Virginia Braun and Victoria Clarke. 2006. Using thematic analysis in psychology. *Qualitative Research in Psychology* 3, 2: 77–101. https://doi.org/10.1191/1478088706qp063oa

37. Marc D Breton, Devin P Shields, and Boris P Kovatchev. 2008. Optimum subcutaneous glucose sampling and fourier analysis of continuous glucose monitors. *Journal of diabetes science and technology* 2, 3: 495–500. https://doi.org/10.1177/193229680800200322

38. Amanda R. Budzowski, Michael D. Parkinson, and Valerie J. Silfee. 2019. An Evaluation of Lifestyle Health Coaching Programs Using Trained Health Coaches and Evidence-Based Curricula at 6 Months Over 6 Years. *American Journal of Health Promotion* 33, 6: 912–915. https://doi.org/10.1177/0890117118824252

39. Marissa Burgermaster, K.Z. Gajos, and L. Mamykina. 2016. Explanations Improve Nutrition Learning Among Lab in the Wild Quiz-Takers. *Journal of Nutrition Education*

and Behavior 48, 7: S52–S53. https://doi.org/10.1016/j.jneb.2016.04.142

40. Marissa Burgermaster, Krzysztof Z. Gajos, Patricia Davidson, and Lena Mamykina. 2017. The Role of Explanations in Casual Observational Learning about Nutrition. In *Proceedings of the 2017 CHI Conference on Human Factors in Computing Systems - CHI '17*, 4097–4145. https://doi.org/10.1145/3025453.3025874

41. Marissa Burgermaster, Filippa Juul, Elliot Mitchell, Elizabeth Heitkemper, Jhack Sepulveda, Amenda Almonte, and Lena Mamykina. 2019. Personal Informatics Technology for Engagement in Community Health (PI-TECH): Mixed Methods Study of Platano, a Motivationally Tailored App for Dietary Diabetes Management (P16-051-19). *Current Developments in Nutrition* 3, Supplement_1. https://doi.org/10.1093/CDN/NZZ050.P16-051-19

42. Christine Buttorff, Teague Ruder, and Melissa Bauman. 2017. *Multiple Chronic Conditions in the United States*. https://doi.org/10.7249/TL221

43. Federico Cabitza, Davide Ciucci, and Raffaele Rasoini. 2019. A Giant with Feet of Clay: On the Validity of the Data that Feed Machine Learning in Medicine. . Springer, Cham, 121–136. https://doi.org/10.1007/978-3-319-90503-7_10

44. Federico Cabitza, Raffaele Rasoini, and Gian Franco Gensini. 2017. Unintended Consequences of Machine Learning in Medicine. *JAMA* 318, 6: 517. https://doi.org/10.1001/jama.2017.7797

45. Angelo Cafaro, Hannes Högni Vilhjálmsson, and Timothy Bickmore. 2016. First Impressions in Human--Agent Virtual Encounters. *ACM Transactions on Computer-Human Interaction* 23, 4: 1–40. https://doi.org/10.1145/2940325

46. Kerri L Cavanaugh. 2011. Health literacy in diabetes care: explanation, evidence and equipment. *Diabetes management (London, England)* 1, 2: 191–199. https://doi.org/10.2217/dmt.11.5

47. Centers for Disease Control and Prevention. 2018. Racial and Ethnic Approaches to Community Health | DNPAO. Retrieved January 3, 2019 from https://www.cdc.gov/nccdphp/dnpao/state-local-programs/reach/

48. Beenish M. Chaudhry, Christopher Schaefbauer, Ben Jelen, Katie A. Siek, and Kay Connelly. 2016. Evaluation of a Food Portion Size Estimation Interface for a Varying Literacy Population. In *Proceedings of the 2016 CHI Conference on Human Factors in*

Computing Systems - CHI '16, 5645–5657. https://doi.org/10.1145/2858036.2858554

49. Beenish M. Chaudry, Kay H. Connelly, Katie A. Siek, and Janet L. Welch. 2012. Mobile interface design for low-literacy populations. In *Proceedings of the 2nd ACM SIGHIT symposium on International health informatics - IHI '12*, 91. https://doi.org/10.1145/2110363.2110377

50. Ming-Yuan Chih, Timothy Patton, Fiona M. McTavish, Andrew J. Isham, Chris L. Judkins-Fisher, Amy K. Atwood, and David H. Gustafson. 2014. Predictive modeling of addiction lapses in a mobile health application. *Journal of Substance Abuse Treatment* 46, 1: 29–35. https://doi.org/10.1016/J.JSAT.2013.08.004

51. Eun Kyoung Choe, Bongshin Lee, Matthew Kay, Wanda Pratt, and Julie A. Kientz. 2015. SleepTight: low-burden, self-monitoring technology for capturing and reflecting on sleep behaviors. In *Proceedings of the 2015 ACM International Joint Conference on Pervasive and Ubiquitous Computing - UbiComp '15*, 121–132. https://doi.org/10.1145/2750858.2804266

52. Eun Kyoung Choe, Nicole B. Lee, Bongshin Lee, Wanda Pratt, and Julie A. Kientz. 2014. Understanding Quantified-Selfers' Practices in Collecting and Exploring Personal Data. *Proceedings of the 32nd Annual ACM Conference on Human Factors in Computing Systems*: 1143–1152. https://doi.org/10.1145/2556288.2557372

53. Konstantina Christakopoulou, Filip Radlinski, and Katja Hofmann. 2016. Towards Conversational Recommender Systems. In *Proceedings of the 22nd ACM SIGKDD International Conference on Knowledge Discovery and Data Mining - KDD '16*, 815–824. https://doi.org/10.1145/2939672.2939746

54. Chia-Fang Chung, Kristin Dew, Allison M Cole, Jasmine Zia, James A Fogarty, Julie A Kientz, and Sean A Munson. 2016. Boundary Negotiating Artifacts in Personal Informatics: Patient-Provider Collaboration with Patient-Generated Data. In *Proceedings of the 19th ACM Conference on Computer-Supported Cooperative Work & Social Computing - CSCW '16*, 768–784. https://doi.org/10.1145/2818048.2819926

55. CIRP. 2019. Report: Smart speaker adoption in US reaches 66M units, with Amazon leading. Retrieved February 12, 2019 from https://techcrunch.com/2019/02/05/report-smart-speaker-adoption-in-u-s-reaches-66m-units-with-amazon-leading/

56. Herbert H. Clark and Susan E. Brennan. 2004. Grounding in communication. In

Perspectives on socially shared cognition. American Psychological Association, 127–149. https://doi.org/10.1037/10096-006

57.   Céline Clavel, Steve Whittaker, Anaïs Ana\"\is Blacodon, and Jean-Claude Martin. 2018. WEnner: A Theoretically Motivated Approach for Tailored Coaching About Physical Activity. In *Proceedings of the 2018 ACM International Joint Conference and 2018 International Symposium on Pervasive and Ubiquitous Computing and Wearable Computers - UbiComp '18* (UbiComp '18), 1669–1675. https://doi.org/10.1145/3267305.3274190

58.   James Clawson, Jessica A. Pater, Andrew D. Miller, Elizabeth D. Mynatt, and Lena Mamykina. 2015. No longer wearing: investigating the abandonment of personal health-tracking technologies on craigslist. In *Proceedings of the 2015 ACM International Joint Conference on Pervasive and Ubiquitous Computing - UbiComp '15*, 647–658. https://doi.org/10.1145/2750858.2807554

59.   J. Codella, C. Partovian, H.-Y. Chang, and C.-H. Chen. 2018. Data quality challenges for person-generated health and wellness data. *IBM Journal of Research and Development* 62, 1: 3:1-3:8. https://doi.org/10.1147/JRD.2017.2762218

60.   Enrico Coiera. 2000. When conversation is better than computation. *Journal of the American Medical Informatics Association 7*, 277–286. https://doi.org/10.1136/jamia.2000.0070277

61.   Heather J. Cole-Lewis, Arlene M. Smaldone, Patricia R. Davidson, Rita Kukafka, Jonathan N. Tobin, Andrea Cassells, Elizabeth D. Mynatt, George Hripcsak, and Lena Mamykina. 2016. Participatory approach to the development of a knowledge base for problem-solving in diabetes self-management. *International Journal of Medical Informatics 85*, 1: 96–103. https://doi.org/10.1016/J.IJMEDINF.2015.08.003

62.   Felicia Cordeiro, Elizabeth Bales, Erin Cherry, and James Fogarty. 2015. Rethinking the Mobile Food Journal: Exploring Opportunities for Lightweight Photo-Based Capture. In *Proceedings of the 33rd Annual ACM Conference on Human Factors in Computing Systems - CHI '15*, 3207–3216. https://doi.org/10.1145/2702123.2702154

63.   Felicia Cordeiro, Daniel A. Epstein, Edison Thomaz, Elizabeth Bales, Arvind K. Jagannathan, Gregory D. Abowd, and James Fogarty. 2015. Barriers and Negative Nudges. In *Proceedings of the 33rd Annual ACM Conference on Human Factors in*

Computing Systems - CHI '15, 1159–1162. https://doi.org/10.1145/2702123.2702155

64. Richard L. Daft and Robert H. Lengel. 1983. Information Richness. A New Approach to Managerial Behavior and Organization Design. *Research in Organizational Behavior*. https://doi.org/10.1128/jb.125.2.608-615.1976

65. Nils Dahlbäck, Arne Jönsson, and Lars Ahrenberg. 1993. Wizard of oz studies-why and how. In *International Conference on Intelligent User Interfaces, Proceedings IUI*, 193–200.

66. Andreea Danielescu and Gwen Christian. 2018. A Bot is Not a Polyglot. In *Extended Abstracts of the 2018 CHI Conference on Human Factors in Computing Systems - CHI '18*, 1–9. https://doi.org/10.1145/3170427.3174366

67. Andreea Danielescu and Gwen Christian. 2018. A Bot is Not a Polyglot: Designing Personalities for Multi-Lingual Conversational Agents. In *Extended Abstracts of the 2018 CHI Conference on Human Factors in Computing Systems - CHI '18*, 1–9. https://doi.org/10.1145/3170427.3174366

68. Thomas Davenport and Ravi Kalakota. 2019. The potential for artificial intelligence in healthcare. *Future Healthcare Journal* 6, 2: 94–98. https://doi.org/10.7861/futurehosp.6-2-94

69. Anthony Christopher Davison and D. V. Hinkley. 1997. *Bootstrap methods and their application*. Cambridge University Press, Cambridge.

70. Pooja M. Desai, Elliot G. Mitchell, Maria L. Hwang, Matthew E. Levine, David J. Albers, and Lena Mamykina. 2019. Personal health oracle: Explorations of personalized predictions in diabetes self-management. In *Conference on Human Factors in Computing Systems - Proceedings*, 1–13. https://doi.org/10.1145/3290605.3300600

71. Anind K. Dey. 2001. Understanding and using context. *Personal and Ubiquitous Computing* 5, 1: 4–7. https://doi.org/10.1007/s007790170019

72. The Diabetes Prevention Program (DPP) Research Diabetes Prevention Program (DPP) Research Group. 2002. The Diabetes Prevention Program (DPP): description of lifestyle intervention. *Diabetes care* 25, 12: 2165–71. https://doi.org/10.2337/diacare.25.12.2165

73. Diabetes Prevention Program Research Group. 2009. 10-year follow-up of diabetes incidence and weight loss in the Diabetes Prevention Program Outcomes Study. *The Lancet* 374, 9702: 1677–1686. https://doi.org/10.1016/S0140-6736(09)61457-4

74.   Sara Belle Donevant, Robin Dawson Estrada, Joan Marie Culley, Brian Habing, and Swann Arp Adams. 2018. Exploring app features with outcomes in mHealth studies involving chronic respiratory diseases, diabetes, and hypertension: a targeted exploration of the literature. *Journal of the American Medical Informatics Association*. https://doi.org/10.1093/jamia/ocy104

75.   Damion M. Dooley, Emma J. Griffiths, Gurinder S. Gosal, Pier L. Buttigieg, Robert Hoehndorf, Matthew C. Lange, Lynn M. Schriml, Fiona S.L. Brinkman, and William W.L. Hsiao. 2018. FoodOn: A harmonized food ontology to increase global food traceability, quality control and data integration. *npj Science of Food* 2, 1: 1–10. https://doi.org/10.1038/s41538-018-0032-6

76.   Devdatt Dubhashi and Shalom Lappin. 2017. AI dangers: Imagined and real. *Communications of the ACM 60*, 43–45. https://doi.org/10.1145/2953876

77.   David Elsweiler, Bernd Ludwig, Alan Said, Hanna Schaefer, and Christoph Trattner. 2016. Engendering Health with Recommender Systems. In *Proceedings of the 10th ACM Conference on Recommender Systems - RecSys '16*, 409–410. https://doi.org/10.1145/2959100.2959203

78.   Daniel A. Epstein, Felicia Cordeiro, James Fogarty, Gary Hsieh, and Sean A. Munson. 2016. Crumbs: Lightweight Daily Food Challenges to Promote Engagement and Mindfulness. *Proceedings of the 2016 CHI Conference on Human Factors in Computing Systems*: 5632–5644. https://doi.org/10.1145/2858036.2858044

79.   Daniel Epstein, Felicia Cordeiro, Elizabeth Bales, James Fogarty, and Sean Munson. 2014. Taming Data Complexity in Lifelogs: Exploring Visual Cuts of Personal Informatics Data. *DIS '14 Proceedings of the 2014 conference on Designing interactive systems*: 667–676. https://doi.org/10.1145/2598510.2598558

80.   Thomas Erickson and Wendy A. Kellogg. 2000. Social Translucence: An Approach to Designing Systems that Support Social Processes. *ACM Transactions on Computer-Human Interaction* 7, 1: 59–83. https://doi.org/10.1145/344949.345004

81.   Alison B. Evert, Michelle Dennison, Christopher D. Gardner, W. Timothy Garvey, Ka Hei Karen Lau, Janice MacLeod, Joanna Mitri, Raquel F. Pereira, Kelly Rawlings, Shamera Robinson, Laura Saslow, Sacha Uelmen, Patricia B. Urbanski, and William S. Yancy. 2019. *Nutrition therapy for adults with diabetes or prediabetes: A consensus report.*

https://doi.org/10.2337/dci19-0014

82. Ahmed Fadhil and Silvia Gabrielli. 2017. Addressing Challenges in Promoting Healthy Lifestyles: The Al-chatbot Approach. In *Proceedings of the 11th EAI International Conference on Pervasive Computing Technologies for Healthcare* (PervasiveHealth '17), 261–265. https://doi.org/10.1145/3154862.3154914

83. Ahmed Fadhil and Gianluca Schiavo. *Designing for Health Chatbots*. Retrieved June 17, 2019 from https://arxiv.org/pdf/1902.09022.pdf

84. Ahmed Fadhil, Gianluca Schiavo, and Yunlong Wang. 2019. CoachAI: A Conversational Agent Assisted Health Coaching Platform. Retrieved June 13, 2019 from http://arxiv.org/abs/1904.11961

85. Ahmed Fadhil, Yunlong Wang, and Harald Reiterer. 2019. Assistive Conversational Agent for Health Coaching: A Validation Study. *Methods of Information in Medicine*. https://doi.org/10.1055/s-0039-1688757

86. Daniel J Feller, Marissa Burgermaster, Matthew E Levine, Arlene Smaldone, Patricia G Davidson, David J Albers, and Lena Mamykina. 2018. A visual analytics approach for pattern-recognition in patient-generated data. *Journal of the American Medical Informatics Association*. https://doi.org/10.1093/jamia/ocy054

87. FiebrinkRebecca and GilliesMarco. 2018. Introduction to the Special Issue on Human-Centered Machine Learning. *ACM Transactions on Interactive Intelligent Systems (TiiS)* 8, 2. https://doi.org/10.1145/3205942

88. Alessio Fioravanti, Giuseppe Fico, Dario Salvi, Rebeca I. García-Betances, and Maria Teresa Arredondo. 2015. Automatic messaging for improving patients engagement in diabetes management: an exploratory study. *Medical & Biological Engineering & Computing* 53, 12: 1285–1294. https://doi.org/10.1007/s11517-014-1237-8

89. William A. Fisher, Jeffrey D. Fisher, and Jennifer Harman. 2003. The Information-Motivation-Behavioral Skills Model: A General Social Psychological Approach to Understanding and Promoting Health Behavior. In *Social Psychological Foundations of Health and Illness*. Blackwell Publishing Ltd, Malden, MA, USA, 82–106. https://doi.org/10.1002/9780470753552.ch4

90. Kathleen Kara Fitzpatrick, Alison Darcy, and Molly Vierhile. 2017. Delivering Cognitive Behavior Therapy to Young Adults With Symptoms of Depression and Anxiety Using a

Fully Automated Conversational Agent (Woebot): A Randomized Controlled Trial. *JMIR Mental Health* 4, 2: e19. https://doi.org/10.2196/mental.7785

91.   Kathleen Kara Fitzpatrick, Alison Darcy, and Molly Vierhile. 2017. Delivering Cognitive Behavior Therapy to Young Adults With Symptoms of Depression and Anxiety Using a Fully Automated Conversational Agent (Woebot): A Randomized Controlled Trial. *JMIR mental health* 4, 2: e19. https://doi.org/10.2196/mental.7785

92.   Annette Flanagin, Tracy Frey, Stacy L. Christiansen, and AMA Manual of Style Committee. 2021. Updated Guidance on the Reporting of Race and Ethnicity in Medical and Science Journals. *JAMA* 326, 7: 621–627. https://doi.org/10.1001/JAMA.2021.13304

93.   Victoria Louise Franklin, Alexandra Greene, ; Annalu Waller, ; Stephen, Alan Greene, and Claudia Pagliari. 2008. Patients' Engagement With "Sweet Talk"-A Text Messaging Support System for Young People With Diabetes. *Journal of medical Internet research* 10, 2. https://doi.org/10.2196/jmir.962

94.   Russell Fulmer, Angela Joerin, Breanna Gentile, Lysanne Lakerink, and Michiel Rauws. 2018. Using Psychological Artificial Intelligence (Tess) to Relieve Symptoms of Depression and Anxiety: Randomized Controlled Trial. *JMIR Mental Health* 5, 4: e64. https://doi.org/10.2196/mental.9782

95.   Patricia Fusch and Lawrence Ness. 2015. Are We There Yet? Data Saturation in Qualitative Research. *The Qualitative Report* 20, 9. Retrieved September 15, 2020 from https://nsuworks.nova.edu/tqr/vol20/iss9/3

96.   Silvia Gabrielli, Kate Marie, and Carolina Della Corte. 2018. SLOWBot (chatbot) Lifestyle Assistant. In *Proceedings of the 12th EAI International Conference on Pervasive Computing Technologies for Healthcare - PervasiveHealth '18*, 367–370. https://doi.org/10.1145/3240925.3240953

97.   Jianfeng Gao, Michel Galley, and Lihong Li. 2018. Neural Approaches to Conversational AI. https://doi.org/10.1145/3209978.3210183

98.   Suat Gonul, Tuncay Namli, Sasja Huisman, Gokce Banu Laleci Erturkmen, Ismail Hakki Toroslu, and Ahmet Cosar. 2018. An expandable approach for design and personalization of digital, just-in-time adaptive interventions. *Journal of the American Medical Informatics Association*. https://doi.org/10.1093/jamia/ocy160

99.   Mitchell L Gordon, Kaitlyn Zhou, and Kayur Patel. 2021. The disagreement

deconvolution: Bringing machine learning performance metrics in line with reality. In *Conference on Human Factors in Computing Systems - Proceedings*. https://doi.org/10.1145/3411764.3445423

100. David A. Gough, Kenneth Kreutz-Delgado, and Troy M. Bremer. 2003. Frequency Characterization of Blood Glucose Dynamics. *Annals of Biomedical Engineering* 31, 1: 91–97. https://doi.org/10.1114/1.1535411

101. Deborah A Greenwood, Perry M Gee, Kathy J Fatkin, and Malinda Peeples. 2017. A Systematic Review of Reviews Evaluating Technology-Enabled Diabetes Self-Management Education and Support. *Journal of diabetes science and technology* 11, 5: 1015–1027. https://doi.org/10.1177/1932296817713506

102. Lisa Grossman, Steven Feiner, Elliot Mitchell, and Ruth Masterson Creber. 2018. Leveraging Patient-Reported Outcomes Using Data Visualization. *Applied Clinical Informatics* 09, 03: 565–575. https://doi.org/10.1055/s-0038-1667041

103. Jonathan Grudin and Richard Jacques. 2019. Chatbots, Humbots, and the Quest for Artificial General Intelligence. In *Proceedings of the 2019 CHI Conference on Human Factors in Computing Systems - CHI '19*, 1–11. https://doi.org/10.1145/3290605.3300439

104. Greg Guest, Arwen Bunce, and Laura Johnson. 2006. How Many Interviews Are Enough? *Field Methods* 18, 1: 59–82. https://doi.org/10.1177/1525822X05279903

105. Varun Gulshan, Lily Peng, Marc Coram, Martin C. Stumpe, Derek Wu, Arunachalam Narayanaswamy, Subhashini Venugopalan, Kasumi Widner, Tom Madams, Jorge Cuadros, Ramasamy Kim, Rajiv Raman, Philip C. Nelson, Jessica L. Mega, and Dale R. Webster. 2016. Development and validation of a deep learning algorithm for detection of diabetic retinopathy in retinal fundus photographs. *JAMA - Journal of the American Medical Association* 316, 22: 2402–2410. https://doi.org/10.1001/jama.2016.17216

106. David Gunning. *Explainable Artificial Intelligence (XAI)*.

107. David Gunning and David W. Aha. 2019. DARPA's explainable artificial intelligence program. *AI Magazine* 40, 2: 44–58. https://doi.org/10.1609/aimag.v40i2.2850

108. Ankit Gupta, Tim Heng, Chris Shaw, Linda Li, and Lynne Feehan. 2018. Towards developing an e-coach to support arthritis patients in maintaining a physically active lifestyle. In *Proceedings of the 12th EAI International Conference on Pervasive Computing Technologies for Healthcare - PervasiveHealth '18*, 392–395.

https://doi.org/10.1145/3240925.3240954

109. Damara Gutnick, Kathy Reims, Connie Davis, Heather Gainforth, Melanie Jay, and Steven Cole. 2014. Brief Action Planning to Facilitate Behavior Change and Support Patient Self-Management. *JCOM* 21, 1.

110. Amanda K Hall, Heather Cole-Lewis, and Jay M Bernhardt. 2015. Mobile Text Messaging for Health: A Systematic Review of Reviews. *Annu. Rev. Public Health* 36: 393–415. https://doi.org/10.1146/annurev-publhealth-031914-122855

111. Yi Han, Melissa Spezia Faulkner, Heather Fritz, Doris Fadoju, Andrew Muir, Gregory D. Abowd, Lauren Head, and Rosa I. Arriaga. 2015. A Pilot Randomized Trial of Text-Messaging for Symptom Awareness and Diabetes Knowledge in Adolescents With Type 1 Diabetes. *Journal of Pediatric Nursing* 30, 6: 850–861. https://doi.org/10.1016/j.pedn.2015.02.002

112. Paul Hansen and Franz Ombler. 2008. A new method for scoring additive multi-attribute value models using pairwise rankings of alternatives. *Journal of Multi-Criteria Decision Analysis* 15, 3–4: 87–107. https://doi.org/10.1002/MCDA.428

113. Steven Haussmann, Oshani Seneviratne, Yu Chen, Yarden Ne'eman, James Codella, Ching-Hua Chen, Deborah L. McGuinness, and Mohammed J. Zaki. 2019. FoodKG: A Semantics-Driven Knowledge Graph for Food Recommendation. *Lecture Notes in Computer Science (including subseries Lecture Notes in Artificial Intelligence and Lecture Notes in Bioinformatics)* 11779 LNCS: 146–162. https://doi.org/10.1007/978-3-030-30796-7_10

114. Mark D. Hayward, Toni P. Miles, Eileen M. Crimmins, and Yu Yang. 2000. The Significance of Socioeconomic Status in Explaining the Racial Gap in Chronic Health Conditions. *American Sociological Review* 65, 6: 910. https://doi.org/10.2307/2657519

115. Katharine J. Head, Seth M. Noar, Nicholas T. Iannarino, and Nancy Grant Harrington. 2013. Efficacy of text messaging-based interventions for health promotion: A meta-analysis. *Social Science and Medicine* 97, 41–48. https://doi.org/10.1016/j.socscimed.2013.08.003

116. Jeffrey Heer and Maneesh Agrawala. 2008. Design considerations for collaborative visual analytics. *Information Visualization* 7: 49–62. https://doi.org/10.1057/palgrave.ivs.9500167

117. Victoria Hollis, Artie Konrad, Aaron Springer, Matthew Antoun, Christopher Antoun, Rob Martin, and Steve Whittaker. 2017. What Does All This Data Mean for My Future Mood? Actionable Analytics and Targeted Reflection for Emotional Well-Being. *Human-Computer Interaction* 32, 5–6: 208–267. https://doi.org/10.1080/07370024.2016.1277724

118. Andreas Holzinger, Chris Biemann, Constantinos S. Pattichis, and Douglas B. Kell. 2017. What do we need to build explainable AI systems for the medical domain? Retrieved July 2, 2020 from http://arxiv.org/abs/1712.09923

119. Kate S. Hone and Robert Graham. 2000. Towards a tool for the Subjective Assessment of Speech System Interfaces (SASSI). *Natural Language Engineering* 6, 3&4: S1351324900002497. https://doi.org/10.1017/S1351324900002497

120. Mohammed (Ehsan) Hoque, Matthieu Courgeon, Jean-Claude Martin, Bilge Mutlu, and Rosalind W. Picard. 2013. MACH: My Automated Conversation coacH. *Proceedings of the 2013 ACM international joint conference on Pervasive and ubiquitous computing - UbiComp '13*: 697. https://doi.org/10.1145/2493432.2493502

121. George Hripcsak and David J Albers. 2013. Next-generation phenotyping of electronic health records. *Journal of the American Medical Informatics Association : JAMIA* 20, 1: 117–21. https://doi.org/10.1136/amiajnl-2012-001145

122. George Hripcsak and David J Albers. 2018. High-fidelity phenotyping: richness and freedom from bias. *Journal of the American Medical Informatics Association* 25, 3: 289–294. https://doi.org/10.1093/jamia/ocx110

123. Paris Hsu, Jingshu Zhao, Kehan Liao, Tianyi Liu, and Chen Wang. 2017. AllergyBot: A Chatbot technology intervention for young adults with food allergies Dining out. In *Conference on Human Factors in Computing Systems - Proceedings*, 74–79. https://doi.org/10.1145/3027063.3049270

124. Eva Hudlicka. 2013. Virtual training and coaching of health behavior: Example from mindfulness meditation training. *Patient Education and Counseling* 92, 2: 160–166. https://doi.org/10.1016/J.PEC.2013.05.007

125. Ellen Isaacs, Alan Walendowski, Steve Whittaker, Diane J. Schiano, and Candace Kamm. 2002. The character, functions, and styles of instant messaging in the workplace. In *Proceedings of the 2002 ACM conference on Computer supported cooperative work - CSCW '02*, 11. https://doi.org/10.1145/587078.587081

126. Faramarz Ismail-Beigi. 2012. Glycemic Management of Type 2 Diabetes Mellitus. *New England Journal of Medicine* 366, 14: 1319–1327. https://doi.org/10.1056/NEJMcp1013127

127. Ying Jin, Zhuoran Yang, and Zhaoran Wang. 2020. Is Pessimism Provably Efficient for Offline RL? Retrieved July 5, 2021 from http://arxiv.org/abs/2012.15085

128. Ulf Johansson, Cecilia Sönströd, Ulf Norinder, and Henrik Boström. 2011. Trade-off between accuracy and interpretability for predictive in silico modeling. *Future Medicinal Chemistry* 3, 6: 647–663. https://doi.org/10.4155/fmc.11.23

129. Ian T Jolliffe and Jorge Cadima. 2016. Principal component analysis: a review and recent developments. *Philosophical transactions. Series A, Mathematical, physical, and engineering sciences* 374, 2065: 20150202. https://doi.org/10.1098/rsta.2015.0202

130. Bart A. Kamphorst. 2017. E-coaching systems: What they are, and what they aren't. *Personal and Ubiquitous Computing* 21, 4: 625–632. https://doi.org/10.1007/s00779-017-1020-6

131. Ravi Karkar, Jasmine Zia, Jessica Schroeder, Daniel A. Epstein, Laura R. Pina, Jeffrey Scofield, James Fogarty, Julie A. Kientz, Sean A. Munson, and Roger Vilardaga. 2017. TummyTrials: A Feasibility Study of Using Self-Experimentation to Detect Individualized Food Triggers. In *Proceedings of the 2017 CHI Conference on Human Factors in Computing Systems - CHI '17*, 6850–6863. https://doi.org/10.1145/3025453.3025480

132. Ravi Karkar, Jasmine Zia, Roger Vilardaga, Sonali R Mishra, James Fogarty, Sean A Munson, and Julie A Kientz. 2016. A framework for self-experimentation in personalized health. *Journal of the American Medical Informatics Association* 23, 3: 440–448. https://doi.org/10.1093/jamia/ocv150

133. Shigeko Kato, Kayo Waki, Sadako Nakamura, Sanae Osada, Haruka Kobayashi, Hideo Fujita, Takashi Kadowaki, and Kazuhiko Ohe. 2016. Validating the use of photos to measure dietary intake: the method used by DialBetics, a smartphone-based self-management system for diabetes patients. *Diabetology International* 7, 3: 244–251. https://doi.org/10.1007/s13340-015-0240-0

134. J. F. Kelley. 1984. An iterative design methodology for user-friendly natural language office information applications. *ACM Transactions on Information Systems (TOIS)* 2, 1: 26–41. https://doi.org/10.1145/357417.357420

135. Keigo Kitamura, Chaminda de Silva, Toshihiko Yamasaki, and Kiyoharu Aizawa. 2010. Image processing based approach to food balance analysis for personal food logging. In *2010 IEEE International Conference on Multimedia and Expo*, 625–630. https://doi.org/10.1109/ICME.2010.5583021

136. Keigo Kitamura, Toshihiko Yamasaki, and Kiyoharu Aizawa. 2008. Food log by analyzing food images. In *Proceeding of the 16th ACM international conference on Multimedia - MM '08*, 999. https://doi.org/10.1145/1459359.1459548

137. Predrag Klasnja, Sunny Consolvo, and Wanda Pratt. 2011. How to evaluate technologies for health behavior change in HCI research. In *Proceedings of the 2011 annual conference on Human factors in computing systems - CHI '11*, 3063. https://doi.org/10.1145/1978942.1979396

138. Predrag Klasnja, Shawna Smith, Nicholas J Seewald, Andy Lee, Kelly Hall, Brook Luers, Eric B Hekler, and Susan A Murphy. 2018. Efficacy of Contextually Tailored Suggestions for Physical Activity: A Micro-randomized Optimization Trial of HeartSteps. *Annals of Behavioral Medicine*. https://doi.org/10.1093/abm/kay067

139. Gary Klein, Paul J Feltovich, Jeffrey M Bradshaw, and David D Woods. 2004. *Common Ground and Coordination in Joint Activity*.

140. A. Baki Kocaballi, Juan C. Quiroz, Liliana Laranjo, Dana Rezazadegan, Rafal Kocielnik, Leigh Clark, Q. Vera Liao, Sun Young Park, Robert J. Moore, and Adam Miner. 2020. Conversational agents for health and wellbeing. In *Conference on Human Factors in Computing Systems - Proceedings*, 1–8. https://doi.org/10.1145/3334480.3375154

141. Rafal Kocielnik and Gary Hsieh. 2017. New Opportunities for Dialogue-based Interaction in Behavior Change Domain. In *CSCW 2017 workshop on Talking with Conversational Agents in Collaborative Action*. Retrieved October 30, 2019 from https://talkingwithagents.files.wordpress.com/2017/02/7-kocielnik1.pdf

142. Rafal Kocielnik, Lillian Xiao, Daniel Avrahami, and Gary Hsieh. 2018. Reflection Companion: A Conversational System for Engaging Users in Reflection on Physical Activity. *Proceedings of the ACM on Interactive, Mobile, Wearable and Ubiquitous Technologies* 2, 2: 1–26. https://doi.org/10.1145/3214273

143. Elizabeth V. Korinek, Sayali S. Phatak, Cesar A. Martin, Mohammad T. Freigoun, Daniel E. Rivera, Marc A. Adams, Pedja Klasnja, Matthew P. Buman, and Eric B. Hekler. 2018.

Adaptive step goals and rewards: a longitudinal growth model of daily steps for a smartphone-based walking intervention. *Journal of Behavioral Medicine* 41, 1: 74–86. https://doi.org/10.1007/s10865-017-9878-3

144. Levente Kriston, Isabelle Scholl, Lars Hölzel, Daniela Simon, Andreas Loh, and Martin Härter. 2010. The 9-item Shared Decision Making Questionnaire (SDM-Q-9). Development and psychometric properties in a primary care sample. *Patient Education and Counseling* 80, 1: 94–99. https://doi.org/10.1016/J.PEC.2009.09.034

145. Mark Kutner, Elizabeth Greenberg, and Justin Baer. 2006. A First Look at the Literacy of America's Adults in the 21st Century. NCES 2006-470. *National Center for Education Statistics*. Retrieved August 23, 2018 from https://eric.ed.gov/?id=ED489066

146. Liliana Laranjo, Adam G Dunn, Huong Ly Tong, Ahmet Baki Kocaballi, Jessica Chen, Rabia Bashir, Didi Surian, Blanca Gallego, Farah Magrabi, Annie Y S Lau, and Enrico Coiera. 2018. Conversational agents in healthcare: a systematic review. *Journal of the American Medical Informatics Association* 25, 9: 1248–1258. https://doi.org/10.1093/jamia/ocy072

147. Liliana Laranjo, Annie Lau, and Enrico Coiera. 2017. Design and Implementation of Behavioral Informatics Interventions. . Springer, Cham, 13–42. https://doi.org/10.1007/978-3-319-51732-2_2

148. Amanda Lazar, Christian Koehler, Joshua Tanenbaum, and David H. Nguyen. 2015. Why we use and abandon smart devices. In *Proceedings of the 2015 ACM International Joint Conference on Pervasive and Ubiquitous Computing - UbiComp '15*, 635–646. https://doi.org/10.1145/2750858.2804288

149. Jisoo Lee, Eric B. Hekler, Emil Chiauzzi, Auriell Towner, and Marcy Fitz-Randolph. 2016. Helping Users Set Rules for Defining Short-Term Activity Goals. In *Proceedings of the 2016 CHI Conference Extended Abstracts on Human Factors in Computing Systems - CHI EA '16*, 2178–2184. https://doi.org/10.1145/2851581.2892488

150. Huitian Lei, Ambuj Tewari, and Susan A. Murphy. 2017. An Actor-Critic Contextual Bandit Algorithm for Personalized Mobile Health Interventions. Retrieved January 31, 2019 from http://arxiv.org/abs/1706.09090

151. Matthew E. Levine, David J. Albers, and George Hripcsak. 2018. Methodological variations in lagged regression for detecting physiologic drug effects in EHR data. *Journal*

of Biomedical Informatics 86: 149–159. https://doi.org/10.1016/j.jbi.2018.08.014

152. Ian Li, Anind Dey, and Jodi Forlizzi. 2010. A stage-based model of personal informatics systems. *Proceedings of the 28th international conference on Human factors in computing systems CHI 10*: 557. https://doi.org/10.1145/1753326.1753409

153. Ian Li, Anind K. Dey, and Jodi Forlizzi. 2011. Understanding my data, myself: supporting self-reflection with ubicomp technologies. In *Proceedings of the 13th international conference on Ubiquitous computing - UbiComp '11*, 405. https://doi.org/10.1145/2030112.2030166

154. Jiwei Li, Will Monroe, Alan Ritter, Michel Galley, Jianfeng Gao, and Dan Jurafsky. 2016. Deep Reinforcement Learning for Dialogue Generation. Retrieved October 21, 2018 from http://arxiv.org/abs/1606.01541

155. Jiwei Li, Will Monroe, Alan Ritter, Michel Galley, Jianfeng Gao, and Dan Jurafsky. 2016. Deep Reinforcement Learning for Dialogue Generation. *EMNLP 2016 - Conference on Empirical Methods in Natural Language Processing, Proceedings*: 1192–1202. Retrieved July 5, 2021 from http://arxiv.org/abs/1606.01541

156. Xiujun Li, Yun-Nung Chen, Lihong Li, Jianfeng Gao, and Asli Celikyilmaz. 2017. End-to-End Task-Completion Neural Dialogue Systems. Retrieved July 5, 2021 from http://arxiv.org/abs/1703.01008

157. Zilu Liang, Bernd Ploderer, Wanyu Liu, Yukiko Nagata, James Bailey, Lars Kulik, and Yuxuan Li. 2016. SleepExplorer: a visualization tool to make sense of correlations between personal sleep data and contextual factors. *Personal and Ubiquitous Computing* 20, 6: 985–1000. https://doi.org/10.1007/s00779-016-0960-6

158. Q. Vera Liao, Yi Chia Wang, Timothy Bickmore, Pascale Fung, Jonathan Grudin, Zhou Yu, and Michelle Zhou. 2019. Human-agent communication: Connecting research and development in HCI and AI. In *Proceedings of the ACM Conference on Computer Supported Cooperative Work, CSCW*, 122–126. https://doi.org/10.1145/3311957.3358607

159. Christine Lisetti, Reza Amini, Ugan Yasavur, and Naphtali Rishe. 2013. I Can Help You Change! An Empathic Virtual Agent Delivers Behavior Change Health Interventions. *ACM Transactions on Management Information Systems* 4, 4: 1–28. https://doi.org/10.1145/2544103

160. Christine Lisetti, Reza Amini, Ugan Yasavur, and Naphtali Rishe. 2013. I Can Help You

Change! An Empathic Virtual Agent Delivers Behavior Change Health Interventions. *ACM Transactions on Management Information Systems* 4, 4: 1–28. https://doi.org/10.1145/2544103

161. Ryan Lowe, Nissan Pow, Iulian Serban, and Joelle Pineau. 2015. The Ubuntu Dialogue Corpus: A Large Dataset for Research in Unstructured Multi-Turn Dialogue Systems. Retrieved November 14, 2018 from http://arxiv.org/abs/1506.08909

162. Gale M. Lucas, Albert Rizzo, Jonathan Gratch, Stefan Scherer, Giota Stratou, Jill Boberg, and Louis-Philippe Morency. 2017. Reporting Mental Health Symptoms: Breaking Down Barriers to Care with Virtual Human Interviewers. *Frontiers in Robotics and AI* 4, OCT: 12. https://doi.org/10.3389/frobt.2017.00051

163. L Mamykina, M E Levine, P G Davidson, A M Smaldone, N Elhadad, and D J Albers. 2016. Data-driven health management: reasoning about personally generated data in diabetes with information technologies. *J Am Med Inform Assoc*: 1–7. https://doi.org/10.1093/jamia/ocv187

164. Lena Mamykina, Matthew E Levine, Patricia G Davidson, Arlene M Smaldone, Noemie Elhadad, and David J Albers. 2016. Data-driven health management: reasoning about personally generated data in diabetes with information technologies. *Journal of the American Medical Informatics Association* 23, 3: 526–531. https://doi.org/10.1093/jamia/ocv187

165. Lena Mamykina, Elizabeth Mynatt, Patricia Davidson, and David Greenblatt. 2008. MAHI: Investigation of social scaffolding for reflective thinking in diabetes management. In *Proceedings of the SIGCHI Conference on Human Factors in Computing Systems (CHI '08)*, 477–486. https://doi.org/10.1145/1357054.1357131

166. César A. Martín, Daniel E. Rivera, Eric B. Hekler, William T. Riley, Matthew P. Buman, Marc A. Adams, and Alicia B. Magann. 2020. Development of a Control-Oriented Model of Social Cognitive Theory for Optimized mHealth Behavioral Interventions. *IEEE Transactions on Control Systems Technology* 28, 2: 331–346. https://doi.org/10.1109/TCST.2018.2873538

167. Nirupa R Matthan, Lynne M Ausman, Huicui Meng, Hocine Tighiouart, and Alice H Lichtenstein. 2016. Estimating the reliability of glycemic index values and potential sources of methodological and biological variability. *The American journal of clinical*

nutrition 104, 4: 1004–1013. https://doi.org/10.3945/ajcn.116.137208

168. David W. McDonald, Stephanie Gokhman, and Mark Zachry. 2012. Building for social translucence: A domain analysis and prototype system. In *Proceedings of the ACM Conference on Computer Supported Cooperative Work, CSCW*, 637–646. https://doi.org/10.1145/2145204.2145301

169. Michael F. McTear. 2002. Spoken dialogue technology: enabling the conversational user interface. *ACM Computing Surveys* 34, 1: 90–169. https://doi.org/10.1145/505282.505285

170. Indrani Medhi, Somani Patnaik, Emma Brunskill, S.N. Nagasena Gautama, William Thies, and Kentaro Toyama. 2011. Designing mobile interfaces for novice and low-literacy users. *ACM Transactions on Computer-Human Interaction* 18, 1: 1–28. https://doi.org/10.1145/1959022.1959024

171. William Mendenhall and Terry Sincich. 1997. A Second Course in Statistics: Regression Analysis. *Journal of the American Statistical Association* 92, 438: 797. https://doi.org/10.2307/2965740

172. Michele Merler, Hui Wu, Rosario Uceda-Sosa, Quoc-Bao Nguyen, and John R. Smith. 2016. Snap, Eat, RepEat: a Food Recognition Engine for Dietary Logging. In *Proceedings of the 2nd International Workshop on Multimedia Assisted Dietary Management - MADiMa '16*, 31–40. https://doi.org/10.1145/2986035.2986036

173. Andreas Michaelides, Jennifer Major, Edmund Pienkosz, Meghan Wood, Youngin Kim, and Tatiana Toro-Ramos. 2018. Usefulness of a novel mobile diabetes prevention program delivery platform with human coaching: 65-week observational follow-up. *JMIR mHealth and uHealth* 6, 5: e93. https://doi.org/10.2196/mhealth.9161

174. Susan Michie, Michelle Richardson, Marie Johnston, Charles Abraham, Jill Francis, Wendy Hardeman, Martin P. Eccles, James Cane, and Caroline E. Wood. 2013. The Behavior Change Technique Taxonomy (v1) of 93 Hierarchically Clustered Techniques: Building an International Consensus for the Reporting of Behavior Change Interventions. *Annals of Behavioral Medicine* 46, 1: 81–95. https://doi.org/10.1007/s12160-013-9486-6

175. B. Middleton, D. F. Sittig, and A. Wright. 2016. Clinical Decision Support: a 25 Year Retrospective and a 25 Year Vision. *Yearbook of Medical Informatics* 25, S 01: S103–S116. https://doi.org/10.15265/IYS-2016-s034

176. Adam S. Miner, Arnold Milstein, Stephen Schueller, Roshini Hegde, Christina

Mangurian, and Eleni Linos. 2016. Smartphone-Based Conversational Agents and Responses to Questions About Mental Health, Interpersonal Violence, and Physical Health. *JAMA Internal Medicine* 176, 5: 619. https://doi.org/10.1001/jamainternmed.2016.0400

177. Elliot G. Mitchell, Elizabeth M. Heitkemper, and Marissa Burgermaster. 2021. From reflection to action: Combining machine learning with expert knowledge for nutrition goal recommendations. *Conference on Human Factors in Computing Systems - Proceedings*: 17. https://doi.org/10.1145/3411764.3445555

178. Elliot G. Mitchell, Rosa Maimone, Andrea Cassells, Jonathan N. Tobin, Patricia Davidson, Arlene M. Smaldone, and Lena Mamykina. 2021. Automated vs. Human Health Coaching. *Proceedings of the ACM on Human-Computer Interaction* 5, CSCW1: 1–37. https://doi.org/10.1145/3449173

179. Elliot G Mitchell, Esteban G Tabak, Matthew E Levine, Lena Mamykina, and David J Albers. 2021. Enabling personalized decision support with patient-generated data and attributable components. *Journal of Biomedical Informatics* 113, 103639: 103639. https://doi.org/https://doi.org/10.1016/j.jbi.2020.103639

180. Volodymyr Mnih, Koray Kavukcuoglu, David Silver, Alex Graves, Ioannis Antonoglou, Daan Wierstra, and Martin Riedmiller. 2013. Playing Atari with Deep Reinforcement Learning. Retrieved July 5, 2021 from http://arxiv.org/abs/1312.5602

181. K W Monsbakken, P O Vandvik, and P G Farup. 2006. Perceived food intolerance in subjects with irritable bowel syndrome – etiology, prevalence and consequences. *European Journal of Clinical Nutrition* 60, 5: 667–672. https://doi.org/10.1038/sj.ejcn.1602367

182. Robert R. Morris, Kareem Kouddous, Rohan Kshirsagar, and Stephen M. Schueller. 2018. Towards an Artificially Empathic Conversational Agent for Mental Health Applications: System Design and User Perceptions. *Journal of Medical Internet Research* 20, 6: e10148. https://doi.org/10.2196/10148

183. Sean A. Munson, Erin Krupka, Caroline Richardson, and Paul Resnick. 2015. Effects of public commitments and accountability in a technology-supported physical activity intervention. In *Conference on Human Factors in Computing Systems - Proceedings*, 1135–1144. https://doi.org/10.1145/2702123.2702524

184. Sean Munson and Sunny Consolvo. 2012. Exploring Goal-setting, Rewards, Self-monitoring, and Sharing to Motivate Physical Activity. In *Proceedings of the 6th International Conference on Pervasive Computing Technologies for Healthcare*. https://doi.org/10.4108/icst.pervasivehealth.2012.248691

185. Inbal Nahum-Shani, Shawna N. Smith, Bonnie J. Spring, Linda M. Collins, Katie Witkiewitz, Ambuj Tewari, and Susan A. Murphy. 2016. Just-in-Time Adaptive Interventions (JITAIs) in Mobile Health: Key Components and Design Principles for Ongoing Health Behavior Support. *Annals of Behavioral Medicine* 52, 6: 446–462. https://doi.org/10.1007/s12160-016-9830-8

186. Inbal Nahum-shani, Shawna N Smith, Katie Witkiewitz, Linda M Collins, Bonnie Spring, and Susan A Murphy. 2014. Just-in-time adaptive interventions (JITAIs): An organizing framework for ongoing health behavior support. *The Methodology Center Technical Report* 073975, 14: 1–37. https://doi.org/10.1023/A:1005618312088

187. Aanand D. Naik, Nynikka Palmer, Nancy J. Petersen, Richard L. Street, Radha Rao, Maria Suarez-Almazor, and Paul Haidet. 2011. Comparative Effectiveness of Goal Setting in Diabetes Mellitus Group Clinics. *Archives of Internal Medicine* 171, 5: 453–459. https://doi.org/10.1001/archinternmed.2011.70

188. Rachael Naphtal. 2015. Natural Language Processing Based Nutritional Application. Massachusetts Institute of Technology.

189. Bonnie A. Nardi, Steve Whittaker, and Erin Bradner. 2000. Interaction and outeraction. In *Proceedings of the 2000 ACM conference on Computer supported cooperative work - CSCW '00*, 79–88. https://doi.org/10.1145/358916.358975

190. Brunilda Nazario. 2013. Portion Size Plate | Recommended Serving Sizes for Portion Control. Retrieved April 15, 2018 from https://www.webmd.com/diet/healthtool-portion-size-plate

191. Duyen T. Nguyen and Susan R. Fussell. 2016. Effects of Conversational Involvement Cues on Understanding and Emotions in Instant Messaging Conversations. *Journal of Language and Social Psychology* 35, 1: 28–55. https://doi.org/10.1177/0261927X15571538

192. Jasmin Niess and Paweł W. Wozniak. 2018. Supporting Meaningful Personal Fitness: the Tracker Goal Evolution Model. In *Proceedings of the 2018 CHI Conference on Human*

Factors in Computing Systems - CHI '18, 1–12. https://doi.org/10.1145/3173574.3173745

193. Wendy Nilsen, Emre Ertin, Eric B. Hekler, Santosh Kumar, Insup Lee, Rahul Mangharam, Misha Pavel, James M. Rehg, William Riley, Daniel E. Rivera, and Donna Spruijt-Metz. 2017. Modeling Opportunities in mHealth Cyber-Physical Systems. In *Mobile Health*. Springer International Publishing, Cham, 443–453. https://doi.org/10.1007/978-3-319-51394-2_23

194. Jon Noronha, Eric Hysen, Haoqi Zhang, and Krzysztof Z. Gajos. 2011. Platemate: Crowdsourcing Nutritional Analysis from Food Photographs. In *Proceedings of the 24th Annual ACM Symposium on User Interface Software and Technology*, 1–12. https://doi.org/10.1145/2047196.2047198

195. Francisco Nunes and Geraldine Fitzpatrick. 2018. Understanding the Mundane Nature of Self-care: Ethnographic Accounts of People Living with Parkinson's. In *Proceedings of the 2018 CHI Conference on Human Factors in Computing Systems - CHI '18*. https://doi.org/10.1145/3173574.3173976

196. Jeanette M. Olsen. 2014. Health Coaching: A Concept Analysis. *Nursing Forum* 49, 1: 18–29. https://doi.org/10.1111/nuf.12042

197. Jeanette M Olsen and Bonnie J Nesbitt. 2010. Health Coaching to Improve Healthy Lifestyle Behaviors: An Integrative Review. *American Journal of Health Promotion* 25, 1: e1–e12. https://doi.org/10.4278/ajhp.090313-lit-101

198. Jayne A. Orr and Robert J. King. 2015. Mobile phone SMS messages can enhance healthy behaviour: a meta-analysis of randomised controlled trials. *Health Psychology Review* 9, 4: 397–416. https://doi.org/10.1080/17437199.2015.1022847

199. Chandra Y Osborn and Leonard E Egede. 2010. Validation of an Information-Motivation-Behavioral Skills model of diabetes self-care (IMB-DSC). *Patient education and counseling* 79, 1: 49–54. https://doi.org/10.1016/j.pec.2009.07.016

200. M. J. Pazzani, S. Mani, and W. R. Shankle. 2001. Acceptance of rules generated by machine learning among medical experts. *Methods of Information in Medicine* 40, 5: 380–385. https://doi.org/01050380 [pii]

201. Cathy Pearl. 2016. *Designing Voice User Interfaces*. O'Reilly Media. Retrieved August 2, 2018 from http://shop.oreilly.com/product/0636920050056.do

202. Monica E Peek, Algernon Cargill, and Elbert S Huang. 2007. Diabetes health disparities: a

systematic review of health care interventions. *Medical care research and review : MCRR* 64, 5 Suppl: 101S–56S. https://doi.org/10.1177/1077558707305409

203. Mor Peleg, Yuval Shahar, Silvana Quaglini, Adi Fux, Gema García-Sáez, Ayelet Goldstein, M. Elena Hernando, Denis Klimov, Iñaki Martínez-Sarriegui, Carlo Napolitano, Enea Parimbelli, Mercedes Rigla, Lucia Sacchi, Erez Shalom, and Pnina Soffer. 2017. MobiGuide: a personalized and patient-centric decision-support system and its evaluation in the atrial fibrillation and gestational diabetes domains. *User Modeling and User-Adapted Interaction* 27, 2: 159–213. https://doi.org/10.1007/s11257-017-9190-5

204. Gabriel Peyré and Marco Cuturi. 2018. Computational Optimal Transport. Retrieved November 28, 2018 from http://arxiv.org/abs/1803.00567

205. Mark Peyrot, Richard R Rubin, Martha M Funnell, and Linda M Siminerio. 2009. Access to diabetes self-management education: results of national surveys of patients, educators, and physicians. *The Diabetes educator* 35, 2: 246–8, 252–6, 258–63. https://doi.org/10.1177/0145721708329546

206. Sara Pinto, Kayo Waki, Luca Chiovato, Pasquale De Cata, Arianna Dagliati, Valentina Tibollo, Giuseppe Ruvolo, and Riccardo Bellazzi. 2018. Smartphone-Based Self-Management of Non-Insulin-Dependent Diabetes: A Japanese System at Use by an Italian Patients' Cohort. *Journal of Diabetes Science and Technology* 12, 4: 903–904. https://doi.org/10.1177/1932296818763884

207. Martin Porcheron, Joel E. Fischer, Stuart Reeves, and Sarah Sharples. 2018. Voice Interfaces in Everyday Life. In *Proceedings of the 2018 CHI Conference on Human Factors in Computing Systems - CHI '18*, 1–12. https://doi.org/10.1145/3173574.3174214

208. Mashfiqui Rabbi, Min Hane Aung, Mi Zhang, and Tanzeem Choudhury. 2015. MyBehavior: Automatic personalized health feedback from user behaviors and preferences using smartphones. In *UbiComp 2015 - Proceedings of the 2015 ACM International Joint Conference on Pervasive and Ubiquitous Computing*, 707–718. https://doi.org/10.1145/2750858.2805840

209. Shriti Raj, Kelsey Toporski, Ashley Garrity, Joyce M. Lee, and Mark W. Newman. 2019. "My blood sugar is higher on the weekends": Finding a role for context and context-awareness in the design of health self-management technology. In *Conference on Human Factors in Computing Systems - Proceedings*, 1–13.

https://doi.org/10.1145/3290605.3300349

210. Alvin Rajkomar, Jeffrey Dean, and Isaac Kohane. 2019. Machine Learning in Medicine. *New England Journal of Medicine* 380, 14: 1347–1358. https://doi.org/10.1056/nejmra1814259

211. Alvin Rajkomar, Eyal Oren, Kai Chen, Andrew M. Dai, Nissan Hajaj, Michaela Hardt, Peter J. Liu, Xiaobing Liu, Jake Marcus, Mimi Sun, Patrik Sundberg, Hector Yee, Kun Zhang, Yi Zhang, Gerardo Flores, Gavin E. Duggan, Jamie Irvine, Quoc Le, Kurt Litsch, Alexander Mossin, Justin Tansuwan, De Wang, James Wexler, Jimbo Wilson, Dana Ludwig, Samuel L. Volchenboum, Katherine Chou, Michael Pearson, Srinivasan Madabushi, Nigam H. Shah, Atul J. Butte, Michael D. Howell, Claire Cui, Greg S. Corrado, and Jeffrey Dean. 2018. Scalable and accurate deep learning with electronic health records. *npj Digital Medicine* 1, 1: 18. https://doi.org/10.1038/s41746-018-0029-1

212. Neesha Ramchandani. 2019. Virtual Coaching to Enhance Diabetes Care. *Diabetes Technology and Therapeutics* 21, S2: S2-48-S2-51. https://doi.org/10.1089/dia.2019.0016

213. Meghan Reading Turchioe, Marissa Burgermaster, Elliot G. Mitchell, Pooja M. Desai, and Lena Mamykina. 2020. Adapting the stage-based model of personal informatics for low-resource communities in the context of type 2 diabetes. *Journal of Biomedical Informatics* *110*, 103572. https://doi.org/10.1016/j.jbi.2020.103572

214. Francesco Ricci, Lior Rokach, and Bracha Shapira. 2015. Recommender Systems: Introduction and Challenges. In *Recommender Systems Handbook*. Springer US, Boston, MA, 1–34. https://doi.org/10.1007/978-1-4899-7637-6_1

215. William Riley, Jami Obermayer, and Jersino Jean-Mary. 2008. Internet and Mobile Phone Text Messaging Intervention for College Smokers. *Journal of American College Health* 57, 2: 245–248. https://doi.org/10.3200/JACH.57.2.245-248

216. William T Riley, Daniel E Rivera, Audie A Atienza, Wendy Nilsen, Susannah M Allison, and Robin Mermelstein. 2011. Health behavior models in the age of mobile interventions: are our theories up to the task? *Translational Behavioral Medicine* 1, 1: 53–71. https://doi.org/10.1007/s13142-011-0021-7

217. Stephen Roller, Emily Dinan, Naman Goyal, Da Ju, Mary Williamson, Yinhan Liu, Jing Xu, Myle Ott, Kurt Shuster, Eric M. Smith, Y-Lan Boureau, and Jason Weston. 2020. Recipes for building an open-domain chatbot. Retrieved April 30, 2020 from

http://arxiv.org/abs/2004.13637

218. Heleen Rutjes, Martijn C. Willemsen, and Wijnand A. IJsselsteijn. 2019. Beyond
      Behavior: The Coach's Perspective on Technology in Health Coaching. In *Proceedings of
      the 2019 CHI Conference on Human Factors in Computing Systems - CHI '19*, 1–14.
      https://doi.org/10.1145/3290605.3300900

219. Thomas L Saaty. 2008. Relative measurement and its generalization in decision making
      why pairwise comparisons are central in mathematics for the measurement of intangible
      factors the analytic hierarchy/network process. *Revista de la Real Academia de Ciencias
      Exactas, Fisicas y Naturales - Serie A: Matematicas* 102, 2: 251–318.
      https://doi.org/10.1007/BF03191825

220. Hanna Schäfer, Santiago Hors-Fraile, Raghav Pavan Karumur, André Calero Valdez, Alan
      Said, Helma Torkamaan, Tom Ulmer, and Christoph Trattner. 2017. Towards Health
      (Aware) Recommender Systems. In *Proceedings of the 2017 International Conference on
      Digital Health - DH '17*, 157–161. https://doi.org/10.1145/3079452.3079499

221. Jessica Schroeder, Jane Hoffswell, Chia-Fang Chung, James Fogarty, Sean Munson, and
      Jasmine Zia. 2017. Supporting Patient-Provider Collaboration to Identify Individual
      Triggers using Food and Symptom Journals. In *Proceedings of the 2017 ACM Conference
      on Computer Supported Cooperative Work and Social Computing - CSCW '17*, 1726–
      1739. https://doi.org/10.1145/2998181.2998276

222. Jessica Schroeder, Ravi Karkar, James Fogarty, Julie A. Kientz, Sean A. Munson, and
      Matthew Kay. 2018. A Patient-Centered Proposal for Bayesian Analysis of Self-
      Experiments for Health. *Journal of Healthcare Informatics Research*: 1–32.
      https://doi.org/10.1007/s41666-018-0033-x

223. Jessica Schroeder, Chelsey Wilks, Kael Rowan, Arturo Toledo, Ann Paradiso, Mary
      Czerwinski, Gloria Mark, and Marsha M. Linehan. 2018. Pocket Skills: A Conversational
      Mobile Web App To Support Dialectical Behavioral Therapy. *Proceedings of the SIGCHI
      Conference on Human Factors in Computing Systems (CHI 2018)*: 1–15.
      https://doi.org/10.1145/3173574.3173972

224. Daniel Schulman, Timothy Bickmore, and Candace L Sidner. 2011. An Intelligent
      Conversational Agent for Promoting Long-term Health Behavior Change Using
      Motivational Interviewing. *2011 AAAI Spring Symposium Series*. Retrieved April 26,

2017 from http://relationalagents.com/publications/AAAI2011-schulman.pdf

225. Joseph Seering, Michal Luria, Geoff Kaufman, and Jessica Hammer. 2019. Beyond dyadic interactions: Considering chatbots as community members. In *Conference on Human Factors in Computing Systems - Proceedings*, 1–13. https://doi.org/10.1145/3290605.3300680

226. Isabel Segura-Bedmar, Paloma Martínez Fernández, and María Herrero Zazo. 2013. SemEval-2013 Task 9 : Extraction of Drug-Drug Interactions from Biomedical Texts (DDIExtraction 2013). 2: 341–350. Retrieved July 22, 2021 from https://e-archivo.uc3m.es/handle/10016/20455

227. Iulian Vlad Serban, Ryan Lowe, Peter Henderson, Laurent Charlin, and Joelle Pineau. 2015. A Survey of Available Corpora for Building Data-Driven Dialogue Systems. *arXiv preprint*. https://doi.org/10.5087/dad

228. Pararth Shah, Dilek Hakkani-Tür, Gokhan Tür, Abhinav Rastogi, Ankur Bapna, Neha Nayak, and Larry Heck. 2018. Building a Conversational Agent Overnight with Dialogue Self-Play. Retrieved July 11, 2019 from http://arxiv.org/abs/1801.04871

229. Diana Sherifali, Virginia Viscardi, Johnny Wei Bai, and R. Muhammad Usman Ali. 2016. Evaluating the Effect of a Diabetes Health Coach in Individuals with Type 2 Diabetes. *Canadian Journal of Diabetes 40*, 84–94. https://doi.org/10.1016/j.jcjd.2015.10.006

230. Ruan Sherry, Jacob OO Wobbrock, Kenny Liou, Andrew Ng, and James Landay. 2016. Speech Is 3x Faster than Typing for English and Mandarin Text Entry on Mobile Devices. *arXiv preprint arXiv:1608.07323* 28, 1: 71–79. https://doi.org/10.1145/2948992.2948998

231. Edward H. Shortliffe, Stanton G. Axline, Bruce G. Buchanan, Thomas C. Merigan, and Stanley N. Cohen. 1973. An Artificial Intelligence program to advise physicians regarding antimicrobial therapy. *Computers and Biomedical Research* 6, 6: 544–560. https://doi.org/10.1016/0010-4809(73)90029-3

232. Katie A Siek, Kay H Connelly, Beenish Chaudry*, Desiree Lambert, and Janet L. Welch. 2009. Evaluation of Two Mobile Nutrition Tracking Applications for Chronically Ill Populations with Low Literacy Skills. In *Mobile Health Solutions for Biomedical Applications*. IGI Global, 1–23. https://doi.org/10.4018/978-1-60566-332-6.ch001

233. David Silver, Julian Schrittwieser, Karen Simonyan, Ioannis Antonoglou, Aja Huang, Arthur Guez, Thomas Hubert, Lucas Baker, Matthew Lai, Adrian Bolton, Yutian Chen,

Timothy Lillicrap, Fan Hui, Laurent Sifre, George Van Den Driessche, Thore Graepel, and Demis Hassabis. 2017. Mastering the game of Go without human knowledge. *Nature* 550, 7676: 354–359. https://doi.org/10.1038/nature24270

234. A Steptoe and G J Molloy. 2007. Personality and heart disease. *Heart (British Cardiac Society)* 93, 7: 783–4. https://doi.org/10.1136/hrt.2006.109355

235. Mirjam Stieger, Marcia Nißen, Dominik Rüegger, Tobias Kowatsch, Christoph Flückiger, and Mathias Allemand. 2018. PEACH, a smartphone- and conversational agent-based coaching intervention for intentional personality change: study protocol of a randomized, wait-list controlled trial. *BMC Psychology* 6, 1: 43. https://doi.org/10.1186/s40359-018-0257-9

236. Melissa S. Stockwell, Elyse Olshen Kharbanda, Raquel Andres Martinez, Celibell Y. Vargas, David K. Vawdrey, and Stewin Camargo. 2012. Effect of a text messaging intervention on influenza vaccination in an urban, low-income pediatric and adolescent population: A randomized controlled trial. *JAMA - Journal of the American Medical Association* 307, 16: 1702–1708. https://doi.org/10.1001/jama.2012.502

237. Elizabeth Stowell, Mercedes C. Lyson, Herman Saksono, Reneé C. Wurth, Holly Jimison, Misha Pavel, and Andrea G. Parker. 2018. Designing and Evaluating mHealth Interventions for Vulnerable Populations. In *Proceedings of the 2018 CHI Conference on Human Factors in Computing Systems - CHI '18*, 1–17. https://doi.org/10.1145/3173574.3173589

238. Pei Hao Su, Paweł Budzianowski, Stefan Ultes, Milica Gašić, and Steve Young. 2017. Sample-efficient actor-critic reinforcement learning with supervised data for dialogue management. In *SIGDIAL 2017 - 18th Annual Meeting of the Special Interest Group on Discourse and Dialogue, Proceedings of the Conference*, 147–157. https://doi.org/10.18653/v1/w17-5518

239. Yueming Sun and Yi Zhang. 2018. Conversational Recommender System. In *The 41st International ACM SIGIR Conference on Research & Development in Information Retrieval - SIGIR '18*, 235–244. https://doi.org/10.1145/3209978.3210002

240. Richard S Sutton and Andrew G Barto. 2018. *Reinforcement learning: An introduction.* MIT press.

241. Kirsten Swearingen and R. Sinha. 2001. Beyond Algorithms: An HCI Perspective on

Recommender Systems. *ACM SIGIR 2001 Workshop on Recommender Systems (2001)*: 1–11. https://doi.org/10.1.1.23.9764

242. Agnieszka Matysiak Szostek, Evangelos Karapanos, Berry Eggen, and Mike Holenderski. 2008. Understanding the implications of Social Translucence for systems supporting communication at work. In *Proceedings of the ACM Conference on Computer Supported Cooperative Work, CSCW*, 649–658. https://doi.org/10.1145/1460563.1460664

243. Esteban G. Tabak and Giulio Trigila. 2018. Explanation of Variability and Removal of Confounding Factors from Data through Optimal Transport. *Communications on Pure and Applied Mathematics* 71, 1: 163–199. https://doi.org/10.1002/cpa.21706

244. Esteban G Tabak and Giulio Trigila. 2017. Conditional expectation estimation through attributable components. *Information and Inference: A Journal of the IMA*: 1–27. https://doi.org/10.1093/imaiai/drn000

245. Guy Tennenholtz. 2021. Offline Reinforcement Learning. *Conference on Health, Inference, and Learning (CHIL 2021)*. Retrieved July 5, 2021 from https://www.chilconference.org/tutorial_T03.html

246. Ambuj Tewari and Susan A. Murphy. 2017. From Ads to Interventions: Contextual Bandits in Mobile Health. In *Mobile Health*. Springer International Publishing, Cham, 495–517. https://doi.org/10.1007/978-3-319-51394-2_25

247. D J Toobert, S E Hampson, and R E Glasgow. 2000. The summary of diabetes self-care activities measure: results from 7 studies and a revised scale. *Diabetes care* 23, 7: 943–50. https://doi.org/10.2337/diacare.23.7.943

248. D J Toobert, S E Hampson, and R E Glasgow. 2000. The summary of diabetes self-care activities measure: results from 7 studies and a revised scale. *Diabetes care* 23, 7: 943–50. https://doi.org/10.2337/DIACARE.23.7.943

249. Chun-Hua Tsai, Yue You, Xinning Gui, Yubo Kou, and John M. Carroll. 2021. Exploring and Promoting Diagnostic Transparency and Explainability in Online Symptom Checkers. In *Proceedings of the 2021 CHI Conference on Human Factors in Computing Systems*, 1–17. https://doi.org/10.1145/3411764.3445101

250. United States Department of Agriculture (USDA). ChooseMyPlate. Retrieved September 16, 2020 from https://www.choosemyplate.gov/

251. Iñigo Urteaga, Mollie McKillop, Sharon Lipsky-Gorman, and Noémie Elhadad. 2018.

Phenotyping Endometriosis through Mixed Membership Models of Self-Tracking Data. Retrieved February 12, 2019 from http://arxiv.org/abs/1811.03431

252. USDA. USDA Food Composition Database. Retrieved April 15, 2018 from https://ndb.nal.usda.gov/ndb/

253. Tiffany C. Veinot, Jessica S. Ancker, Heather Cole-Lewis, Elizabeth D. Mynatt, Andrea G. Parker, Katie A. Siek, and Lena Mamykina. 2019. Leveling Up. *Medical Care* 57: S108–S114. https://doi.org/10.1097/MLR.0000000000001032

254. Tiffany C Veinot, Hannah Mitchell, and Jessica S Ancker. 2018. Good intentions are not enough: how informatics interventions can worsen inequality. *Journal of the American Medical Informatics Association.* https://doi.org/10.1093/jamia/ocy052

255. Cédric Villani. 2009. *Optimal transport : old and new.* Springer.

256. Kayo Waki, Kiyoharu Aizawa, Shigeko Kato, Hideo Fujita, Hanae Lee, Haruka Kobayashi, Makoto Ogawa, Keisuke Mouri, Takashi Kadowaki, and Kazuhiko Ohe. 2015. DialBetics with a multimedia food recording tool, food log: Smartphone-based self-management for type 2 diabetes. *Journal of Diabetes Science and Technology* 9, 3: 534–540. https://doi.org/10.1177/1932296815579690

257. Kayo Waki, Hideo Fujita, Yuji Uchimura, Koji Omae, Eiji Aramaki, Shigeko Kato, Hanae Lee, Haruka Kobayashi, Takashi Kadowaki, and Kazuhiko Ohe. 2014. DialBetics: A Novel Smartphone-based Self-management Support System for Type 2 Diabetes Patients. *Journal of Diabetes Science and Technology* 8, 2: 209–215. https://doi.org/10.1177/1932296814526495

258. David S. Wald, Shahena Butt, and Jonathan P. Bestwick. 2015. One-way Versus Two-way Text Messaging on Improving Medication Adherence: Meta-analysis of Randomized Trials. *The American Journal of Medicine* 128, 10: 1139.e1-1139.e5. https://doi.org/10.1016/J.AMJMED.2015.05.035

259. Danding Wang, Qian Yang, Ashraf Abdul, and Brian Y. Lim. 2019. Designing theory-driven user-centric explainable AI. In *Conference on Human Factors in Computing Systems - Proceedings*, 1–15. https://doi.org/10.1145/3290605.3300831

260. Christopher J C H Watkins and Peter Dayan. 1992. Q-Learning. 8: 279–292.

261. CJCH Watkins. 1989. Learning from delayed rewards. Retrieved July 18, 2021 from https://www.academia.edu/download/50360235/Learning_from_delayed_rewards_201611

16-28282-v2pwvq.pdf

262. Nicole Gray Weiskopf and Chunhua Weng. 2013. Methods and dimensions of electronic health record data quality assessment: Enabling reuse for clinical research. *Journal of the American Medical Informatics Association* 20, 1: 144–151. https://doi.org/10.1136/amiajnl-2011-000681

263. Barry D Weiss, Mary Z Mays, William Martz, Kelley Merriam Castro, Darren A DeWalt, Michael P Pignone, Joy Mockbee, and Frank A Hale. 2005. Quick assessment of literacy in primary care: the newest vital sign. *Annals of family medicine* 3, 6: 514–22. https://doi.org/10.1370/afm.405

264. Joseph Weizenbaum. 1966. ELIZA – a computer program for the study of natural language communication between man and machine. *Communications of the ACM* 26, 1: 36–45. https://doi.org/10.1145/357980.357991

265. M L Wheeler, A Daly, A Evert, and others. 2014. Choose Your Foods, Food Lists for Diabetes. *Chicago, IL: Academy of Nutrition and Dietetics/American Diabetes Association.*

266. Ruth Q. Wolever and David M. Eisenberg. 2011. What is health coaching anyway? Standards needed to enable rigorous research. *Archives of Internal Medicine 171*, 2017–2018. https://doi.org/10.1001/archinternmed.2011.508

267. Ruth Q. Wolever, Leigh Ann Simmons, Gary A. Sforzo, Diana Dill, Miranda Kaye, Elizabeth M. Bechard, Mary Elaine Southard, Mary Kennedy, Justine Vosloo, and Nancy Yang. 2013. A Systematic Review of the Literature on Health and Wellness Coaching: Defining a Key Behavioral Intervention in Healthcare. *Global Advances in Health and Medicine* 2, 4: 38–57. https://doi.org/10.7453/gahmj.2013.042

268. Susan K Wood. 2014. Individual differences in the neurobiology of social stress: implications for depression-cardiovascular disease comorbidity. *Current neuropharmacology* 12, 2: 205–11. https://doi.org/10.2174/1570159X11666131120224413

269. Wei Xu. 2019. Toward human-centered AI: A perspective from human-computer interaction. *Interactions* 26, 4: 42–46. https://doi.org/10.1145/3328485

270. Longqi Yang, Yin Cui, Fan Zhang, John P. Pollak, Serge Belongie, and Deborah Estrin. 2015. PlateClick. In *Proceedings of the 24th ACM International on Conference on*

Information and Knowledge Management - CIKM '15, 183–192.
https://doi.org/10.1145/2806416.2806544

271. Longqi Yang, Cheng-Kang Hsieh, Hongjian Yang, Nicola Dell, Serge Belongie, Curtis Cole, and Deborah Estrin. 2016. Yum-me: A Personalized Nutrient-based Meal Recommender System. *ACM Transactions on Information Systems* 36, 1: 7. https://doi.org/10.1145/3072614

272. David Zeevi, Tal Korem, Niv Zmora, David Israeli, Daphna Rothschild, Adina Weinberger, Orly Ben-Yacov, Dar Lador, Tali Avnit-Sagi, Maya Lotan-Pompan, Jotham Suez, Jemal Ali Mahdi, Elad Matot, Gal Malka, Noa Kosower, Michal Rein, Gili Zilberman-Schapira, Lenka Dohnalová, Meirav Pevsner-Fischer, Rony Bikovsky, Zamir Halpern, Eran Elinav, and Eran Segal. 2015. Personalized Nutrition by Prediction of Glycemic Responses. *Cell* 163, 5: 1079–1095. https://doi.org/10.1016/j.cell.2015.11.001

273. Saizheng Zhang, Emily Dinan, Jack Urbanek, Arthur Szlam, Douwe Kiela, and Jason Weston. 2018. Personalizing Dialogue Agents: I have a dog, do you have pets too? Retrieved July 18, 2019 from http://arxiv.org/abs/1801.07243

274. Brian J Zikmund-Fisher, Aaron M Scherer, Holly O Witteman, Jacob B Solomon, Nicole L Exe, Beth A Tarini, and Angela Fagerlin. 2016. Graphics help patients distinguish between urgent and non-urgent deviations in laboratory test results. *Journal of the American Medical Informatics Association* 24, 3: ocw169. https://doi.org/10.1093/jamia/ocw169

275. Nutrition API by Nutritionix. Retrieved March 26, 2018 from https://www.nutritionix.com/business/api

276. Facts Up Front. Retrieved September 15, 2018 from http://www.factsupfront.org/

277. Twilio Studio. Retrieved October 14, 2020 from https://www.twilio.com/studio

278. Trello. Retrieved October 14, 2020 from https://trello.com/

279. WordBoard Keyboard for iPhone & iPad. Retrieved October 14, 2020 from https://www.bytesizeapps.net/wordboard_keyboard/

280. Amazon Lex – AWS Chatbot AI. Retrieved October 14, 2020 from https://aws.amazon.com/lex/

281. 2021. Chronic Diseases in America | CDC. Retrieved July 1, 2021 from https://www.cdc.gov/chronicdisease/resources/infographic/chronic-diseases.htm

Appendix for Chapter 3: Aim I

A. Data set descriptive statistics

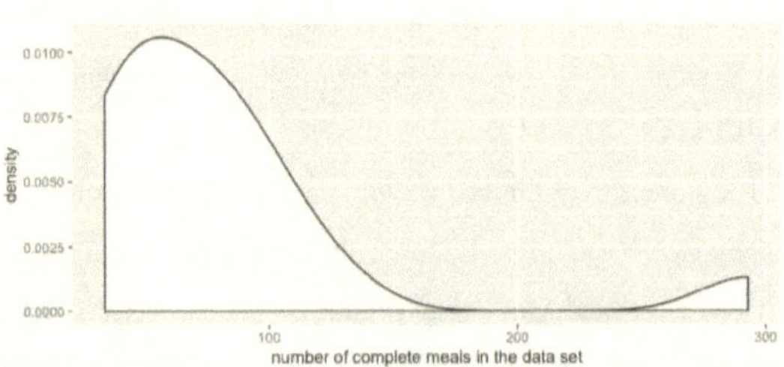

Supplementary Figure A. Kernel density estimate of the number of users with n-many meals in the data set. The mass of the distribution sits near the median of 67 meals logged, with a long tail of users logging considerably more meals.

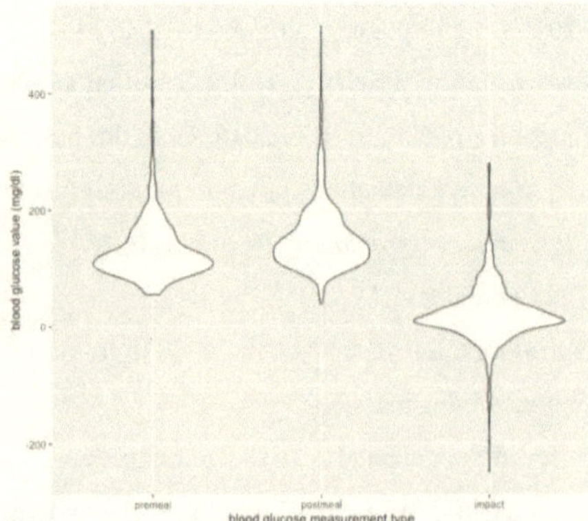

Supplementary Figure B. Violin plots showing the distribution of blood glucose readings across all users. Users varied considerably in their blood glucose levels before and after meals.

Supplementary Table A. Count of meals of each meal type for users A and B.

User ID	Meal Type	Count
A	Breakfast	13
	Lunch	10
	Dinner	23
	Other	12
	Overall	58
B	Breakfast	16
	Lunch	19
	Dinner	44
	Other	9
	Overall	88

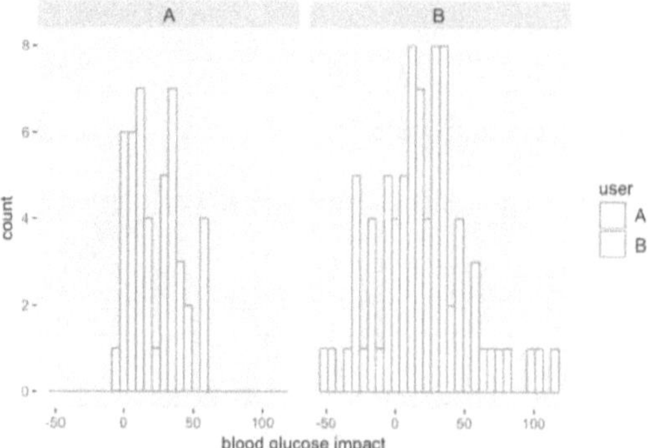

Supplementary Figure C. A histogram of BG impacts for users A and B. User A had less variability in BG impacts compared to user B.

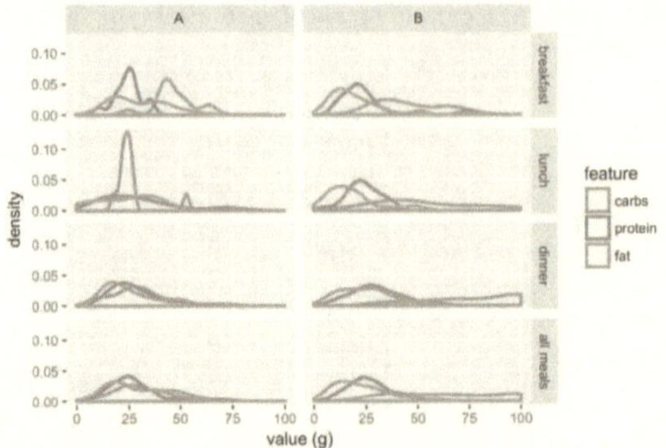

Supplementary Figure D. Kernel density estimate plots of macronutrient consumption for users A and B. There is variability in macro consumption between and within each user. Note that nutrition evaluations only allowed up to 100 grams of each macronutrient, and user B regularly ate 100 grams or more of carbohydrates at dinner.

B.   Controlled experiment materials

This section contains supplementary figures with example materials used in the controlled experiment.

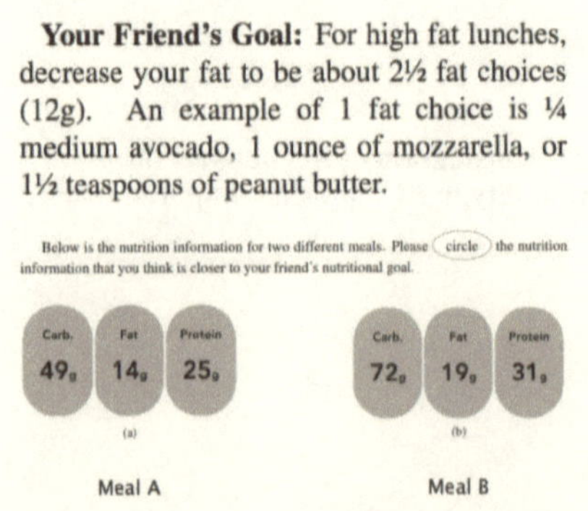

Supplementary Figure E. An example item from the goal comprehension task

Your Friend's Goal: For high carb lunches, replace 1 carb choice with 1 heart healthy fat choice. For example, replace 1 apple with 1 ounce of feta or 1 ounce of mozzarella.

(a) Tuna with mayo, celery, 2 hard boiled eggs, carrots

(b) Tuna with mayo, celery, 1 hard boiled egg, 1 pear

Supplementary Figure F. An example item from the goal/image matching task

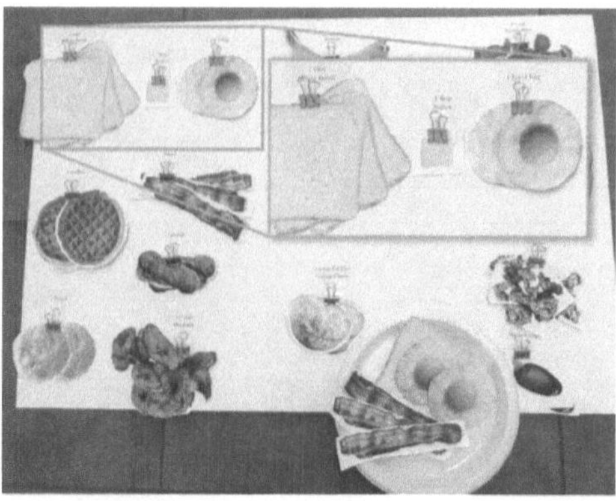

Supplementary Figure G. The "virtual buffet" for breakfast meals.

Appendix for Chapter 4: Aim II

A.   **Supplementary scripted dialogs from t2.coach**

Supplementary Table B. An example exchange with t2.coach for goal setting based on Brief Action Planning (BAP)

User	Message	BAP Step/Skill
t2.coach	Hi! I have an update for you. Are you ready to talk about your goals? Y. Yes, right now N. No, remind me in 24 hours	Follow-up
client	Y	
t2.coach	You met your goal to "Make ½ my meal non-starchy vegetables" 75% of the time last week. Great job! Are you ready to start working on a new goal? (Y/N)	Celebrate success
client	Y	
t2.coach	What goal would you like to work on for the next week? A. Do 30 minutes of your favorite aerobic exercise per day B. Choose whole fruits C. Choose low fat foods M. See more	Behavioral Menu
client	C	
t2.coach	Here are a few ideas to help you meet that goal, which would you like to try? A. Choose fish instead of meat B. Avoid meats high in fat like spareribs, cow or pig feet, and ox tail C. Choose whole beans instead of refried M. See more	SMART behavioral plan
client	B	
t2.coach	Would you like me to remind you to "Avoid meats high in fat like spareribs, cow or pig feet, and ox tail" at 8:00 AM? Y. Yes N. No	Establish accountability
client	Y	

User	Message	BAP Step/Skill
t2.coach	Okay, let me summarize: Your goal is to "Choose low fat foods" Your plan is to "Avoid meats high in fat like spareribs, cow or pig feet, and ox tail" I will not send you a reminder. Do you agree? Y. Yes N. No	Elicit a commitment statement
client	Y	
t2.coach	Ok, I'll check in with you tomorrow. Keep a positive attitude and stay strong. You are already on the road to learning more about your body. Goodbye!	Establish accountability

Supplementary Table C. An example daily check-in dialog, based on Brief Action Planning (BAP)

User	Message	BAP Step/Skill
t2.coach	Hello Tom! Did you meet your goal to "Choose low fat foods" today/yesterday? Y. Yes N. No	Follow-up
client	Yes!	
t2.coach	Great job! Do you want to "Avoid meats high in fat like spareribs, cow or pig feet, and ox tail" again today/tomorrow, or try something new? Y. Yes, repeat this plan tomorrow N. No, try something new	Recognize success
client	Y	
t2.coach	Okay, I will remind you again at the same time. Every day is a new opportunity to learn about how your body works and how to control blood sugar values. Goodbye!	Establish accountability

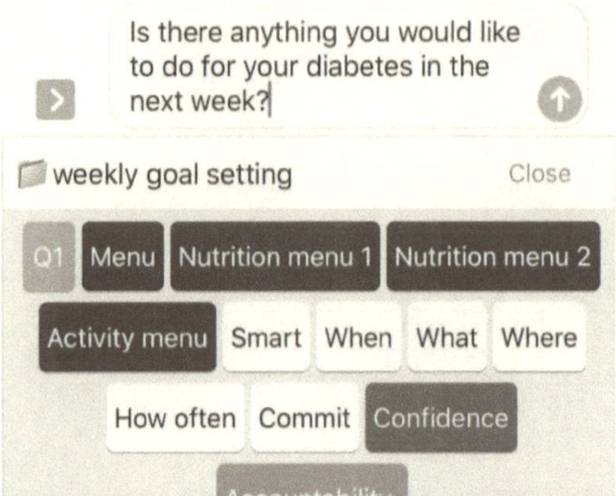

Supplementary Figure H. A screenshot of the WordBoard application [279], configured to allow human coaches to quickly type and send messages from the t2.coach script.

B. Post-study measures

Supplementary Table D. Selection of items from the Subjective Assessment of Speech Systems Interfaces (SASSI; [119]). Each item was answered on a Likert scale from 1 (Strongly Disagree) to 5 (Strongly Agree).

Subcomponent	Question
1	The system (t2.coach) is accurate
1	The system did not always do what I wanted
2	The system is useful
2	The system is friendly
3	It is clear how to send messages to the system
3	I felt confident using the system
4	I felt tense using the system
4	The interaction with the system is repetitive
5	The interaction with the system is boring
5	I always know what to say to the system

Supplementary Table E. Selection of 7 items adapted from the Shared Decision-Making Questionnaire (SDM-9 [144]). Underlined section are rephrased from the original measure

to adapt the context to health goals instead of treatment decisions. Each item was answered on a Likert scale from 1 (Strongly Disagree) to 5 (Strongly Agree).

Question
t2.coach wanted to know exactly how I wanted to be involved in choosing a health goal
t2.coach told me that there are different options for choosing a health goal
t2.coach precisely explained the advantages and disadvantages of the health goal choices
t2.coach helped me understand all the information.
t2.coach asked me which health goal I prefer.
t2.coach and I thoroughly weighed the different health goal choices.
t2.coach and I selected a health goal together.

C.   Supplementary qualitative results

Supplementary Table F. Prevalence of themes across participants in both groups. Gray cells indicate the presence of the theme for a given participant.

	Chatbot	Human Coach
Theme 1: Participants in both groups felt like they were working with a health coach		
Theme 2: Human coaching has advantages		
Theme 2a: Participants received expressions of empathy from the coach		
Theme 2b: Expanded scope of support		
Theme 3: The consistency and predictability of the chatbot		
Theme 3a: Perseverance in pursuing goals		
Theme 3b: Choice and autonomy		
Theme 4: Expectations for personalized and continuous support		

Supplementary Table G. Prevalence of themes from interviews with human coaches. Gray cells indicate the presence of the theme for a given participant.

	Coach #1	Coach #2	Coach #3	Coach #4
Theme 2: Human coaching has advantages, but encounters barriers with text messaging	■	■	■	■
Theme 2b: Text messaging created barriers to effective communication	■	■	■	■
Theme 2c: Coaching without nuance and context	■	■	■	■
Theme 2d: Attempts for deeper engagement sometimes backfired	■	■	■	
Theme 2d: Coaches want a rewarding experience, too, but rarely received it	■	■	■	■

Supplementary Table H. Illustrative quotes from each group of participants for each sub-theme related to the experience of working with a health coach

Sub-Theme	Human Coaching	Chatbot
Setting actionable goals	*"Yeah the goals were – the goals weren't hard to meet or anything. They were basically suggestions pointing me in the right direction." P13 (HC)*	*"I did find a friend. She does walk with me… I do walk with a friend and we did from here to [], walking." P8 (Chatbot)*
Increased Motivation	*"I like it better than you know, you try to work on the key issue like motivate it for me. It gives me motivation and teach me" P15 (HC)*	*"Yeah, but it gave me motivation to doing more, like, you know, days I just didn't feel like doing, you know. So, this one gave me motivation." P8 (Chatbot)*
Learning and knowledge	*"The coaching was very informative for you, you know, okay, let's try this and let's try that, okay you know what you are supposed to eat, what's vegetables, what's fruits… you know, my eating habits and stuff like that." P14 (HC)*	*"Like a teacher… You know a teacher teaches… Okay and that's what a coach does too but a coach is more open because they work in many areas at one time." P9 (Chatbot)*

Sub-Theme	Human Coaching	Chatbot
It Felt Conversational	*"You know, you text somebody and they take your – you know, it's like you're talking to somebody." P15 (HC)*	*"The communication helps a lot – being able to communicate with someone my plan and then the feedback from the Coach." P11 (Chatbot)*
Building a relationship	*"Well, you know, once the coach was done, I missed it. I know that because I knew once I got started with the coach, I started to looking forward to chat with the coach…" P17 (HC)*	*"Yes, it was nice to talk to somebody, you know, about diabetes because I don't even want to talk to stuff like that this with my girl." P6 (Chatbot)*
Increased Mindfulness	*"This program helped me to be a little more conscious of the time and hence I guess helped me to focus my attention on eating at a set time" P17 (HC)*	*"I get a message every morning, it was like telling for me to select the goal for the day, so it was like 'okay, today I'm gonna eat more fruits,' in my breakfast oatmeal or put more vegetables in my dinner." P10 (Chatbot)*
Accountability	*"The person is making sure you're doing what you said you are going to with your goals and that was good, that is why I like that" P14 (HC)*	*"It just gave me a note of, a sign of accountability… once you put it in writing you can't erase it… Somebody else has a copy of what you have done. So you got to" P9 (Chatbot)*

Appendix for Chapter 5: Aim III

A.   Goal attainment and difficulty analysis

Supplementary Table I. Summary of goal attainment and user-expert agreement over 3000 meals. Goals used as case studies in Aim 3 are indicated in bold.

Goal name	Meal count	Goal attainment	User-expert Agreement
Choose foods without added sugar	433	81%	85%
Replace ½ carb choice with 'free foods'	44	70%	77%
Water instead of sugary beverages	317	62%	72%
Decrease your protein to 1½ protein choices	11	55%	55%
Decrease your carbs to 2½ carb choices	13	54%	54%
Eat more fruits and/or vegetables	491	54%	66%
Choose low fat foods	410	51%	57%
Decrease your fat to 3½ fat choices	28	50%	54%
Replace ½ carb choice with 'free foods'	12	50%	67%
Low glycemic index	152	48%	66%
Choose lean proteins	**1047**	**48%**	**61%**
Drink water instead of sugary beverages	430	46%	56%
Decrease your carbs to 2 carb choices	**11**	**45%**	**55%**
Decrease your protein to 2 protein choices	36	44%	44%
Drink water	567	44%	64%
Variety of fruits and vegetables	762	44%	61%
Include more vegetables	308	43%	88%
Make ¼ of my meal protein	159	36%	48%
Choose whole grain carbs	242	31%	56%
Half fruits and vegetables	**369**	**31%**	**65%**
Vegetable fats	126	30%	44%
Reduce portion size	387	29%	53%
Choose whole fruits	385	26%	66%
Whole fruits	172	25%	94%
Include more fruit	238	22%	89%
Make ¼ of my meal carbs	515	21%	37%
Choose plant proteins	108	20%	59%
Choose plant proteins	379	16%	49%
Decrease your carbs to 2½ carb choices	25	16%	44%
Choose whole grains	456	15%	70%
Low fat dairy	207	11%	81%

B.   Crowdsourced corpus descriptive statistics

The complete corpus of micro-coaching dialogs is available on GitHub at

https://github.com/elliotgmitchell/micro-coaching-corpus.

Supplementary Figure I and Supplementary Figure J summarize the length of messages

from crowd workers in the corpus, with word count and character counts. There is a diversity of

response lengths, and importantly, all of the responses are fewer than 160 characters, suggesting

they are a reasonable length for SMS messaging.

Supplementary Figure K shows how the count of food items parsed by *Nutritionix*

increases as conversations increase in length. The number of food items identified increases most

after the first turn, and then gradually increases in subsequent turns.

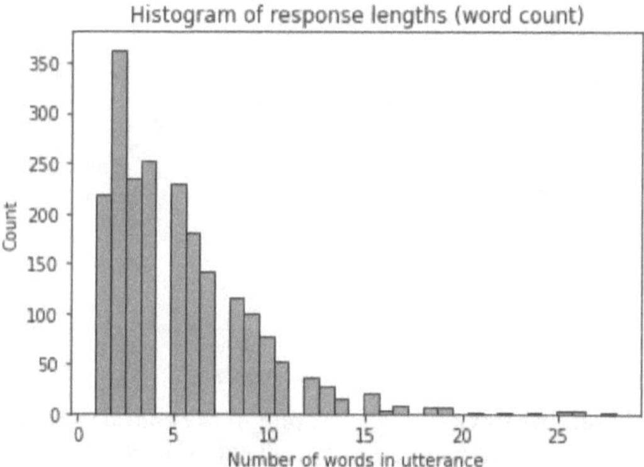

Supplementary Figure I. Histogram of crowd worker response lengths (word count)

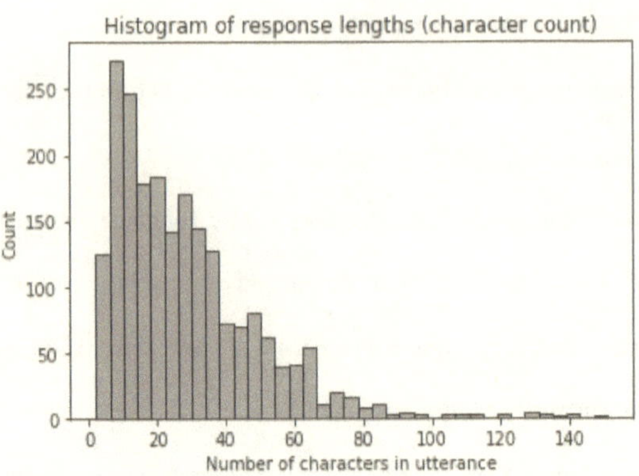

Supplementary Figure J. Histogram of crowd worker response lengths (character count)

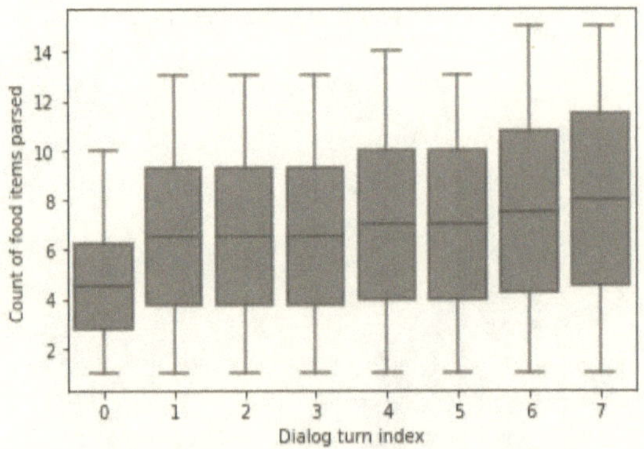

Supplementary Figure K. Box-and-whisker plot of the cumulative count of food items parsed by the depth of the conversation.

Supplementary Table J. Questions for each goal in the "scripted" chatbot condition.

Goal	Question type	Question text
Choose lean proteins	`what_else`	What else will you have with your meal?
	`any(lean protein)`	Will you have any lean proteins with your meal, like chicken breast or egg whites?
Eat no more than 2 portions of carbs (30g)	`what_else`	What else will you have with your meal?
	`how_much(carbs)`	What portion of carbohydrates like rice, pasta, or bread will you eat? For example, one fist is about one cup
	`how_much(fruit)`	What amount of fruit will you eat? For example, one fist is about one cup
Make ½ my meal fruits and/or non-starchy vegetables	`what_else`	What else will you have with your meal?
	`how_much(fruit)`	What amount of fruit will you eat? For example, one fist is about one cup
	`how_much(non-starchy veg)`	What amount of non-starchy vegetables will you eat? For example, one fist is about one cup
	`how_much(protein)`	All fruit and vegetables have amounts?
	`how_much(carbs)`	What portion of carbohydrates like rice, pasta, or bread will you eat? For example, one fist is about one cup